CW01066895

McMULLAN TO O'LEARY
claret & blue managers

Dave Woodhall

First published in Great Britain in 2003 by
Heroes Publishing.
P.O. Box 1703, Perry Barr,
Birmingham B42 1UZ.

ISBN 0-9543884-1-0

Cover photo - Colorsport
Printed by Blueprint, Pontypridd.

"We were playing away, somewhere in the North-East, and we'd taken this fifteen-year old apprentice up with us. Before the game we were in the dressing room and, as was our custom, a whisky bottle was being passed round.

"Some of the players took a drink before running out onto the pitch, then when they'd all gone Vic took a big swig out of the bottle. The young apprentice asked him why he'd drunk so much of the whisky.

"Vic turned to him and said 'Son, when you're the manager of this club, you'll know why'."

Jim Cumbes, Aston Villa goalkeeper 1972-76

Acknowledgements

First of all, thanks to those past and present managers of Aston Villa who freely gave of their time to answer questions that often ranged from the inane to the plain hero-worshipping. Tommy Cummings, Tommy Docherty, Graham Turner, Graham Taylor, Dr. Josef Venglos, Ron Atkinson, Brian Little and David O'Leary. Gentlemen, thank you all. Without your co-operation this book would have been impossible.

Thanks also to those who agreed to be interviewed, in no particular order, Dennis Jackson, Harry Burrows, Alan Deakin, Brian Godfrey, Jim Cumbes, Chris Nicholl, Dennis Mortimer, Gary Shaw, Tony Morley, Allan Evans, Steve McMahon, Paul Birch, Ian Olney, Sir William Dugdale, Neil Moxley, Leon Hickman, Kevin McCarra and Martin Swain.

Others who have helped in the production of this book include Peter Page and Andy Wainwright (proofreaders extraordinaire), Simon Page, Bryan Swain, Phil Mepham, Terry Weir, everyone at the local archives section of the Birmingham Central Library, Andrew Cowie of Colorsport and Andrew Searle of Parrs Wood Press.

My final thanks are to those without whom....

Neil Rioch, who provided me with a comprehensive list of ex-players, all of whom helped enormously. That the Aston Villa Former Players Association is such a successful organization is no surprise, considering its chairman. If ever you get the opportunity to watch the Old Stars or attend one of their fund-raising events, please take it.

Rosina Barton, who gave so much help for the chapter which more than any other deserves to be remembered for all time.

And finally Bernie, for putting up with another year of angst, tantrums, worry, panic and childishness, thereby proving yet again that she truly is far too good for me.

Contents

1

Jimmy McMullan

May 1934 - October 1935

Aston Villa, like most English clubs, did not feel that a team manager was a necessary member of staff for many years after they were founded in 1874.

Players were signed and teams selected by a combination of the committee and captain. Tactics and skill training were matters left to the players themselves, while such organised sessions as there were consisted of fitness work under the auspices of the first team trainer. The all-conquering Villa team of the late nineteenth and early twentieth centuries refined these methods into a system whereby Joe Grierson and secretary George Ramsay behaved much as a manager and a director of football would do today. Grierson was the first trainer in the game to adapt his team's tactics to outwit the opposition rather than merely playing the same way in every match, while Ramsay was responsible for finding players best suited to fit into the Villa's style. Six championships and four FA Cups during Grierson's 22 years with the club bore witness to the success of their partnership.

Grierson's departure led to a tailing off in the Villa's pre-eminence, but Ramsay retained his authority until retiring in 1926. When he left Villa Park, the club originally advertised for a secretary-manager. After a fruitless search, assistant secretary Billy Smith was promoted to the position of secretary, and although his duties included many of those that would be considered managerial, Smith was not officially credited with such a role. However, as the years passed and success continued to elude the Villa, there were mutterings that the board of directors should consider following the example of other clubs in employing someone whose role would be solely devoted to playing affairs.

The first sign that the Villa board were considering the appointment of a team manager came in early February 1934, when the Villa News suggested that such an appointment was in the offing, stating that "Nothing but the best in the way of a manager will do for Aston Villa". Public opinion supported this decision, although the Sports Argus cautioned that the move was, "Excellent – provided the new manager is allowed to perform his duties without interference". As if predicting the charge often levelled at Villa boards from that day onwards, the reporter continued; "When Villa appoint a manager, I hope they will permit him to manage and support him." And as a letter from a supporter to the Birmingham Mail pointed out, "The best thing the directors have done for the team is relinquish control of it."

This was followed by an advertisement in the Sporting Chronicle & Athletic News of 5th February which announced that:

Aston Villa Football Club, Ltd.,
invite applications for the post of team manager.
Qualifications:-
Must be an expert judge of football players, a skilful coach, and
thoroughly competent adviser.

The Birmingham Mail carried a story that suggested George Jobey of Derby County had been offered the position. Jobey at first denied that any approach had been made, but later confessed that the Villa board had indeed asked him to become the club's first manager and that he had turned down their offer out of loyalty to Derby. Also linked with the post was Arsenal player David Jack, one of the most famous names in football, and it was reported that the board had received hundreds of applications for the position, including several from Villa players.

They may have been breaking with tradition in appointing a team manager, but the Villa board certainly had one eye on the past when wondering how the position should be filled. The Scottish influence at Villa Park had long been established and in the main hugely successful, so it was little surprise that the first incumbent in what would soon become one of the hottest seats in football was a man from north of the border.

Jimmy McMullan was born in Denny, Stirlingshire in 1895. He started his career with local club Denny Hibs, then spent a short period with Third Lanark before moving to Partick Thistle in 1913. Thistle at that time were still more than a match for their Old Firm rivals and McMullan made a name for himself as a typical Scottish half-back - talented while fierce in the tackle despite being no more than 5' 5" tall. With a rare positional sense and the ability to play the long or short ball with defence splitting accuracy, McMullan would have been an asset to any midfield whatever the era.

The end of the First World War saw McMullan gain his first international recognition, with four appearances in Victory Internationals. The following season he made three appearances for the Scottish League, and went on to play sixteen times in total for his country, seven of these games coming against England. Only once did he finish on the losing side in a full international.

McMullan was unlucky with injuries, missing out on Thistle's epic Scottish FA Cup final win over Rangers, although he was a runner-up in two English finals following a move to Manchester City in 1926 for a fee of £4,700. Two years after signing for City, McMullan joined the ranks of Scottish footballing immortals when chosen to captain Scotland in the Home International at Wembley. With the likes of Hughie Gallagher and Alex James in a side that was later christened the Wembley Wizards, McMullan led the Scots to a 5-1 victory that ranks as one of Scotland's finest sporting hours.

In total, McMullan made 242 appearances for Manchester City before moving to Oldham Athletic as player-manager in May 1933. In his only season at Boundary Park, McMullan led the Latics to tenth place in the second division, a particularly commendable position in the light of the recession that was hitting the Lancashire cotton mills at the time, severely affecting Oldham's finances. Incidentally, Oldham's near-neighbours Manchester United finished the season in twentieth place in the second division, only avoiding relegation to Division Three North by virtue of beating relegated Millwall in the final game of the season.

Jimmy McMullan was appointed Villa manager on 11th May 1934, originally on a one-year contract that would later be extended to two years. His first signing was Portsmouth centre-half Jimmy Allen for a record fee of £10,775. McMullan may have ostensibly been in charge of team affairs, but there was little doubt the real power at Villa Park lay elsewhere. Billy Smith remained in control of the day to day running of the club, regarding himself as the monarch of his Villa Park kingdom. "Billy was the real boss at Villa Park" was the comment of the great Pongo Waring many years later.

Revealingly, Waring told the story of how McMullan was one day giving a team talk in the dressing room, using cups on a table to add emphasis to his tactical planning. Smith burst into the room and, after surveying the scene for no more than a few seconds, sent table and crockery crashing to the floor. Pointing to the pitch, he exclaimed, "That is where you play football, not in here," and walked straight out again. Waring, himself no great lover of authority, never saw eye to eye with his manager, and the two men once had a lengthy argument over whether the legendary centre-forward was fit enough to take part in a training session. Spying the manager was carrying a sheaf of papers, Waring shouted at him, "You're only the office boy around here!" and there is no doubt McMullan was regarded in a similar light by many of the Villa Park hierarchy.

It must be acknowledged here that most clubs took a similar view of their team manager during this period. At around the same time as McMullan arrived at Villa Park, league champions Arsenal appointed George Allison to succeed the legendary figure of Herbert Chapman, who had died a few months previous. Allison's title was secretary-manager, and he came from a background in journalism and broadcasting, with no previous managerial experience. That the pre-eminent club of the era, with three league championships in four years to their name, could make such an appointment was further proof that the major clubs of the time still regarded the team manager as no more than a minor figure.

During his first summer in charge at Villa Park, McMullan made several purchases. Jimmy McLuckie, the manager's old team-mate at Manchester City, arrived as a defensive half-back whilst up front George Beeson was signed as the season was getting underway. What was to prove a far more significant signing, though, was that of a youngster from non-league Berkhamstead Town by the name of Frank Broome. Unknown he may have been upon his arrival, but Broome gave many years of sterling service to the Villa.

Despite the new arrivals, Villa failed to improve on the previous season's league position. 1934-35 saw them finish in thirteenth spot for the second season in a row, with fewer goals scored and many more conceded than during the previous campaign. Off the field, it was reported the club had made a loss of £2,515, the first time such a situation had occurred, save for the war years when league football had not been played. Whatever worries supporters may have had during the summer of 1935, they were nothing compared to the shocks that they would endure over the coming twelve months.

There may have been a bigger sensation in the history of football than the relegation of Aston Villa in May 1936. Possibly there has not. That the most famous club in the world was destined for the second division was a story that at the time was unparalleled. The way in which they went down just added to the drama.

The defensive strength upon which the Villa's post-war stability had been built had gone. Gibson, Talbot and Tate, the most famous and effective half-back line of the period between the wars, had been broken up and their replacements were just not good enough to cope with the forwards of the day. The team changed formation to accommodate a third defensive back, yet this was seen as the wrong move. It certainly did nothing to overcome the Villa's defensive frailties. Villa conceded 110 goals in 42 league games and it seemed every first division centre-forward regarded a game with the Villa as his own personal benefit match. W.G. Richardson scored four for the Albion at Villa Park when the Villa's oldest rivals ran out 7-0 winners. "The final humiliation of the once great Aston Villa," was how the Birmingham Mail saw it. Yet there was still more to come.

Spurred on by the local press, the Villa board had authorised the spending of what was then a colossal amount in order to preserve Villa's first division status. Over £35,000 was spent in three months as the club battled in vain to reverse the slide. Unfortunately, for Jimmy McMullan, this investment came too late. He had resigned his position in October, following a 4-2 defeat away at Leeds, ironically a game which onlookers described as one of Villa's best performances of the season. This had left the club lying bottom-but-one in the first division and they slumped to the foot of the table on the following Saturday after a 6-2 thrashing at home to Grimsby Town, for whom Pat Glover scored four.

The Sports Argus contributor 'Linesman' added a touch of mystery to the departure of McMullan, when he wrote on the Saturday following the manager's departure, "Here one treads indelicate ground, and the motives which influenced the writer from announcing the fact a week ago still militate against any comment on the subject of his regime." As has often been the case, there was obviously more to the resignation of the Villa manager than first met the eye. Few were surprised at his departure, though, and supporters made little comment on McMullan's leaving. Readers' letters to the editor that local newspapers had been publishing with ever-increasing frequency during the season reserved what criticism there was for the directors, who were still seen as the men who picked the team. In particular, they faulted the way in which players had been played out of position and the team appeared to have been built around centre-half Jimmy Allen, who had been chosen to take the third defensive role adopted with such singular lack of success.

McMullan, one of the finest half-backs of his day, was not the last great player unable to make the transition to top-level management. After leaving the Villa he spent some time at Notts County, then moved to Sheffield Wednesday in November 1937. At the foot of the second division on his arrival, Wednesday stayed up and just failed to get promotion two seasons later. With the outbreak of war, McMullan was kept on as part-time manager at Hillsborough, and his contract was finally terminated in 1942. At the end of the war, McMullan was unable to find further employment in football and he drifted out of the game, dying in November 1964 at the age of 69.

Jimmy McMullan is a largely forgotten figure at the Villa. As the club's first manager, he deserves his place in history, and in playing a part in their first relegation his name should perhaps live on in infamy. In truth, McMullan made little impact during his eighteen months at Villa Park. His match record was a poor one. Moreover, his relationship with the players was not all it could have been and his transfer purchases, although extensive, were unable to keep the Villa in division one. It is unkind to say that McMullan was solely responsible for relegation - his time as manager coincided with the start of Villa's distress, a precursor of the slow, steady decline that would almost end in extinction three decades later. But regardless of who was to blame, the buck now stopped at the manager's office door. Maybe the Villa board had realised that whatever his other duties may have included, the manager was now always available to take the blame for any failings on the pitch.

With McMullan gone, Villa now had to look for his replacement. Today, a club would appoint a successor within days, no doubt following a media frenzy surrounding the appointment. Back in the thirties, though, they did things a little differently.

2

Jimmy Hogan
August 1936 - September 1939

Post-the departure of Jimmy McMullan, things reverted to 'normal' around Villa Park. The team was once more in the hands of an alliance consisting of directors and secretary Billy Smith plus Frank Barson, who had returned to the club as coach of the Combination side, and had been handed further duties when the manager left.

However, these three men were unable to turn round the fortunes of the team, and relegation was confirmed with a defeat at Villa Park in the final game of the season. Blackburn Rovers were already doomed to relegation, but they still managed to run out 4-2 winners. Both teams were the only original members of the Football League to have been in the top flight since its formation in 1888.

The local press regarded the Villa's relegation as a cataclysmic event, far outweighing trivialities elsewhere such as the Spanish Civil War and Italy's invasion of Abysinnia, both of which acted as precursors to the Second World War. "A civic, if not a national, disaster" was how the Birmingham Mail had put it and there was plenty of comment from supporters of other clubs, who pointed out that much less had been made when Birmingham, Wolves and the Albion had been relegated in previous years. It has to be said that they had a point. Modern supporters of the other local sides complain now that the Midlands press is biased towards the Villa; quite what they would have made of the events of 1936 does not bear thinking about. As relegation grew ever more imminent, all attempts at impartiality were forgotten as the Mail and Argus concentrated on the Villa's fight to stay in the first division.

This did not, however, prevent supporters from rounding on the board in the most vigorous manner. The Shareholders Association called an Extraordinary General Meeting at which they moved for two extra members to be appointed to the board. This proposal failed, but at the club's AGM the following week they were successful in the removal from the board of chairman J.E. Jones. Former player Howard Spencer had resigned as a director a few days earlier, on the grounds of ill-health, and became a vice-president of the club. One of the vacant seats was filled by Chris Buckley, while the other saw the return of the grand old man of Villa Park, Fredrick Rinder. This magnificent servant to the club had originally been forced to resign as a director in 1924, following criticism of his spending on the Trinity Road stand. At that time, he had stated; "One should never forget that we are not talking about a mere business. This is the Aston Villa Football Club and it deserves nothing short of the best. I hope and pray the new brood can give it that."

Rinder's return at the age of 79 was proof Villa had been led in his absence by men who failed to understand the full implications of their position. Rinder had always been of the opinion that Aston Villa were no ordinary club and could not be run as such. His initial successors had, it was said, "invited disaster by attempting to fit square pegs into round holes". Rinder immediately sought to rectify matters by appointing a manager who would share his vision.

During the months following Jimmy McMullan's resignation, the board had been in no hurry to appoint a successor. They had, though, assured the expectant supporters that they wanted "a first-class manager to take charge of everything at Villa Park." On August 15th 1936 they got their wish.

Jimmy Hogan is arguably the most important figure in the development of European football. As a coach he was without parallel, as an innovator he provided the inspiration for the central European teams that came to overtake England in the period immediately following the Second World War.

Born in Nelson, Lancashire, in October 1882, Hogan harboured thoughts of training for the priesthood before becoming a footballer. He first signed at the age of eighteen for his home-town club, then in the Lancashire Combination, before moving to Rochdale and then Burnley, of the second division, in 1903. Two years later he moved to Fulham and was instrumental in their Southern League successive championship wins of 1906 and 1907, after the second of which they were promoted to the Football League. He then played for Swindon Town and Bolton Wanderers, with whom he won a second division championship medal, before moving in 1910 to the Dutch side Dordrecht where, at the age of twenty-eight, he became the youngest Englishman to coach a foreign side.

After two years at Dordrecht, during which time he also coached the Dutch national side, Hogan returned briefly to Bolton, who still held his player registration. In 1912 he had met Hugo Meisl, the son of a wealthy Jewish businessman from Vienna. Meisl had left the family business to pursue his love of football and became a leading figure in the Austrian Football Federation, offering Hogan the post of coaching the Austrian Olympic squad.

Hogan was an immediate success, his scientific approach to training striking a chord with the university students who made up the majority of Austria's top footballers. When the First World War broke out, Hogan and his family were interned. His pregnant wife and two children were allowed to return home in March 1915, but Hogan stayed in Vienna under virtual house arrest until 1916, when he was sent to Budapest to coach the MTK club who subsequently won every Hungarian championship from 1917 until 1925.

When the war ended Hogan returned to Britain, only to be treated icily by the FA, who regarded him as somewhat of a traitor despite having been, in effect, a prisoner of war during hostilities. After a time out of the game, Hogan once more headed for the continent, spending time in Switzerland as coach to Young Boys and then Lausanne. He then moved to Hungaria (the new name of MTK) in Budapest, before being invited to become head coach with the Central German Football Association. That he was accepted in such a role less than a decade after the end of the war spoke volumes for the reputation he enjoyed throughout Europe. Hogan went on to coach the Dresden side with considerable success; one of the young players he unearthed being Helmut Schoen, who later managed West Germany to the 1974 World Cup. However, the rise of fascism in Germany was now causing Hogan some problems, not least because of his friendship with Hugo Meisl, and he moved to France where he coached Racing Club de France before returning to Lausanne in protest at his players' lack of professionalism

By 1932 Hogan was asked to coach the Austrian national side, now known as the wunderteam, for a game against England that they unluckily lost 4-3 at Stamford Bridge. It was during this time that Hogan watched several English games and noted that the tactic of long balls to the centre-forward was inevitably stifled by any reasonably competent defender.

Hogan spent the 1934-35 season as manager of Fulham. However he found that his methods were, as yet, unwelcome in his homeland. English football was still convinced that footballers were born, rather than made, and that time between matches was better spent improving players' fitness than improving their ball skills. Hogan suffered from appendicitis during this time, and while recovering found himself sacked by Fulham in February 1935.

Returning to Austria, Hogan was asked to coach the country's amateur team for the 1936 Olympic Games in Berlin, where they lost 2-1 to Italy in the final. Frederick Rinder was in attendance in his capacity as FA representative with the British football team and wasted no time in persuading Hogan where his future lay.

On August 15th 1936 Jimmy Hogan was appointed Villa's second manager, on a three-year contract at £1,000 per annum. He had also been sought by the Arsenal board, and it was proof of the respect Villa still commanded that, despite relegation, their managerial target had chosen the club in preference to the opportunity of managing the foremost team of the era. Indeed, on the day he began work at Villa Park, Hogan stated that, "In all my years on the Continent I have had two examples of classic English sides - Newcastle United and Aston Villa." Fredrick Rinder, for his part, said "I would stake my reputation" - and Rinder's reputation was greater than that of any Villa man before or since - "on the new manager".

Of the new appointment, full-back George Cummings would later say, "It was a shock when Villa appointed Jimmy Hogan." New chairman Fred Normansell declared that Hogan was in sole charge of the team and scouting. It was also announced that James Whittall, formerly of Arsenal, would now also be scouting for the Villa and that Frank Barson would revert to training the youth teams. Hubert Bourne would replace Harry Cooch as first-team trainer. The manager's job was steadily growing in importance.

The new manager's first training session with his charges, held at the Alexander Sports Ground in Perry Barr, was a revelation to those used to the traditional English methods of playing. The Birmingham Mail reporter who had been invited along wrote in wonder that Hogan, belying his 53 years, had proved himself capable of masterly ball control, which few of his players could emulate. His secret, it was said, was that he did not ask of his players anything that he could not do himself. However, he stressed that he was not teaching them. "Of course they know how to do it. The system

I adopt is to get into the training the type of work which occurs in every game of football."

This may sound obvious now, but to players used to an endless routine of fitness training interspersed with the odd tactical lecture, it was revolutionary. Warming to his theme, Hogan explained the formula that had made him the greatest coach in Europe. "Then of course, there is the tactical aside of the game, in which a player has two things to think of when in possession of the ball – where to put the ball and where to put himself. The great difference in modern English football and Continental football is that every move is made with one of two ideas - where to be defensively and how to get the ball into the opponents' goal by the shortest route possible." Such talk found favour with the Mail, who spoke of the need for the Villa to find a style which suited them and for all the club's players to reflect credit on the club - shades of the philosophy of Ramsay and Grierson which had won so much over forty years previous.

George Cummings thoroughly approved of the new manager: "Jimmy's methods certainly brought a breath of fresh air to Villa Park and he certainly gained the respect of all the players. He introduced the Friday team talks when we'd all get together and talk about the previous match and the one coming up. We were all encouraged to chip in and there were no holds barred on occasions." Cummings also found that the manager was willing to practice what he preached. "One day he came to training wearing a brand-new tracksuit. We had a practice game and he was running down the wing with the ball so I charged him into the mud. He got up and wanted to know why I'd done it. I pointed out that he'd always told us to get rid of the ball first time so it was hardly my fault if he wasn't following his own instructions."

Eric Houghton was equally enthusiastic. "I wouldn't have missed my spell under Jimmy Hogan for anything," said the man who thought Hogan worth employing even in his later years. "His teaching and coaching was always based on common sense."

Despite his obvious tactical genius, Hogan was not an immediate success at Villa Park. Supporters expecting an immediate return to the first division were boosted by a return of ten points from the first six games of the 1936-37 season. However, the team failed to cash in on such a start and eventually finished the season in ninth place in the table. Although many aired their misgivings at the appointment of Hogan, they were silenced when Villa celebrated 1937-38, the fiftieth anniversary of the Football League they had founded, by running away with the second division championship. A good FA Cup run saw the team get to the semi-final for a record fourteenth time, while a Villa Park average gate in excess of 42,000 proved that the good times were returning.

During the summer of 1938 Villa were invited to take part in a tour of Germany. With Hogan in charge of the team it was only natural that they should be asked to play in Europe. However, this tour would go down in Villa Park folklore. Over the years, the true picture of what exactly happened when the Villa players were asked to give the Nazi salute has become cloudy. It appears that in the first game of the tour they were asked to give the salute and refused, claiming that they were a club side and not a national one. Coming the day after an England team, which included Villa player Frank Broome, had given the salute prior to an international, the players' stance caused a diplomatic storm. After virtually being ordered by the FA and the Foreign Office to give the salute in their next match they did so - after a fashion. As Eric Houghton explained many years later, in Rogan Taylor's book Kicking and Screaming, "The next time they said we'd got to give the Nazi salute, you see, so we had a meeting and said that, for peace and quietness we'd give the Nazi salute. At the next place, I think it was Stuttgart, both teams gave the Nazi salute, so we went to the centre of the field and gave them the two-finger salute and they cheered like mad. They thought it was all right." Despite modern attempts to cast the players and the club in a poor light over the incident, they deserved the highest praise for the way in they manoeuvred out of a potential problem.

Villa's first season back in the top flight saw the team finish in a creditable twelfth position, although the season was blighted by the death on Christmas Day 1938 of Frederick Rinder. The future was certainly bright; the team was young and contained some of the most promising players in the game. With Jimmy Hogan's coaching methods providing extra impetus, the general feeling around Villa Park was that the club could go on to emulate at least the talented, if ultimately unsuccessful, side of the early thirties. In the words of Alex Massie, "The relegation side of 1935-36 was the worst I ever played in. And the promotion team of two years later was the best." Hogan himself, writing in the final Villa News & Record of the season, talked of how much the players had learned during their first season back in the top division, and spoke optimistically that "during the next two years we should reap the reward of our labours and be among the league and Cup honours again." Indeed, Hogan was later to describe his Villa side as "the best I have ever coached."

However, possibly in retaliation for Eric Houghton & co showing what they had thought of him twelve months earlier, Adolf Hitler had other ideas. The outbreak of war saw the abandonment of the league programme after just three games of the 1939-40 season and the Villa directors announced that the club would close down for the duration. This announcement was greeted unfavourably by the press and supporters – many of whom pointed out that other clubs, most notably the Blues, were continuing to operate, albeit in reduced circumstances and by playing friendly matches against non-league opposition.

But no matter. The Villa were temporarily out of business and the squad moved either into the forces or to do other essential war work. With no players to manage, Hogan found himself out of a job and moved back to Burnley, who employed him in whatever back-room position he could find himself useful.

Jimmy Hogan's record as Villa manager was a highly respectable one. He must also go down as the great 'If Only' manager of Aston Villa. If only he had been appointed a few years earlier, then that first, earth-shattering relegation of 1936 might never have happened. If only the Second World War had not broken up his promising young team...

When the War ended, Jimmy Hogan first embarked upon a lecture tour of the country, spent a brief period with Brentford, and then went on to coach Celtic. There he ran up against the problem he had always encountered during his time in Britain - namely attempting to teach new ideas to players who were convinced the methods they had always used were the best, even though Celtic had spent the previous season struggling against relegation. "Jimmy was outstanding," recalls Tommy Docherty, then making his name as a wing-half with the Glasgow club. "He would demonstrate the sort of stuff he wanted you to do, always working on the skill side of football. He wasn't a great player but he was a great coach."

Hogan left Celtic after two fruitless years and spent the last period of his career back at Villa Park, where he coached the youth team from October 1953 before retiring in 1959, at the age of 76. Dennis Jackson was one of the players who felt the benefit of Hogan's experience. "I think the Villa gave him a bit of work to help him out. He spent a lot of his time in Eric Houghton's office, working in there. Then again, you could tell just what a massive wealth of knowledge he had. I used to go round the schools with him, when he was coaching the young lads, and the way he talked to them you could tell that here was a man who had been a great coach. I used to wonder what it must have been like to work with him at his peak. He was a lovely feller, a man who knew everything there was to know about training footballers."

Sadly, Hogan's legacy was felt far away from Villa Park. On the day in November 1953 that Hungary signalled to the world that English dominance of the game was over with a 6-3 victory at Wembley, Jimmy Hogan was the proudest spectator in the ground. He attended in the company of a group of Villa youth players who he had taken to the game in the knowledge that they would receive a footballing masterclass. He was not mistaken. The finest team in the world had been influenced by a former manager of Aston Villa; the pity was they didn't play in claret and blue.

One of Hogan's successors as Villa manager, Josef Venglos, said of Hogan, "He was a great influence on European football. He was one of the first men to strike the balance between the physical English training and the tactical side of the game that European coaches were working on."

In retirement Hogan moved back to the area of his birth and acted as a scout for the Villa who, to their credit, had continued to pay Hogan a pension from the time he had left the club at the outbreak of World War Two. In 1970, the 88 year-old Hogan was in attendance when Villa beat Manchester United in the second leg of the League Cup semi-final at Villa Park.

In his later years, Hogan finally received the accolades due to such a genius. Matt Busby called him a footballing legend, while Eric Houghton's description was of, "A great man in every way." After suffering ill-health, Jimmy Hogan died in Burnley in January 1974 at the age of 91. Thus ended the remarkable career of a manager respected throughout Europe yet who, as the saying goes, was for so long truly a prophet without honour in his own country.

3

Alex Massie

August 1945 - July 1949

A classic example of a late developer in football, Alex Massie was born in Possilbank, Glasgow, on March 13th 1905. His early playing career took in Partick Thistle, Ayr United and Bury, but after failing to make the grade with any of these, he moved to America to play for Bethlehem Steel of Pennsylvania. After a spell in the USA, during which time he achieved the notable feat of playing in three leagues in two years, Massie found himself playing in Ireland, spending a season with Dublin Dolphins, before asking Hearts for a trial in 1930.

This was to be the turning point in his career, for Massie's time at Tynecastle saw him become captain of Scotland before moving to Villa for a fee of £6,500 during the unsuccessful spending spree the club embarked upon during the 1935-36 season. Massie would have had an immediate idea of the task facing him when, in his second match for the Villa, Ted Drake scored all Arsenal's goals in their 7-1 victory at Villa Park.

Massie settled at right-half in the Villa side and gave sterling service both pre-war and during the war years when Villa played a series of friendlies and then took part in the wartime competitions that culminated with the team winning the Football League (North) War Cup in 1944. In total he played eighteen times for Scotland. "The best one-footed player I've ever seen and one of the best skippers I played under," was the verdict of long-serving Villa player Harry Parkes. During wartime the club had reverted to the system of directors running the club with the help of the first-team trainer, the long-serving Hubert Bourne. However, the resumption of peacetime football saw the club in need of a team manager again and the job was given, by popular acclaim, to Alex Massie who, at the age of 42, was still playing for the Villa in the Football League (North) competition that had been intended to act as a stop-gap until the league proper could be restored.

It was announced that Massie was to become team manger on 22nd August 1945. "The first hint I received was a conversation with Fred Normansell when he said to me 'Billy Smith, you and I could run Villa fine'. I didn't go into the job with my eyes closed. I knew I had landed the post for services rendered on the field," he was later to say. Ten days later Massie played his last competitive game, at home to Luton in the league. The league proper resumed in August 1946. Concern had been expressed as early as 1940 that the Villa team would be too old after the war to make a real impact and this proved to be the case. In addition to an ageing team, Massie also faced the twin problems of too much interference from directors and the lack of authority that often afflicts former players when they come to take charge of their former team-mates. With these he had varying success. As he put it, "I thought I could break down the barriers. I was wrong. The directors, especially Fred Normansell, thought I had enough authority, but I never had full control."

Yet Massie certainly appeared to enjoy the job, at least in the early stages of managing the team in their old first division slot. "I think I prefer managing to playing," he told the local press, adding that there had only been one or two occasions when he wished he had never been given the job.

Concern had already been expressed that Massie was being thwarted in the job he had been given. One supporter had written to the Sports Argus, asking "Is Manager Massie given a free hand to manage and choose the team, and if not, why not?" The local press were unable to state to what extent Massie was finding the board interfering with his job, but they agreed that the manger should stand or fall by his own judgement. When the league programme was finally finished in June – bad weather during the winter months had necessitated an extension to the season – Villa had finished in eighth place, having won 18 of their 42 games. This was a reasonable position, with the team generally doing better away from home than they did at Villa Park.

Nobody, though, was particularly convinced that the club was moving on the right lines. As the 1947-48 season started, there were worries about the average age of the team, and it was pointed out that Villa had eighteen players on their books who had been with them when war broke out, far and away the largest number of any club in the first division. "Villa need practically a new team," reported the Argus as an early season game ended in defeat.

That's not to say that Massie was complacent. Indeed, he travelled the country searching for new players, and in particular drawing on his many contacts north of the border as the need for new talent grew ever more obvious. Yet despite no great investment, Villa finished a respectable sixth in the first division, and the club recorded a healthy profit of £26,000. But still the doubts remained that, with no new signings, the team would begin to struggle.

And struggle, they most certainly did. By mid-September there were serious concerns that the team would be relegated, and nobody was kidding themselves that if they did go down, that it was the sort of slump that could be dismissed as a temporary blip as had happened in 1936. If the Villa found themselves in the second division, they would languish for some considerable time. Supporters were up in arms as the team slumped into the bottom four although, as ever, the directors took the blame and the manager's performance generally passed without comment. There was a lack of character about the team and on the field they looked slow both in thought and deed.

It was not as though the Villa weren't trying to sign players – in one week in September alone they made unsuccessful enquiries about six potential new signings. But they were having to face the unpalatable fact that the name Aston Villa was no longer enough to force clubs into parting with their brightest stars. The days when Villa could handpick the players they wanted, and be able to afford the inflated fees invariably asked of such a supposedly wealthy club, were over.

Eventually Villa were able to move into the transfer market, spending over £50,000 in total on Con Martin from Leeds, Welsh international Ivor Powell from Queens Park Rangers and former Blues winger Ambrose Mulraney from Kidderminster Harriers. However, these new signings failed to have the desired effect and the Villa slumped to bottom-but-one in the table early on in February.

Villa then made their final big-money signing of the season, forward Colin Gibson from Newcastle. The Argus bemoaned the fact that Villa were having to resort to spending heavily; "What has happened to the old Villa knack of finding and developing young players who develop to greatness?" they asked. However, Gibson proved to be the player Villa were looking for and 26 points from the final 17 games saw them race up the table to finish in tenth position - a position that seemed impossible a few months earlier. The first team were rewarded by the directors for their turnaround in form with a post-season trip to Ireland, which was a huge success both with the players and the Irish crowds who treated the arriving Villa party like royalty.

It was revealed during the summer that despite record receipts of over £135,000, the club had recorded a loss of £1,400, in contrast to the large profits made in the two previous seasons. It must be said though, that such a deficit was a small price to pay for keeping the Villa in the first division.

Whether through financial constraints, or because they thought that sufficient funds had been spent during the previous season, the board did not sanction any more signings during the close-season of 1949. This action, or rather inaction, aroused little comment either in the press or amongst supporters, so it came as a bombshell when the Birmingham Mail of 30th July announced that Alex Massie had resigned as Villa manager. It was later revealed that he had handed in his letter of resignation to the board a month earlier, but had been asked to stay on to oversee players' trials which had been taking place during that time.

It was widely reckoned that, rather than a sudden decision, Massie's resignation was the culmination of several months of friction between him and the board, revolving round the influence that the directors wished to exert upon the playing staff. In announcing his resignation, Massie stated, "The Villa board have treated me generously and I am parting from the club on amicable terms. I wish the club and players every success in the future." However, he went on to say that his departure was "The outcome of differences on matters of policy." Massie was certainly annoyed by the way in which Trevor Ford was repeatedly going over his head to chairman Fred Normansell. There had also been a difference of opinions between the manager and director Joe Broughton over the time players were allowed to stay up during a training break at Saltburn some seven months earlier.

The club were eager to stress that they remained on good terms with their former manager, and that they were not as yet inviting applications for the vacancy. Their statement that they "may not have another manager" was seen by many as proof that the board had been attempting to reassert their influence over playing matters and that this was the reason for Massie's departure. For their part, supporters offered few opinions over the news, with one long-time follower of the club commenting that the club had won all its honours without a manager, so there seemed little point in appointing a successor to Massie. That during his reign the Villa had never looked like adding to their trophy haul would no doubt have put further pressure on to the manager's shoulders.

Commenting on his future, Massie said, "I do not know whether I will stay in football or not. I have had a great feeling of relief now that I have handed over the burden of team manager at Villa Park". Again, this was seen as a veiled attack on those who had made his time in the manager's office at Villa Park a difficult one. In fact, Massie went on to spend some time commenting on football matters for the Birmingham Mail before becoming manager of Third Division (South) side Torquay United from 1950-1951.

Massie moved to Hereford, where he took charge of Hereford United, then of the Southern League during 1952. His last position in football came when he moved to Welwyn Garden City, whose amateur side he coached for a time. Massie died in September 1977, at the age of 72.

Massie had been a fine footballer. Like his predecessor in the Villa hot seat, Jimmy McMullan, he was another of the generation of Scottish ball artists who had thrilled the crowds when moving south. Similarly, he found the transition from dressing room to manager's office a hard one to make. As George Cummings said many years later, "Some say it was the biggest mistake of Alex's life to take over the Villa managership."

Massie was not helped by the fact that he had come by the job at an inopportune time. The Villa's top players had lost their best years to the war and their replacements were not of comparable quality. His transfer dealings were on the whole good ones; Con Martin, to give just one example, going on to become one of the finest Villa servants of the immediate post-war period. But Villa were finding it difficult to attract anything like the quality of player they had signed before the war. It may have been imperceptible to all but the expert eye, but Villa under Alex Massie were well and truly on the slide.

Massie's breed of artistic football was also lost on the Villa crowds of the time, who wanted to see more strong-arm stuff as a way of getting the club out of relegation trouble. Such a philosophy was anathema to Alex Massie.

Despite such indifferent league form, Massie was Villa manager when they took part in two of the most memorable games ever seen at Villa Park. Each round of the FA Cup was played over two legs in 1945-46 and the quarter-final saw Villa facing highly-fancied Derby County. Villa lost 3-4, with Derby going through on aggregate after a 1-1 draw at the Baseball Ground in the return leg; the tie was notable for the crowd at Villa Park – 76,588, a record that will almost certainly never be broken. Two years later Villa went out of the competition in the third round, losing 4-6 to Manchester United at home in a match that is regarded by those present as the greatest cup-tie ever played. Massie's half-time team talk was reported to have consisted merely of the statement "We're going to lose but let's show them we can·play some decent football".

Massie also suffered interference from the board, who had not yet come to terms with the fact that the club's power was on the wane. "I often had more say in running the side when I was skipper than as manager", he stated on one occasion. This was the era when such forceful managerial characters as Arthur Rowe of Spurs and Manchester United's Matt Busby were beginning to prove that the days when the manager was a minor figure at a football club were over. Yet the Villa board seemed at times to regard Massie as little more than a lecturer on tactics, and chief scout. Frank Moss told the story of how Massie said to him one Friday afternoon, "I suppose they'll let me pin the team sheet up this week". Many years later, at a Lions Club forum, Massie was asked who his best signing was. The forthright reply came back, "Don't you mean who was the best player that was bought for me?" Massie stated that he had little influence in transfer policy; "Virtually all transfers in my four years were conducted by Billy Smith and Fred Normansell," and in fact only found out that the Villa had bought Ivor Powell for a record fee when asked for his comments by a newspaper reporter.

Looking back, Alex Massie was not one of the most successful managers the Villa have ever employed. His success on the field was limited and during his time in charge the club steadily slipped further behind those who, not so many years previous, they would have regarded as inferior. His signings had little long-term success and the club's youth policy was undergoing one of its many periods when discoveries of genuine Villa class were few and far between. He had inherited a club struggling to rebuild after the Second World War and his successor still faced a large reconstruction job. Yet for all his apparent lack of success, Alex Massie would not be the first Villa manager to have to struggle with a board who, well-meaning though they undoubtedly were, had found it hard to come to terms with running a football club in a rapidly-changing world. "I was bitter at the time, but now I don't blame the directors," Massie would say many years later. "They had always run the club and couldn't visualise any other set-up." And neither would he be the last to have to cope with such a problem.

4

George Martin

December 1950 - August 1953

Villa began the 1949-50 season without a manager. In truth, the directors were in no particular hurry to appoint one. "The matter will simply fade away unless and until Villa strike the rocks," was the prophetic comment of a Sports Argus writer who gave the world-weary sigh of one who had seen it all before. The board seemed to give the impression that the club's great triumphs had occurred while they (or rather, their predecessors) had been in sole charge; therefore it followed that harking back to tradition would see a return to their previous glories. They had, of course, failed to realise that football had changed dramatically during the intervening half a century. Veteran trainer Hurbert Bourne was still involved with the first-team, with Ivor Powell replacing the long-serving George Cummings as captain.

Villa finished the season in twelfth place in the league. They had not been particularly bad, neither had they shown signs of anything resembling progress. After a third round FA Cup defeat at the hands of Middlesbrough, the Argus's ever-astute Argus Junior had cautioned that "Villa will be courting disaster unless the directors brush up on their planning and remodel their policy on long-term lines." Still there was no call for a manager, although a letter from a supporter who signed himself 'True Villain' asked, "When are the directors going to have a manager again?"

The AGM was a fairly straightforward affair. Chairman Fred Normansell was returned unopposed, as were the other members of the board. There was some disquiet at the team's performances, with one shareholder asking why the club did not employ a coach to provide greater tactical awareness; but on the whole, those in attendance were reasonably happy. A profit of £15,000 was declared and club president, Sir Patrick Hannon, stated that members of the club were "a body of friends working in harmony". Yet again the image given to the world was one of complacency and a reluctance to bring in fresh manpower and ideas.

The start of the 1950-51 season was not greeted with great enthusiasm and trouble soon arrived at Villa Park. Despite a reasonable
start to the season, results soon started going badly. It became clear
that the Villa faced a relegation battle, and the local press were once
again keen to pin the blame on a board of directors seen as out of
touch and set in their ways. They were reminded that it had been
over twelve months since the resignation of Alex Massie, who, it was
said, had "little scope while supposed to be in command", and that
events in the meantime had not been a good advertisement either
for the club, or for the idea that they could do without a manager.

The board still gave the impression they believed the traditions of
the Villa were proof enough that a manager was not needed. The
supporters had other ideas – and not only did they clamour for a
team boss, they also demanded one who would be more than the
type of figurehead the club had appointed in the past. There were
calls for a boycott of home games, which were not helped by the
transfer listing and subsequent departure of Trevor Ford, the Villa's
finest forward since the war. That Ford had been sold, to
Sunderland for £30,000, was bad enough. That he had asked for a
transfer as he felt that the Villa were on a downward slope, was further proof that the club was heading for serious trouble.

Reports that Dave Mangnall of Queens Park Rangers had been
approached to take the manager's job were denied by Fred
Normansell, who insisted that the directors were not even considering making such an appointment. This was the club's only public
pronouncement on the position, which was in keeping with their
policy of secrecy. In fact, so secretive were they that they had only
themselves to blame when they faced yet more accusations of complacency and incompetence.

So it came as something of a surprise to outsiders when it was
announced on December 15th 1950 that Newcastle United manager
George Martin was to become the manager of Aston Villa. It was
later made public that negotiations with his former club had been
taking place for three weeks.

Like two of his three predecessors, Martin was a Scotsman. 48
years old, he hailed from Hamilton and had started his career with
his home-town team, later moving to Hull City, Everton and
Middlesbrough before finishing his playing days with Luton Town.

Martin's chief claim to fame at this point was that he had scored in Luton's 12-0 win over Bristol Rovers in 1936, when Joe Payne had set a record by scoring ten of Luton's goals.

Martin became manager of Luton at the end of World War Two, moving to Newcastle in 1947 and leading the St James' Park side to promotion to the first division in his first season there. However, Martin had been working without a contract at Newcastle for several months and his departure was no great shock.

In a complete break with their accepted practice, the board had announced that Martin was to be given the title of club manager, rather than be called team manager, as had his predecessors. This may seem a minor point now, but at the time it was a revolutionary step. For the first time a Villa manager was given wider responsibilities than those of merely looking after the playing affairs of the first team, although it was mentioned that the board would still have to approve his team selections. It was hoped that such approval would invariably be a formality.

The announcement that Martin was to have wider powers than any previous Villa manger was regarded as a progressive one. It certainly seemed to quell disquiet amongst supporters, who could not have failed to be impressed by Martin's words upon taking the Villa Park hot seat. The new incumbent spoke well of the Villa and of the club's traditions. Indeed, such was his obvious affection for life in Aston that the Birmingham Mail pointed out how the club was held in greater esteem elsewhere and how this seemed to have a greater effect on other clubs than it did the Villa. Recalling his playing career, when he had scored on his every appearance at Villa Park, Martin pointed out that he had always enjoyed playing at what he considered to be his lucky ground.

George Martin's management philosophy recalled that of previous Villa boss Jimmy Hogan. "It's a ball game, so practice with the ball as much as possible. Bring variety into the game – avoid repetition in style and method," he advised. "A competitive element is important and never be afraid to try out new ideas." The Villa supporters, who had feared that yet again the club was falling behind the times, warmed to these words, although Martin offered further caution. "I am not a magician," he warned, "There must be co-operation, I'm a great believer in team spirit, and hard graft will help the Villa improve."

The local press approved of Martin's appointment. They gave the usual warnings that the manager should be left to manage, and asked for him to be given time by the supporters, pointing out that there was much preliminary work to be done before results would be seen. Martin was under no illusion as to the size of his task. "I'm not afraid of it," he said, knowing that he was charged with the two-pronged task of saving the club from relegation as well as re-introducing the stylish football for which Villa had traditionally been known. It was noted that Newcastle under Martin had been renowned as one of the best footballing sides in the first division.

Villa had been in the bottom five in the table when Martin was appointed; just a single point away from the relegation places. His arrival saw a slight improvement in the team's fortunes, aided by the signing in March 1951 of Danny Blanchflower, one of the finest Villa players of the post-war period. Martin had been a long-time admirer of Blanchflower while still at Newcastle, and persuaded the Villa board to pay £14,000 to Barnsley for the services of the Northern Ireland international wing-half. At this point Villa supporters were convinced that their team was doomed. In fact, it was said that those at the club were more convinced of impending relegation than were neutral observers, who reckoned that the Villa had little chance of going down. Obviously, the spectre of 1936 had burned deep into the Villa Park psyche.

A final league place of fifteenth was distorted by the fact that Villa finished top of four clubs on the same number of points, with relegation only avoided in the last two weeks of the season. No-one was under any illusion that Villa were anything other than also-rans in the first division, but there was relief that Martin had got them playing with a bit more of what could be described as the old Villa style.

His efforts in keeping Villa in the first division had led to Martin being described in glowing terms in some quarters. The Sports Argus referred to the "medicine man duties he had to fulfil," although they commented that Martin "does not claim to possess a magic wand" and warned Villa supporters that success would not come easily to the club. Looking to the future, the manager stated that he intended to improve the Villa's youth policy, and told supporters that the club had received over 200 applications for trials to be held at the start of the forthcoming season; the manager had personally sifted through each one.

There was some optimism at Villa Park as 1951-52 began, even though the manager sprang a surprise when playing his namesake, centre-half Con, in goal for the opening matches of the season when injuries ruled out all of the club's senior 'keepers. Despite this set-back, Villa made their best start to a season for 19 years, topping the table after ten matches. However, this form was not to last and amidst concerns that they lacked a quality goalkeeper and that the players were unable to last the full ninety minutes, the team slipped back into mid-table. There were the usual claims that the board were interfering in the work of the manager, with one supporter asking of Martin, "You know your job. What is holding you back? I cannot believe it is money." There was also an underlying problem at the club obvious to anyone who looked in depth.

Charles Harrold, writing in the Argus during March 1952, suggested that while the football at Villa Park was satisfactory, there was a disturbing lack of consolidation taking place. The Villa, he argued, were in a good position but the players were getting old and five or six new signings had to be made if the team were not to go backwards. Looking at Martin's reluctance to spend, he posed the question as to whether the Villa were as wealthy as everyone presumed and pointed out that a net figure in excess of £120,000 had been spent on players during six post-war years.

Martin, he wrote, had made a good start at Villa Park. He had brought about an improvement in discipline, team spirit and standard of play. However, he was reminded that the Midlands had waited over twenty years to see a Villa revival and that if such a thing were to happen, then there would be plenty more hard work to be carried out.

Supporter reaction to Harrold's article was mixed. Maurice Goodall, a supporter since 1897, pointed out he had "followed the fortunes of the mediocre teams which have so sullied the grand old claret and blue. I share your unease at the apparent lack of effort to consolidate while there is still time." However, 'Staunch Villa Fan' countered that team building takes time and that the present Villa side was "the best we have had for years". Which, bearing in mind the deficiencies of the post-war period, was not really saying much. Meanwhile, 'Tired Supporter' articulated the feelings that everyone who has ever followed a football club must at some time have thought, "I have finished supporting Villa until the present policy is altered." Others must have felt the same, because the attendance of 17,251 for the 4-1 victory over Fulham on 5th April 1952 was Villa's lowest gate for many years.

Villa finished the 1951-52 season in sixth place, although few gave the club much chance of improving on this position during the forthcoming season. The summer of 1952 was a quiet one on the transfer front, with Martin growing frustrated by the lack of available targets. One player who was signed by the Villa, though, was eighteen-year old Northern Irish winger Peter McParland, who joined the club from Newry.

The team got off to a poor start to the season, and supporter discontent was rife from the off. The team were being referred to as 'Aston Veteran's', and Villa Park was becoming known throughout Birmingham as the 'Hall of Memories'. Also coming in for some criticism was George Martin, and in particular his selection policy, which seemed to make repeated changes to allow players to alter positions.

Charles Harrold, again, in the Argus, continued his attacks on the club's hierarchy. In an article entitled 'The Tragedy of Aston Villa', he pointed out that the club had repeatedly failed to provide anything in the way of a long-term plan or even a strategy for improvement. He argued that whenever the Villa ran into problems, they usually managed to get themselves out of trouble - just about - then sat back with an air of complacency to await the next calamity.

Harrold was still a supporter of the manager; "George Martin brought discipline and inspiration, Villa avoided the drop and played their best football since the war but did not build." He added that such essentials to modern-day football such as a youth policy and coaching had passed the Villa and that no-one seemed to possess the will or the ability to change this state of affairs. He was certainly correct about the club's youth policy. Those formerly in charge in this area, veteran players George Cummings and Bob Iverson, had not been replaced when they had left the club and those who were left to oversee the club's juniors were so disillusioned that they had given up trying to do their jobs. The Villa, according to at least one director, were "not interested in juniors."

Unlike the previous season, Harrold's article provoked a series of letters from supporters who agreed with him. The club was badly in need of overhaul, although Martin escaped criticism. Comments from supporters in reply to the Argus article were similar to those aired about the Villa both before and after George Martin was in charge; "The trouble is above Mr Martin", "if given full control he could be one of the best managers in the country," "the directors must be held responsible," "the only thing that seems to matter is 'we've made a profit, so everything's alright'," and most succinct of all, "I had great hopes of Mr Martin, but I am afraid Mr Normansell still rules at Villa Park." There was even a report that one noted local coach had offered his services free of charge to help train the club's junior sides, but after his offer was accepted by Martin he was then turned down by chairman Fred Normansell, with the rejoinder that the Villa would in the future be buying all their players.

The general feeling was that Martin was not enjoying the control he had been promised at the time of his appointment, although it was believed that the job of running a club of Villa's stature was too much for one man and there were calls for the return of Jimmy Hogan to act as first team coach.

With Normansell still dominating the Villa Park scene, there were repeated calls for a boycott of Villa Park, as this, some supporters claimed, was the only way in which the board would take any notice of their unhappiness.

Charles Harrold, who by now was becoming the largest thorn in the side any Villa board had ever known, made a further attack when he stated that, "It is beyond my comprehension to understand how it is that men in the honoured position of officials of the club can let the state of affairs continue." As ever, he exempted Martin from criticism when he went on to say that, "It is no good haggling over who does what. The board have the final say and have Villa's failures in their hands."

Villa finished the season in eleventh place in the league. They lost more games than they won, but had the consolation that the football played was still of a reasonable standard. However, this did not save the club from renewed criticism throughout the summer. Supporters spoke of an air of defeatism that was hanging over the club, and the AGM was described as the longest, and liveliest, for years.

Responding to accusations of interference in transfers, Fred Normansell stated that, "No player has been signed without the full sanction of the board and George Martin is always consulted." The

club had made a negligible loss of just over £300 during the previous twelve months, although the board's reluctance to look ahead
was emphasised when the chairman pointed out that the club would
not be installing floodlights, as the £10,000 cost was thought to outweigh any advantages the new system might have possessed.

Asked to speak to the meeting, George Martin made an impromp-
tu speech in which he emphasised that the club had struggled to
overcome the long-term injuries suffered by Tommy Thompson and
Johnny Dixon, and that hundreds of boys were undertaking trials at
Villa during the summer. He finished with the words, "If you give
me time I don't think you will regret it," and was warmly received
by those present.

However, George Martin was not to be given any more time. On
17th August, it was announced that Martin had been dismissed as
Villa manager. In a statement he later released to the press, he stated that Fred Normansell had asked him to resign on 6th August.
When asked for a reason, Normansell said that Martin's "style did
not fit" but would not elaborate on this rather cryptic comment.
Martin refused to step down and demanded a meeting with the
board. This took place a week later, and again no further explanation was given as to why the board wanted Martin to resign. Once
more he refused to leave and was handed a letter from the club's
solicitors before the meeting had ended stating that his agreement
with the club had been terminated.

It had been clear for some time that Martin was at loggerheads
with the board. The Birmingham Mail's Tom Blunt spoke of several
off-the-record conversations he had had with Martin in the weeks
leading to his departure from Villa Park, in which he had made it
plain that he was not happy at Villa Park, although he stated that he
would not resign. It was believed that the speech he had made at the
AGM, where his logical approach and popularity had contrasted
with the board's inability to deal with criticism, had brought matters
to a head. Indeed, speculation was rife at that very meeting that Eric
Houghton had already been offered the job of Villa manager.

Public sympathy was with the dismissed manager, who was
regarded as a scapegoat for what was rapidly becoming a discredit-
ed Villa board. As J.P. Leeson wrote in a letter to the Argus, "During
the mediocre years the only constant factor has been the composi-
tion of the directorate." The Mail, meanwhile, wrote that Villa had

"dropped overboard a man who, with the right kind of encouragement would have put them back among the best".

Martin had been popular with both supporters and players. He had been a believer in working hard, and had been a close student of human nature. He was also talented in other areas, Villa's Irish international centre-forward Dave Walsh commenting that, "He might have become famous as a sculptor, and his singing attracted the attention of a top London impresario."

After leaving the Villa, Martin initially moved out of football, setting up in business in Liverpool. He returned to Luton in 1961 as chief scout, and managed the club from February 1965-November 1966 before retiring from football. He died in Luton in 1972, at the age of seventy.

Whilst undoubtedly a disciplinarian, he had never been a dictator, preferring to treat his players with respect rather than strictness. Indeed, Martin allowed those playing for the first-team to smoke in the run-up to a game, believing that engendering a good atmosphere amongst the team would outweigh the risks involved. He also took the players away for training during the season, Letchworth Hall in Hertfordshire being a favourite place for a change of scenery. However, the team did not always train in a completely professional manner. Peter McParland, for example, once said, " Players turned up at any old time and the way they trained was a farce – just walking around the track or even going for a smoke." Supporters, on the other hand, enjoyed the fact that Martin had got the team playing in the manner in which an Aston Villa team always should.

He did not, though, get on with all his players. Leslie Smith spoke of the time when he fell out with his manager after insisting that he was still unfit when Martin thought he was able to play. Their argument led to the England international asking for a transfer, to which Martin gave the unsympathetic reply, "Who would want you at your age?"

Martin's record as Villa manager was a reasonable one. He saved the team from relegation, then took them as high in the league as they had finished for almost two decades. His transfer dealings on the whole were good, and in Blanchflower and McParland, to name but two, he signed players who would fit into any all-time Villa XI without looking out of place.

Martin's biggest failing is one common to many Villa managers - he was at the helm during a time when the club was in decline. As Danny Blanchflower later said, "The players ran Aston Villa; the whole place was crying out for leadership and guidance."

The board was old-fashioned, unable to deal with the ways of modern football and complacent enough to believe that they were still living in the days when the very name Aston Villa was on its own a guarantee of success. George Martin was unable to overcome that barrier, but then again, few managers could have. As Dave Walsh said, "George Martin would have been a great manager if he'd been given a completely free hand."

Ironically, the Birmingham Post story that told of Martin's dismissal was immediately above the headline 'Mr Eric Houghton Resigns'. On the same day that Martin had been sacked, the former Villa stalwart had asked to be released from his contract as manager of Notts County. The position of the two stories in the newspaper may have been coincidental; the timing of both events almost certainly was not.

5

Eric Houghton

September 1953 - November 1958

In the aftermath of George Martin's dismissal, the Sports Argus carried a prophetic warning. Martin's successor, they wrote, would have to be able to persuade the board that a junior system and scouts were essential. It had been thought that Martin's appointment as club manager with full control would have been a turning point. However, the promise of true revival had failed, and it was to be hoped that lessons had been learnt. It was still felt that, even after years of neglect, the right man could revive the Villa. That 'right man' was not hard to track down.

William Eric Houghton was born in Billingsborough, Lincolnshire on 29th June 1910, when Villa were the reigning League champions. He was recommended to the club by his uncle Cecil Harris, after a brilliant season in schools football, during which he scored 88 goals. He was reputed to cycle fourteen miles to play for Lincoln City and was one of the fittest players of his era. Eric signed for the Villa in August 1927 (there is a story that he turned up for a one-day trial with enough clothes to last a fortnight, so sure was he of being signed up by the club) and made his debut two and a half years later. In 1930-31 the Villa scored 128 goals in finishing division one runners-up, with Eric himself responsible for thirty of these. "The hardest shot I ever faced," was how West Bromwich Albion and England international goalkeeper Harold Pearson remembered his clashes with Houghton.

Such form attracted the attention of the England selectors, who awarded him seven caps in the early thirties. In total he made 392 appearances for the Villa, scoring 170 goals, many of them as a result of those fearsome free kicks.

Eric left the Villa after the war in order to play for and then manage Notts County, who won the third division (north) in his first season in charge. He was also a talented cricketer, who played for Aston Unity in the Birmingham League and captained the Warwickshire

2nd XI for several years. But there was never any doubt where Eric's heart belonged. On 31st August 1953, Houghton left County. Three days later he was back at Villa Park. Fred Normansell, on behalf of the board, issued a statement saying that "Mr W.E. Houghton has been appointed team manager in charge of the players and training staff." He also took this opportunity to state that the club's long-term coaching and scouting policies were to be overhauled. As Charles Mattheson wrote in the Argus on the following Saturday, "Our Eric has come home".

With the appointment of Eric Houghton, Villa reverted to the title of team manager, although times had changed and the phrase meant less that it had done in the past. There were the usual hopes that the board would allow the new man to get on with his job with the minimum of interference, while the appointment undoubtedly fired the imagination of supporters who hoped that Houghton the manager would produce a team as exciting as the side of the early thirties in which he had been such a key figure. Supporters, it was felt by the Evening Mail, "will not expect him to be an absolute dictator threatening death and destruction." Instead, they would have remembered Houghton the sportsman, the epitome of a loyal claret and blue clubman.

Charles Harrold, whom the Villa board must have become used to, such was his barbed and usually accurate criticism of their actions, wrote in the Argus that, "Manager Houghton has to be given the chance to see what he can do - he has a host of jobs to tackle from organising junior development to strengthening the senior side." Harrold also warned, " People do not appreciate the magnitude of the task. It is too big for one man and unless the board pull all the way and give him a lead, it may not be accomplished." And in a statement which would bear strong parallels with Graham Taylor's declaration upon first arriving at Villa Park over 30 years later, Harrold declared that "The first team aren't good enough, the reserve strength isn't there, there is little coming on amongst the youngsters and there is not a great deal of money available to improve positions." Houghton, though, he readily conceded, had "made a start. He is keen and enthusiastic and ready to work hard."

The new manager certainly made an immediate impact, motivating the players into what was described as real football, with idea and understanding. As often happens, the teams he picked seemed to have greater confidence under a new manager, and there was no doubt Houghton had got off on the right foot. He certainly produced a masterstroke when bringing Jimmy Hogan back to Villa Park as scout and youth coach. Even at the age of seventy, Hogan's influence and eye for a player was to bear fruit before long. Also arriving at Villa Park was the former Blues and England centre-forward Joe Bradford, who was to work as a scout alongside former trainer Hubert Bourne

However, after a promising few weeks, Villa drifted back into a familiar mediocrity. There were calls for a boycott of games, one commentator pointing out that if gates fell, the directors might be shaken out of their complacency. The oft-stated criticisms were levelled again, namely that the club were happy to bob along aimlessly until finding themselves in trouble, at which point they would spend heavily in an attempt to safeguard their place in the first division, and that once this short-term objective was achieved they would once more return to their slumbers. The club had "been on the brink of relegation so many times it would be a relief if it came," was the opinion of a Mail letter-writer who signed himself "Fifty years of Villa history".

February 1954 saw the equivalent of an entire reserve team being told that they could leave the club. The general comment of the local press was that they would be glad to leave. Yet throughout these problems, Eric Houghton retained his popularity both amongst supporters and with his playing staff, who regarded him with devotion. The end of the season saw the Villa finishing in thirteenth place in the league with 47 points. It had not been a memorable campaign, and things had been made worse by the fact that the Wolves had won the league and Albion the FA Cup, as well as finishing runners-up in the league. In the competition to be Pride of the Midlands, Villa were now a distant third.

The summer of 1954 saw the Villa announcing a loss of almost £5,000, while it was revealed that gate receipts had dropped below £100,000 for the first time since the war. The Villa were no longer amongst the aristocrats of English football, and they were unable to buy their way into the higher echelons they had once considered theirs by right.

Houghton had spent much of his time during the season battling to improve matters. A second youth team had been introduced, and

the policy he had advocated on his appointment for bringing youngsters into the club was slowly beginning to take shape. However,
such a policy would never have the immediate impact on results
that the supporters were demanding. Their opinions were familiar
ones by now. "Bring back football worthy of the name Aston
Villa"….. "Buy out the directors"…… "Give Jimmy Hogan more
responsibility". This latter cry showed the desperation of supporters, for Hogan was well into his seventies by now; yet there were
those who wanted him to be made responsible for all team selection
and coaching, with Houghton given charge of non-playing affairs.
And as ever, the question of Who Manages at Villa Park? was raised,
with cries for Alex Massie and George Martin to give their versions
of the way in which managers were expected to go about their business at the club. Indeed, there was the first sign of a split amongst
the directors, however minor it may have appeared, with one of the
board being quoted as saying, "No-one at Old Trafford dare question Matt Busby on team policy and selection". Even in the inner
sanctum, it appeared, there were small signs the directors were
starting to realise their old belief that they knew best was out-dated.

These words, though, would have been little comfort to Eric
Houghton, who himself was coming under heavy fire from supporters who called for a change of manager, for someone with greater
vision and initiative to come in and be given total control of running
the club.

1954-55 was a better season on the field for the Villa, at least in
terms of their final league place. An indifferent performance for
most of the season was followed by eleven wins in the final fifteen
matches, enabling the team to finish in sixth place. This late run
might normally have encouraged optimism for the season ahead,
but such notions were long since beaten back by reality at Villa
Park. As Peter Morris said in his centenary book 'Aston Villa – The
First Hundred Years', "The Villa had no basic style on which to
endure. They appeared to play their games as the indifferent card
player plays each hand – on instinct – and blindly rode their luck
when the breaks came".

More significantly, the season had seen the departures of two of
Villa's finest players since the war. Tommy Thompson joined
Preston for £17,000, while Danny Blanchflower moved to Spurs,
where he proved himself one of the greatest footballers of the era.

Both men had left because they could see that Villa Park was no longer a place for ambitious players, Blanchflower in particular being heavily critical of the way the club had been run during his time there. However, nobody could doubt the dedication of Eric Houghton. Such was his commitment to the Villa that on Christmas Eve 1954 he had signed Tommy Southren from West Ham for £12,000, the deal being completed at midnight on Euston station.

The summer of 1955 saw several changes amongst the backroom staff at Villa Park. Former Notts County man Bill Moore linked up with his old manager as first team trainer, while the previous incumbent of that position, Jimmy Easson, became team coach.

Disappointingly, the Houghton/Moore partnership failed to reap instant reward. After a reasonable start to the 1955-56 season, Villa's form slumped dramatically. They were bottom of the league for long periods, and after losing to Spurs with three games left, the situation appeared hopeless. Three points adrift, having played two games more than the clubs above them, the Villa seemed destined for relegation. Instead, three straight wins in the remaining games meant that the Villa finished the season in twentieth place in the first division, goal average separating them from relegated Huddersfield Town. Yet again, when threatened with disaster, the Villa had resorted to the tried and sometimes successful method of buying their way out of trouble. David Hickson had cost £17,000 from Everton early in the season and he was later followed by Sheffield Wednesday's Jackie Sewell, Jimmy Dugdale from the Albion and finally the Wolves pair of Les Smith and Nigel Sims. Over £50,000 was spent on avoiding relegation and no doubt the directors considered it money well spent. Supporters, though, were not so easily satisfied. An Extraordinary General Meeting had been called for March, and although the directors were able to triumph over a no-confidence motion with ease, and regain their seats at the following AGM in the summer, things were still not rosy between board and fans.

As is often the case with the Villa, success was to come when least expected. To the keen eye, there were definite signs of optimism during what appeared to be a stormy period. Long-serving Con Martin was granted a free transfer, which may have been down to the fact that, with 26 players signing amateur terms, the club were hopeful that their youth policy was finally paying dividends.

Included in this number were the entire Aston Boys side, signed en masse in the hope that they could provide the backbone of a successful youth team. As the 1956-57 season progressed, these players began to make their mark in the club's lesser sides. Tom Duckworth, writing admiringly of the "youth revolution" in the Argus of January 1957, noted that the previous week had seen a Villa reserve team where all the players were "under the age of twenty" (the term 'teenager' had not yet been coined). Passing without comment in this team was a seventeen year-old wing-half from BSA Tools by the name of Ron Atkinson.

It was noticeable that Houghton was willing to answer questions regarding team selection put to him by supporters in the local press. Such an initiative would be unthinkable even in the media-friendly modern eras and was a further example of the warm relationship Eric Houghton usually shared with the fans.

Villa finished a distinctly average tenth in the first division in 1956-57. They never looked in any danger of relegation, but neither did they look at any time worthy of any higher than a mid-table placing. Nevertheless, the 1956-57 season will go down in Villa folklore alongside winning the double, the European Cup and any of the club's other numerous triumphs. And it was primarily down to the abilities of the manager.

Luton Town were beaten in the FA Cup third round, after a replay at Villa Park. The next two rounds saw Middlesbrough and then Bristol City despatched with ease. The sixth round away to high-flying Burnley saw a titanic struggle on a mud-caked pitch with Villa holding the Lancashire side to a 1-1 draw before winning 2-0 at home. 2-1 down with five minutes to go against the Albion at Molineux, Villa looked doomed to semi-final disappointment. Peter McParland netted an equaliser and a replay at St Andrews saw Billy Myerscough score the goal that took Villa to Wembley, where they would face Manchester United, league champions and arguably the greatest team in Europe. Nobody outside the Midlands gave the Villa a chance. But they had not reckoned on a piece of managerial genius. And as Houghton himself said just days before the final, "What have we got to lose?" Dennis Jackson, in the party for the cup final but knowing that he stood little chance of making the team, takes up the story:

"I was in the squad for the 1957 cup final, and I could see just how well he did for that match. He tried to find us a pitch that was similar to Wembley and he found the Cadbury sports ground at Bournville. Then we moved to Hendon Hall on the outskirts of London on the Thursday before the match and we trained there on the Thursday and Friday morning, then we trained at Wembley on the Friday afternoon."

"Bill Moore was a good motivator, he got the players up for that match and they all respected him; he was very disciplined. As for Eric, well, I sat next to him on the bench and as the lads were kicking in he sent me back for his pipe and his cigarettes. He never smoked all that much, but that day he had about 60 fags in one pocket and his pipe in the other. He was brilliant that day".

History records that the club won the FA Cup for a record seventh time, thanks to two goals from Peter McParland and an injury to Ray Wood which meant that the United goalkeeper had to leave the field with a broken cheekbone – caused by an over-exuberant but entirely fair shoulder-charge by McParland midway through the first half. Wood returned to the action shortly after the interval but could only watch helplessly as McParland's goals brought the cup back to Aston. Whether or not they would have beaten a full-strength United side is open to debate, but Dennis Jackson has no doubts. "The players were raring to go and after twenty minutes I knew we'd win. The lads all knew each other and they played really well on the day. That was down to Eric, players believed in him because he was such a nice fella. He'd have a go at people but they could rely on him. He was like a father-figure to us."

After such a triumph, great things were expected for the following season; but it was not to be. Villa finished in fourteenth place, their total of 39 points just four more than they had accumulated during the almost-disastrous campaign two seasons earlier. The old Villa problem of complacency had struck again with a vengeance, and this time the directors could point out that there could be little wrong with the club if there was silverware in the trophy cabinet. In hindsight, the departure of Bill Moore in November 1957 was a grave setback. The dressing room was never the same place. Indeed, Houghton later said that he should have left at the same time as his trainer. "They worked well together," said Harry Burrows, who joined the club as a sixteen year old during the cup-winning summer of 1957. "There seemed a very good spirit amongst the players at that time, but it was never the same once Bill left".

1958-59 started badly and got worse. Supporters by now were directing their fire at everyone concerned with the club. Loyal servant or not, Eric Houghton drew more than his share of criticism. "Stop saying 'Something has to be done'," was the despairing cry of one supporter after yet another defeat. "Nothing ever is done". However big the problems may have been on the pitch, the underlying difficulties were worse. The AGM was held later than usual, in September, by which time the season had started, and badly at that. Chairman Chris Buckley, commenting on the club's reserve strength, admitted, "There is nobody good enough to get into the first team. We cannot do any more until we find the money to buy some players." For manager Houghton, who all through his time at Villa Park had professed himself satisfied with the progress of the youth and junior sides of the operation, this must have been a devastating blow.

For his part, the manager remained optimistic. "A really good wing-half and inside-forward would fill the side's most pressing needs. With these positions filled the club should be able to pull round," he stated. Supporters pointed out that Danny Blanchflower and Tommy Thomson were two such players.

At the end of September, Villa were bottom of the table, although they could at last unveil one new signing when Ron Wylie joined from Notts County for a fee of £9,000. The Houghton magic was still working, with the new arrival saying, "I owe a lot to Mr Houghton." However, Wylie was to find repaying the debt to prove harder than he imagined.

Floodlights were still a novelty at Villa Park, and so the crowd for the friendly with Heart of Midlothian on 19th November 1958 was higher than it might otherwise have been. Those present would not have realised that they were witnessing the end of an era, for as the match ended, Eric Houghton announced to a stunned home dressing room that he was leaving Villa Park. Typical of the man, he had made his decision on the previous day, but had not made it public so as not to affect the players before the game. "There were several players bidding for a first-team place and I didn't want to say anything to upset their prospects," was how Eric described events.

"A complete shock," was the reaction of one unnamed player. "We hardly realised what had happened before he walked out again."

Peter McParland confirmed the shock that the news brought, "He'd never said one word about leaving," he said, later paying tribute to his former manager. "The blame for our position is down to us and I'm sad and upset that the boss is carrying the can." McParland also gave what was probably the most accurate comment anyone could ever pass about Eric Houghton. He was, the Irish international winger stated, "a Villa fanatic. He lived, dreamt and slept Aston Villa seven days a week. All his time was devoted to Aston Villa".

Harry Burrows was in agreement. "He was a real father figure to us younger players," he says. "We might have been called Mercer's Minors later on, but that team started out with Eric".

Houghton's departure may have been a shock to the players, but the manager himself had grown resigned to the fact that his departure was imminent. It later transpired that he had been asked to resign at a board meeting the day before the game with Hearts, and when he had refused, his employment had been terminated. Chris Buckley later stated that, "The board decided there would be a reorganisation of administration at Villa Park and consequently.... Mr Eric Houghton terminated his service with the club"

When asked if the news had come as a surprise, Houghton's response was, "Not really, I read about it recently" – a reference to a newspaper story that Jimmy Murphy, then manager of Wales and Matt Busby's assistant at Manchester United, had been asked to take over a "famous Midlands first division club". Murphy later confirmed the story, stating that he had refused to take the job as the club in question (which he admitted was Villa) already had a manager at the time. Although Murphy did not reply to Villa director Bill Lovesey's challenge to name the man who had offered him the job, the board did not come out of this particular episode with any great credit.

Houghton, though, was plainly tiring of the rancour that the job was attracting. The previous Saturday had seen Villa surrender a three-goal lead to go down 6-3 to Leicester City at Filbert Street, after which the manager was observed to be as upset as anyone could ever remember seeing him, later bemoaning what he called the lack of responsibility and carefree attitude of his players.

Dennis Jackson, however, has another theory as to why Eric left the Villa. "He left after a row with the chairman over the money he

got for the cup final, it wasn't what he'd been promised. It all started during the tour of Germany in 1957 after we won the final and
was never sorted out. Chris Buckley had a row with him and it all
went on from there." This was later borne out by Houghton himself,
who stated that he had been promised a £2,000 bonus by Fred
Normansell several years earlier in the event of Villa reaching the
cup final, yet had eventually been paid less than half that amount.

Houghton made a statement in which he said his big regret was
he, "...would not see the crop of youth develop. For the first time in
years we have our own youngsters who are being brought up to play
the right kind of football. These boys will pay dividends in about
two years time. Just wait and see". To those already in the first team
squad, he urged, "If you feel sympathy for me, go out there and do
your best to get the Villa away from the bottom of the table. The club
is bigger than the individual in all circumstances."

In an interview with the Birmingham Mail's Eric Woodward,
Houghton, somewhat surprisingly, did not make the obvious excuse
for his departure. "I don't want to sling any mud about – I am not
that kind of chap. I've had a reasonably free hand and selected the
team." he said, before going on to discuss his future. "I have no
future plans to manage another club. I have never applied for a job
and have no intention of starting now." Disappointed though he no
doubt was to have been relieved of his responsibilities, Houghton
also seemed glad to escape the bitterness and in-fighting that was
increasingly overtaking Villa Park. "I often wondered what something like this would feel like. I thought it would break my heart.
Instead I feel twice as young. It was as if all that worry had been lifted from my shoulders. It would take a lot to get me back into football." And as if echoing those thoughts, his wife was quoted as saying, "If Eric goes back into football he goes alone. I've had enough".

The programme for the following week's match, at home to
Preston, featured a message of thanks to Eric from the board, which
concluded with the words, "We don't know what he plans for the
future, but in whatever sphere it is, we wish every success to a great
but ever-modest sportsman." For their part the team, with Ron
Wylie making his debut, paid their own tribute with a 2-0 win thanks
to what the Argus reporter described as "The new-look side he
moulded before he left".

Houghton later cast light on the difficulties he had encountered when managing at Villa Park. "The secretary was always powerful. Fred Normansell was a good leader and a likeable chairman. On his death the position changed and I felt my days were numbered. I went from attending board meetings in full to being invited to give a report. I felt like an office boy."

It would be hard to find anyone who has ever had a bad word to say about Eric Houghton. Tom Duckworth, writing in the Argus, stated: "I doubt whether there has ever been anyone better liked at the club. His first thought was always the club." The only criticism, and it was oft-repeated in the days following his departure, was that Eric had too nice a streak in him. He was, in the words of Peter McParland, "Too nice to be a football manager"

Dennis Jackson, restricted to a handful of first team appearances during Houghton's reign, said of his treatment of all the players in his charge, "In those days you had the first team squad and you had the rest - the reserves and the young players. There were no splits in the dressing room; in 1957 the team were all solid for each other in all those hard matches in that run and that's what kept us going. And that was down to Eric. He was a joker; he'd have a laugh with the players. He was great. We worried a bit about upsetting Bill because he came down hard on anything, but Eric was more easygoing. They worked in tandem really well.

"Eric used to moan about Chris Buckley having to see the team sheet on a Friday afternoon and sometimes he'd want to change the players round. Bill went barmy about that, but Eric was more of a diplomat about it. I never heard him complaining about the board interfering with the players he wanted to sign. He always seemed to have a reasonably free hand and he was content with it all. You couldn't really fault him in the time I was there. Anyone who can win the FA Cup and beat the Manchester United of that time in the final couldn't have been a bad manager."

After a period out of the game, Eric returned in unusual circumstances, and he lost no time in surrounding himself with some familiar faces. Dennis Jackson was one of them. "He took over at Rugby Town who were in the Southern League. I was playing for Millwall at that time, about 1963, and he turned up one day and wanted to sign me. He offered more than I was on at Millwall, more probably than the Villa team were on at that time, and I was off back with him. In fact, the team he had at Rugby was unbelievable. There was Stan Crowther; Ronnie Clayton he signed from Arsenal, Bill Holden from Burnley who'd played for England the year before. The money helped, but the main reason they signed for Rugby was down to Eric."

As a manager, Eric Houghton was yet another to find he was unable to overcome the general feeling of decline and decay that had set in at Villa Park. Peter McParland wrote, "Relegation... that was a word which rang frequently in my ear during my first six years at Villa Park. Virtually every season we were struggling."

Good, sometimes great, players wanted to leave and the Villa name was no longer enough to attract adequate replacements. League performances were poor and only in the cup did flashes of the Villa of old shine through. The Villa board, as had been the case for decades, were interfering, complacent and simply not up to the challenges of running a club of the size and history of Aston Villa. Eric Houghton performed his task without anger and with a great deal of dignity. After leaving Villa Park he refused to comment in public on the goings-on at the club, even when offered large sums of money by the newspapers. The club, he believed, must always come first, although many years later Eric did hint at the problems he had faced at the Villa: "If I had my time again I would not give a manager's job the slightest consideration. You just can't win - directors should never interfere with the manager from the playing point of view."

After his retirement from football Eric worked for the Villa Supporters Association as a full-time organiser and was later elected to the board under Doug Ellis before becoming the club's only permanent vice-president. In his later years he acted as an unofficial public relations man for the club, never meeting a supporter without displaying the warmth and patience that had become legendary. Eric died in May 1996, at the age of 85, and his passing was a cause for deep and sincere mourning not only at Villa Park, but throughout football.

There may have been better Villa players than Eric Houghton. There may have been better managers. But there has never been anyone who gave more unquestioning, unconditional service during a lifetime of devotion to the cause of Aston Villa FC. Eric Houghton was one of the greatest servants the club will ever know.

6

Joe Mercer
December 1958 - July 1964

"Hurry up and appoint the manager, Villa," was the opening sentence of the Argus report on the 1-1 draw with Manchester City on 6th December 1958, a game that was witnessed by around 18,000 frustrated Villa supporters. The report continued, "Whoever the new boss is, he has a big job on his hands".

Newspaper coverage of football was changing in the fifties, with more readers letters appearing and supporter opinions canvassed as editors began to realise that supporters wanted to do more than turn up and watch the match without comment. Villa fans were asked who they would like to be the new manager and the narrow favourite was former Villa captain Billy Walker, then doing sterling service with Nottingham Forest. Also mentioned was Bill Moore, who had become manager of Walsall after being sacked as Villa trainer the previous summer, as well as former players Frank Barson and Frank Broome.

In the end, the new manager was appointed just over two weeks later, and in a sequence of events that would be considered bizarre in modern times. On 22nd December Joe Mercer, then manager of Sheffield United, announced to his board that he would be applying for the Villa job. On the following day Chris Buckley stated that the club had not as yet received Mercer's application, but left no doubt that once it arrived, the job would be offered to the Sheffield United boss. Nobody stopped to think what would happen if the letter were lost in the post; but no matter, it arrived safely at Villa Park and, on Christmas Eve 1958, Mercer travelled to a fog-bound Birmingham, where he apparently got lost in the one way system, finally arriving at a city centre hotel to meet the Villa board. At the culmination of this meeting, Chris Buckley announced: "Mr Mercer will have full managerial control." This was a first for the Villa. Every other appointment had been given the title 'team manager' with the exception of George Martin, and he could hardly have been said to have enjoyed a free hand in playing affairs. Mercer was the first Villa manager to be assured that he was in total control of the club's playing affairs. As Buckley pointed out, "Mr Mercer has a big job... he is a big enough man to take it on." And as if to acknowledge the size of the task, Mercer was given a contract of five years length at a reported £3,000 a year - the most lucrative in the club's history.

Mercer himself was full of enthusiasm for the task ahead, saying, "It is not a challenge, but there is something to do and that is what appealed to me." The local press approved of the appointment, calling Mercer a "great personality", who would nevertheless be unable to perform miracles straight away.

Joe Mercer was born in August 1915 in Ellesmere Port, Cheshire. He began his professional playing career as a wing-half with Everton, winning the league championship in 1938-39, but like many of his contemporaries, Mercer's career was interrupted by Word War Two. He moved to Arsenal in December 1946 for a fee of £7,000, despite having started up in business on Merseyside as he believed that his playing days were drawing to a close.

Mercer captained Arsenal to the league championship in 1953 before retiring the following season after a freak collision with a team-mate during a league match. He made five appearances for England and had captained his country in wartime internationals. Were it not for the war, Mercer would have won many more caps, and was regarded as one of the finest wing-halves of all time.

As a manager Mercer began his career with Sheffield United. Arriving at Bramall Lane too late to save them from relegation in 1955-56, Mercer worked wonders on a limited budget and the club were firm favourites for promotion back to the first division when he walked out on them. As soon as he arrived at Villa Park, Mercer made his philosophy clear. "I am coming here with full control and that is the beginning and end of it," he stated, going on to say, "Money must be found if the players are there, although if the youth players are good enough they will get every opportunity."

The players were in favour of the appointment. Dennis Jackson remembers the impact that Mercer's arrival had on the playing staff. "We'd seen him play, and he was a hell of a player. We all respected him for that. Joe had such wide experience; he'd played for Arsenal with their great team and he'd obviously picked up a lot of knowledge there. He'd got a modern outlook as regards tactics and how the game should be played."

Mercer's first action was to appoint his deputy from Bramall Lane, Dick Taylor, as assistant manager. Wolverhampton-born Taylor was an FA staff coach, and he echoed Mercer's thoughts when stating, "There's a lot of young talent here, but it doesn't seem to be coming through quickly enough".

Villa, bottom of the league when Mercer arrived, steadily improved. They eased out of the relegation places and reached the FA Cup semi-finals where they were unlucky to go down to eventual winners Nottingham Forest, managed by Billy Walker. In contrast to previous relegation struggles, there was no great air of desperation around Villa Park. As Alan Deakin, then beginning to ease himself into first-team contention, recalls, "We never thought we'd get relegated. You never thought the Villa would go down then. Joe never thought it, he was always positive."

However, just three points from eight games took Villa back into the danger zone and the final match of the season, against the Albion, has gone down in the folklore of the rivalry between the two teams. With Villa leading by a goal from Gerry Hitchens, Albion's Ronnie Allen equalised with just minutes remaining. Joe Mercer had left the ground by then, to attend a banquet honouring Billy Wright's hundredth England cap.

In fact, the game at the Hawthorns may not have been quite so important as it has been made out to be. Manchester City, Villa's rivals to stay in the first division, had kicked off fifteen minutes later than the match at the Hawthorns had commenced, and, with goal average so narrow between the two sides, would almost certainly have been able to add another goal to the single one with which they beat Leicester City had they needed to.

But no matter. Villa, seemingly safe a few weeks earlier, had suffered relegation for the second time in their history. No-one was blaming Joe Mercer, of whom one director said, "He has worked so hard to get the club out of trouble with limited resources." Well, almost no-one. A Sheffield United supporter, remembering that his own team were relegated during the manager's first season in charge, sent a telegram to Villa Park saying, "Congratulations, Mercer. You've done it again".

The close-season was filled with the usual fall-out that accompanies a Villa Park disaster. The local papers were filled with letters from gloating Albion and Blues supporters; a stormy AGM heard the club was now £87,000 in debt. In fact, supporters were even fighting amongst themselves, as the Shareholders Association had split into two quarrelling factions to match the two, often disagreeing, supporters' clubs. But Mercer was still very much the fans' choice. He talked of "clearing away the dead wood" (Sixteen players had been made available for transfer at the end of the season) and stated, "I look forward to the day when a style runs through all our teams that is recognised as Aston Villa".

Chairman Chris Buckley had promised Mercer £25,000 to spend on new players when the manager first took over. Mercer, though, decided that the money would be better invested in a training ground, and Villa consequently developed the most modern facilities in the country at the Hercules Sports Ground, three hundred yards from Villa Park.

Villa regained their place in the top division at the first time of asking. With Gerry Hitchens scoring 41 goals, including five in an 11-1 victory over Charlton Athletic, Villa were crowned second division champions and reached the FA Cup semi-final, where, for the second season in succession, they were knocked out by the eventual winners - this time Wolves. Mercer was entitled to feel proud of his achievement, particularly as the youth programme, by which he had set great store, was beginning to bear fruit. The Central League side regularly featured half a dozen or more youngsters, while hundreds of young players attended trials at Villa Park during the close-season. Gates were up for the second successive season during the promotion year and supporters were looking forward to the Villa making a realistic assault on the championship for the first time in a quarter of a century. Mercer, though, ever a realist, merely stated, "We shall be happy to establish ourselves in division one and consolidate our position". He did, however, concede that the promotion side was a much better one than the team which had been relegated twelve months previous. Further confirmation of the spirit of optimism surrounding Villa Park came from the legendary Frank Barson, who commented, "Leave everything to Joe Mercer and Villa will soon be a great club again."

There was more good news for the sporting public of Birmingham that summer, as speedway returned to Perry Barr for the first time in several years, under the auspices of co-promoters Phil Hart and a young local businessman by the name of Doug Ellis.

The team lived up to expectations, and were in the top six going into the new year. "We are poised on the threshold," stated Mercer in 1961. Whilst commentators spoke of the Villa's whole-hearted effort and team spirit, Mercer declined to accept sole credit for the way in which the club was transforming itself. "The spirit was there from the start," he modestly insisted. However, there was no hiding the delight with which he acknowledged, "I am quite happy at the way things are going. We are making progress."

Certainly, the players were happy with life at Villa Park. Dennis Jackson summed up the mood of the dressing room: "Joe Mercer, he was very popular. He brought some wonderful players through, and everybody loved him. He'd do things like, we'd be going away for a match and on Friday afternoon he'd get all the players together and he'd say 'Right, who wants to do what? Anybody want to go racing?' And he'd go with them, because that was his big passion outside football. Or if they wanted to go anywhere else, or go to a show, he'd let them. Anything to keep his players contented."

However, the players knew when Mercer was unhappy. Alan Deakin recalls what life was like if the team were playing poorly. "Joe would come in the dressing room, his face was like thunder, and if it was winter and he had his coat on he'd take it off slowly, hang it on the peg. Then he'd turn round and thump! - whoever he was picking on would be for it. I think that was what made him ill in the end, he got so wound up about how we were playing."

Villa ended the season in ninth place, with 43 points. The last game, at home to Sheffield Wednesday, was one of those events which would prove significant in a way in which nobody present could have guessed. Playing his final game for the Villa was that magnificent, long-time servant to the club Johnny Dixon, who scored the last goal in a 4-1 victory. Making his debut at left-back was Charlie Aitken, who went on to have an even longer career in claret and blue.

During the summer, Villa parted company with Gerry Hitchens, who moved to Internazionale for £80,000. His replacement was Derek Dougan, for whom Villa paid Blackburn Rovers just £15,000, with Mercer pointing out that "If he dedicated himself he could become better than Hitchens." However, Dougan proved a less than adequate replacement for one of the great Villa centre-forwards.

"He was a hell of a player at home, but away from home sometimes you'd only get 80%," was the opinion of one of Dougan's colleagues.

1961-62 started with Villa making history yet again, when a 3-2 aggregate victory over Rotherham United saw them winning the inaugural League Cup in a two-legged final which had been held over from the previous season. Once more, things seemed on the up at Villa Park. The team, now dubbed the 'Mercer Minors', were regarded as the most promising collection of young players in the country. The club's debts had been virtually wiped out, and plans were unveiled for new double-decker stands on the Witton End and Witton Lane areas of the ground which were to be ready for the World Cup of 1966.

However, such optimism was soon tempered by a run of bad form that prompted the first real criticism aimed at Joe Mercer since his arrival. A 0-0 draw with Sheffield United in January 1962 saw the crowd slow-handclapping the team's performance, which was described by one supporter as "the worst exhibition in over forty years". There were calls for big money signings and for promising youngsters to be given a run in the first team. Mercer responded by saying, "These people have a perfect right to express their opinions. My own favourite hobby is to pick the England team".

But there was no disguising the displeasure of the Villa Park crowd when the team embarked on a record five game run without scoring a league goal and the popular Peter McParland was sold to the Wolves for £30,000. In letters to the local press, E Willetts (who described himself as a season ticket holder for forty years) demanded to know "how Joe Mercer keeps his job", whilst A. Sergant called for the appointment of Johnny Dixon as manager. P. Price was of the opinion that "the present team must be the worst for forty years" (forty years obviously being a period of great significance for Villa supporters of the early sixties) and G. Turner believed that a "team manager was only a gimmick", pointing out that Villa's greatest triumphs were built around strong leadership from the directors. It was, however, said by many supporters that Villa's fortunes under Mercer were more favourable than for some time, although there was criticism of the way in which he had apparently changed the team's style of play to suit the disappointing Derek Dougan.

Ironically, in view of the criticism which they had received, the team finished the season in seventh position, two places higher than they had done the previous season and with one more point. Mercer defended his tactics throughout the season, claiming that the team had been forced through circumstance to play more defensively than he would have liked. He also informed supporters that money was available for the right players.

It was felt that 1962-63 would be the season in which the promise that had been evident during Mercer's time at Villa Park would bear fruit. The team were tipped as potential champions and whilst such talk may have been over-ambitious, there was a very real feeling that the Villa were now one of the finest sides in the country. They certainly started off well enough, and with half the season played were fifth in the table, six points off the lead. In addition, November 1962 saw the youngest-ever Central League team in the club's history, with an average age of just 18, beat Preston 4-0.

However, with the team seemingly set for great things, fate took a hand. The winter of 1963 was one of the coldest on record and at one point Villa had played a league game against Blackburn despite the poor conditions. The match finished goalless, but attempts to make the pitch playable caused severe damage to the turf and meant that Villa Park was still unfit when other grounds had recovered from the bad weather, causing a severe fixture backlog. The Villa youngsters were unable to cope, suffering eleven consecutive league defeats, and the Mercer Minors never recovered from this setback. "We had a good nucleus," Harry Burrows remembers. "Joe had brought about five of us into the team and three had already played under-23 internationals. But when you have a lot of youngsters they will always go through a bad patch."

Alan Deakin is another of the Mercer Minors who well remembers how the fates conspired during this period. "We beat Spurs, we beat Manchester United, we beat most of the top teams. We were fourth in the league with a very young side; then we played one match in about two months. We had something like eight players aged 21 and under in the team, and once you're on a winning streak you feel so confident, you feel fitter. We were all young kids and we might have got better. As it was, once that break came, we all started dropping off one by one with injuries, Mick Wright broke his leg, John Sleeuwenhoek had cartilage problems, I broke my leg and had trouble with my knee. We had too many youngsters and the older players we had weren't the kind who would help you along; they were more interested in playing their own game. Cracking players, but they were very much individuals."

An eventual league position of fifteenth was much worse than they deserved, and a defeat in the League Cup final at the hands of the Blues was the final insult to the supporters, who had started to turn against Joe Mercer. Despite the elevation of Alan Deakin to the captaincy of the England under-23 team and the promising debuts of George Graham and England youth international Lew Chatterley, things were starting to take a distinctly downward turn.

The Villa began the 1963-64 season without the figure of Derek Dougan, sold to Peterborough for what would prove a bargain £16,000. There were calls for the club to buy big and Mercer accepted that "the team is not good enough... we have got to do something about it." However, he still claimed that there was the nucleus of a good side at Villa Park. Mick Wright became the youngest of the Mercer Minors, when making his debut at the age of sixteen, and the club still meant enough for Stan Crowther, forced to retire at 28, to say, "Villa is the kind of club that maybe no-one should ever leave". Nonetheless, supporters were beginning to lose patience. "Some say that we should leave Mr Mercer alone," commented one letter to the Argus. "Forty thousand of us have left him alone for four long years." Gates were down, the team made its worst home start in history with five defeats in the first six games at Villa Park and an air of despondency settled around the place.

One bright spot came with a 4-0 Villa Park win over Manchester United, amidst stormy scenes which saw Dennis Law sent off for kicking Alan Deakin as the Villa player lay on the floor and condemnation from Villa supporters towards the United fans' loud and aggressive chanting.

The disenchantment that was growing at Villa Park took on fresh impetus following an FA Cup third round defeat at the hands of fourth division Aldershot Town. A 0-0 draw preceded a 2-1 defeat at the Recreation Ground; Villa described as "outplayed" and "inept in both games" by the local press. As supporters called for a boycott of home games, Mercer continued with his calls for them to have patience, stating once more that he was desperately looking to sign new players. This latter comment drew the retort from one weary supporter that "Villa are watching players - watching them sign for other clubs." The cup saga with Aldershot led to Mercer bearing the brunt of criticism from the supporters who watched both matches, first with disbelief and then anger at the way in which the most famous cup-fighting side in the country had been humiliated by a team from three divisions below. They hurled insults, and the odd missile, at Mercer and subjected the team to the slow handclap that was the most vocal insult any team's followers would resort to in those days. "You should never lose these cup games," says Harry Burrows of the tie, "but it happens all the time".

"It hurt like hell," Mercer said later and there was no doubt that the pressure was growing on this most genial of managers. Indeed, Alan Deakin remembers that for Mercer, the pain of losing to Aldershot was more intense than it might have appeared at first. "Joe came into the dressing room after the match, and he went berserk. He kicked the kit skip; all these cups went flying and the story went round that he broke his toe. That was the beginning of the end for Joe."

Mercer later told of a game at Villa Park shortly after the Aldershot defeat when he bore the brunt of the crowd's displeasure: "I walked down from the stand to the trainer's bench. Vulgar abuse followed me all the way. I could hear every word of their vulgar epithets… apples and orange peel hit me."

Ironically, even though Mercer was losing the confidence of the Villa supporters, he enjoyed a tremendous reputation throughout the rest of football. As early as August 1962, Mercer had been tipped for the job of England manager as successor to Walter Winterbottom. The job had then gone to Alf Ramsey, who subsequently gave Mercer control of the England under-23 team and effectively used the Villa boss as his right-hand man.

Villa eventually scrambled out of the relegation places and finished the 1963-64 season in nineteenth place, an escape which was not regarded too kindly by supporters who expected better, particularly as Villa had lost 3-0 at home to the Blues towards the end of the season. There was, at least, a partial excuse for this defeat, in the shape of thirteen players missing through illness or injury.

Mercer had been travelling the length of the country in his quest for players in addition to supervising coaching sessions and having to cope with the myriad of other problems to which the Aston Villa manager is invariably subjected. The outcome was inevitable.

Several days after the season ended, it was announced that Mercer had been forced to take time off from the management of the Villa. A specialist described his problem as "hypertension brought about by illness and overwork," and it was later revealed that Mercer had suffered a stroke. Public sympathy was with Mercer, whose duties were temporarily taken by his assistant, Dick Taylor.

Some weeks after his illness was first announced, Mercer was described as making good progress, and he was reported as looking forward to returning to Villa Park in the near future. However, on 10th July it was announced that the manager would be stepping down from his position by mutual consent.

There were several theories as to why Mercer left the Villa. Most observers seemed to think that, like many Villa managers before and since, he had tired of the in-fighting and the perpetual state of civil war which seemed to exist between board, management and supporters. The eminent Villa historian Peter Morris, writing in his book 'The Team Makers', theorised that the board had already made the decision to get rid of Mercer and tactfully waited until he had recovered his health before informing him of their decision. A third shade of opinion was that the club were in deep financial straits (with gates down yet again, a record loss of £53,806 had been announced and the club had an overdraft of £110,000). Mercer's dismissal was seen as part of a number of economy measures covering everything from players' wages to the club's telephone bills.

For his part, Mercer bore no malice towards the Villa or the supporters who had criticised him, speaking of "four happy years, except for the past eighteen months." About the treatment he had received from the crowd at Villa Park during this later unhappy period, he said, "The crowd are entitled to complain. They just cannot appreciate the difficulties."

Mercer had already mentioned the problems that were besetting his management in a television interview filmed before his departure. "The strain was greater than ever. I tried to fight it but it got to the stage where I pinned up the team sheet and said; 'God bless this ship and all who sail in her. May God save them'."

Mercer was too much of a gentleman to broadcast his true feelings, but he did show some bitterness towards those who had criticised him. "On the way up it was Good Old Joe. The reaction set in; I got depressed when people stopped believing in me".

Harry Burrows is certain that the board acted prematurely in allowing Mercer to leave "We'd had a bit of a bad run, but if they'd have persevered he'd have got it right. And after Joe left it just went downhill. He was a good tactician; he got us playing the way football was evolving, with the wingers deeper."

However, Alan Deakin disagrees with his erstwhile team-mate: "He'd have found it difficult if he'd continued. I wouldn't say the board weren't ambitious, but they didn't want to spend money. You have to buy players at some stage: I don't know whether they'd have given him anything or whether the money was there. Possibly Joe had too many young players in the team, but we were going great guns at one time. There were a few injuries, some of the players lost form a bit and I don't know whether he could have improved things."

Mercer's time was best summed up in the Birmingham Post: "A period first of splendid hopes – then increasing disappointment," a feeling echoed by Tom Duckworth in the Sports Argus: "The partnership hailed as the finest move Villa have ever made ended in disappointment and disillusion." Perhaps Mercer's Villa career, and the handicaps he had to work under, were best summed up in a quote he gave several years later: "We were too concerned with solvency at Villa Park."

Mercer took twelve months away from football, during which time he was nursed back to health by his wife, Nora. It was thought at one point that he would never return to the game, but in July 1965, Mercer was approached by Manchester City, then in the second division, to become their manager. His family, understandably, were against his taking the job, but Mercer was adamant.

His decision proved to be the most fortunate in the club's history. Mercer, with Malcolm Allison as his assistant, took City to promotion in his first season. This success was followed by all three domestic trophies and the European Cup-Winners Cup in the next few years before Mercer was forced into the role of general manager following a boardroom upheaval in 1971.

Unhappy in his new role, Mercer moved to Coventry City, where he managed in partnership with Gordon Milne until being asked to take the England job on a temporary basis following the sacking of Sir Alf Ramsey in February 1974. The man who had once said that his hobby was picking the England team now had the opportunity to do so for real. Mercer's time as caretaker manager of the national side reflected his footballing philosophy – his orders to the team were in essence, "Go out and enjoy yourselves." And for seven matches, they did.

Back at Coventry, Mercer moved into the boardroom, where he performed the elder statesman role with his usual dignity. Honoured with the OBE in the New Year's Honours List of 1976, Mercer retired from football in 1981, at the age of 66, but continued to serve on a variety of panels and committees within the game.

Joe Mercer died on 9th August 1990, his seventy-fifth birthday, mourned by the whole of football. He was a true gent, a man for whom no-one had an unkind word. Indeed, it was said that Joe had achieved the impossible in football – he was liked by everyone.

Mercer's reign as Villa manager really was a case of the right man at the wrong time. He produced some magnificently-talented youngsters, yet they were unable to make the breakthrough into the highest echelons. While Mercer's time at Villa Park provided the first real cause for optimism since before the Second World War, the club's inability to cope with a rapidly-changing football world meant that the players he needed to bring in to complement his youngsters were unavailable. For the first time in their history, Villa could not rely on a mass of supporters filing through the turnstiles regardless of league position and the team's performance. With supporters until then regarded as the most loyal in football beginning to stay away, the money was no longer available to enable the board to finance Villa's traditional methods of spending their way out of trouble as and when necessary. In addition, the Villa name no longer commanded the attention of players looking to further their careers. Had Mercer been able to sign a couple of forwards to complement his talented young defence, things might have been so different. As it was, the Birmingham Post, at the time of Mercer's departure, spoke of "the big myth of British soccer - that Aston Villa are still a major force." Looking at Mercer's career post-Villa, it's not hard to imagine that in different circumstances he could have made that myth reality.

7

Dick Taylor

July 1964 - May 1967

When Joe Mercer was first taken ill, his role was taken temporarily by his assistant, Dick Taylor, When it was subsequently announced that Mercer was leaving Villa Park, Taylor remained in short-term charge of the first team. "Everything is up to him," was the comment from Chris Buckley on Taylor's chances of being given the job permanently.

Wolverhampton-born Taylor was 45 years old when he was appointed Villa manager. He had an unspectacular playing career with Grimsby and Scunthorpe before moving into coaching. He and Mercer had first met at a get-together of FA coaches at Lilleshall in 1956, and Taylor subsequently became Mercer's assistant at Sheffield United. When Mercer left to join the Villa, Taylor had been offered the manager's job at Bramall Lane, but chose to move to Villa Park as Mercer's number two. He soon gained the respect of the Villa playing staff, as Dennis Jackson recalls. "Dick was an FA staff coach, one of only three in the country at the time and he was absolutely brilliant. He was a great coach, very, very good and the lads respected him. He and Joe knew each other from the England set-up as well and they got on very well. They agreed on things and they agreed on how football should be played, so that helped a lot."

Taylor had emphasised the need for hard work on his arrival at Villa Park as assistant manager, and this ethic was strengthened when he took charge of team affairs. He also made what could have been seen as a veiled criticism of Mercer's tactics, when he said: "Perhaps we have had too much of a defensive attitude. The players must be more adventurous; perhaps they have stopped believing in their own abilities". With the whole club in decline, it was understandable the players had adopted a defeatist attitude, but Taylor was nothing if not a footballing philosopher. "I must try to bring out the players' own thoughts so that they can create and produce better football." First of all, though, he had to find the right players.

The economies that had bitten at Villa Park had seen the playing staff pruned. Veterans Vic Crowe and Nigel Sims had left on free transfers, whilst among the other departures was half-back George Graham, who moved to Chelsea for what would later prove to be the unforgivably bargain price of £6,000. First team trainer Ray Shaw was replaced by Bill Baxter while Johnny Dixon took over the reserves, who the previous season had won the Central League under the tutelage of Taylor.

The players who started the season under Taylor's management were keen to see how the former assistant would handle promotion. Alan Deakin recalls, "Morale was quite low at the time. Dick tried to instil confidence, telling us what he intended to do, but he made the training interesting, I'll give him that. He'd been Joe's right hand man and he played more games in training, you still did running but you'd have a laugh and a joke as well, so because you were enjoying it, you didn't notice how many miles you were running."

It was generally reckoned that the Villa would do well in 1964-65, or at least improve on their poor showing of the previous season. However, such optimism proved unfounded. The team recorded just two points from the first seven league games, and despite the arrival of Arsenal's right-winger Johnny McLeod for a club record fee of £40,000, had just six points from fourteen games, including a 0-7 reverse at Old Trafford.

In the midst of this disappointment, Taylor remained upbeat, continually asserting there was money available for new players while at the same time bemoaning the fact that injuries had cost him dearly and too many experienced players had been allowed to leave. Alan Deakin, for one, found that Taylor's approach was an improvement on the style of play he had been used to under Joe Mercer. "Joe had always been a defensive type of manager. He'd been teaching me to tackle, whereas Dick let me get forward a bit more. He liked to see the game played properly."

But Taylor was not immune from criticism. Harry Burrows, who left Villa after a dispute over wages, believes Taylor was the wrong man for the job: "He was a coach, really. The step up to manager was too great for him at the time. Dick just didn't have the experience to be manager. If they were going to get rid of Joe Mercer they might as well have had a completely clean sweep and started again. Dick wasn't really strong enough to take on the board."

Alan Deakin agrees. "Whatever Joe did, Dick must have taken some of the blame but it was easy for the directors to say 'Okay Dick, take over.' No fuss, no bother, no interviewing. I'd have thought that once a manager goes then his staff should all go as well because they're all to blame."

The FA Cup third round tie against second division Coventry at Villa Park was seen as a "battle between the old world and the new". Coventry, for so long strugglers in the lower divisions, had been reborn under the visionary leadership of Jimmy Hill, and were marketing themselves as a modern football club. In the end, they went down to a 3-0 defeat, but such a margin of victory fooled none of the 47,656 crowd that Villa were on the right lines. The revelation that Villa's average league gate was scarcely two-thirds of the break-even figure of 36,000 was more typical of the situation facing Dick Taylor as he struggled to keep the Villa in the first division.

Villa finished the season in sixteenth spot, and the lack of money at Villa Park was emphasised by the decision to sell Ron Wylie, both the Villa and the Midlands Footballer of the Season, to Blues for a bargain £15,000. As the new season started, the Sports Argus came out with a neat summation of events: "Average is not a word I associate with Aston Villa". However, before long, average would be an unattainable goal.

The team got off to a reasonable start in 1965-66 and were ninth in the league after ten matches. This, though, failed to placate supporters who were still demanding fresh faces. With goalscoring a problem, the inevitable slump began and defeat to Leicester in the FA Cup third round led to a fresh torrent of abuse from supporters. Taylor was adamant that progress was being made. "Players who don't look like making the grade will go," he said. "We clearly need more power and aggression." Obviously, the desire for attractive, attacking football the manager had promised at the start of his reign had been overtaken by a grim reality that every match was now a battle for survival. As Taylor conceded, "Pure football is now out."

Supporters had been fairly quiet during Taylor's time in charge, but they were once more up in arms. Gates regularly dipped below 20,000 and there were calls for new blood and, more importantly, new money, to be injected into the club. As 'Astonian' wrote in the Sports Argus, "The present Villa image is of a weary, sick old man, dreaming of the past but getting badly pushed around by lively youngsters." And so it was proving. Spurs, Liverpool, Leeds United - clubs which had scarcely been in existence when Aston Villa were lords of all they surveyed - now regarded games with the Villa as little more than a training exercise with two points virtually guaranteed. Taylor had spent some money, including £30,000 on winger Barry Stobbart from Manchester City and £23,000 for centre-forward Tony Hateley from Notts County. But what little was available was often squandered on players who were of lesser quality than the players they were replacing, and certainly not up to the standard expected of Aston Villa players. Villa finished sixteenth in the table for the second year in succession. Taylor promised yet another clear out and an overhaul of the youth policy. However, such details were soon overtaken by events.

The 1966-67 season was, without doubt, one of the most cataclysmic in the history of Aston Villa. The team began the season badly, and things got worse from then on. Tony Hateley demanded a transfer and eventually moved to Chelsea for £100,000 after scoring 86 goals in 148 appearances. The board, under new chairman Norman Smith, made the short-sighted decision to sell the club's training ground on Trinity Road to property developers, leaving the coaching staff having to scratch around for places on which to train. For any professional club, this was an unsatisfactory state of affairs. For Aston Villa, it was unbelievable.

That the Villa, winners of the FA Cup a record seven times, were 100/1 to make it eight victories, told its own story. That they went out of the competition in the fourth round was no great surprise - although there was the consolation of knowing they had played well in going down to a single goal defeat against Liverpool at Anfield. Despite the Villa staying for the most part out of the relegation places, there was a feeling that the drop was inevitable. "When Villa went down in 1935-36 it was a national disaster," said supporter George Smith. "Should they fall again it could be with a sigh of relief." A. Taylor remarked that, "Appeals for support in an attempt to escape relegation is becoming an annual event." A run of one point from nine games saw Villa slide into the relegation zone. Defeat at the hands of Everton in the penultimate game of the season confirmed Villa's fate. The crowd, who had responded to rallying cries from the local press to support the team in their hour of need, reacted in what was now becoming the traditional manner;

slow hand-clapping, besieging the directors box and calling for the board to resign.

Dick Taylor's reaction to relegation was to say, "Dramatic action is needed immediately. The entire policy of the club must change. The problem has got to be looked straight in the face." Such comment was undoubtedly tempting fate and the board's response was entirely predictable. Meeting three days after relegation was confirmed, they decided to sack Taylor, together with chief scout Jimmy Easson and Johnny Dixon, at that time reserve team coach and still as popular amongst supporters as he had been during his days as Villa skipper. Indeed, Taylor may have been one of the last to learn of his fate. Alan Deakin recalls, "We were playing away and we were sitting around talking to Dick about what was going to happen the next season. We found out later that it had been in the papers in Birmingham that he'd already been sacked."

If the directors thought dispensing with the services of such men would get themselves off the hook they were mistaken. Villa supporters knew full well who were at fault. In the words of C.W. Haughton, "Villa's board are the guilty men. Those they sacked are the can carriers." Shareholders Association chairman Dr G. Campbell echoed these words: "They sack the staff instead of sacking themselves". However, the players may have been more aware. "I think it was the right time for him to go, he wasn't happy," remains the verdict of Alan Deakin

Taylor, as expected, had plenty to say on the subject, first of all showing sympathy for Easson and Dixon, whose sackings were widely perceived as unnecessary. Of his own plight, Taylor could only reflect, "The manager's head always goes, irrespective," although he willingly accepted his share of the responsibility for the club's poor form. In response to chairman Norman Smith's recent comments that shortage of funds had never prevented Taylor from signing a player, the former manager commented, "From the time I took over as manager I had to apply economy measures on all spending. Several times I made bids for players but was turned down because I could not offer enough." Taylor wished the club all the best; "I hope the public get the standards they deserve," and couched his final shot at the board in diplomatic language: "They have their ideas. I have mine"

Club vice-chairman Bruce Normansell stressed that the club was looking for a big name replacement for Taylor, stating that the successful applicant would receive a top salary and would be in full control of all playing matters. However, he admitted the board were not willing to accept new investment. Any new investor would, he felt, "want full control, and I doubt very much that that is on".

After leaving the Villa, Dick Taylor, in common with a number of the club's departing managers over the years, moved out of professional football altogether. He didn't, though, move far from Villa Park, eventually opening a sports shop in Witton Road and becoming Villa's kit supplier. Alan Deakin remained in contact with his former boss, and the two men would often meet up in Taylor's shop. "I used to go in there with my son, to buy his ball and his boots. Dick would always be letting him have stuff cheap or giving it away. He loved to talk football, we'd be in there for hours, in the back room for hours talking football."

Dick Taylor may have left the Villa in 1967, but there was to be a postscript to his work many years later. During his time at Scunthorpe, Taylor had become friendly with the football reporter on the local newspaper, his namesake Tom Taylor. Dick also struck up a friendship with Tom's son, Graham, and as the youngster's career progressed, it was one of Dick's greatest ambitions that Graham Taylor become manager of the Villa. Indeed, it was Dick who first spoke to Graham about taking the Villa job following the dismissal of Billy McNeill and then tipped off Doug Ellis that his friend was unsettled at Watford and might be amenable to a change of club. It can therefore be argued that Dick Taylor's greatest service to the Villa came twenty years, almost to the day, after he left the club. Upon his retirement from business, Taylor remained living in the Birmingham area, and died in January 1995 at the age of 76.

Dick Taylor was yet another Villa manager who found himself unable to swim against the tide of history. The club was in serious, long-term decline, and the only people who failed to appreciate the seriousness of the situation were the directors. Their attitude seemed to be one of denial of the fact that Aston Villa could be in real trouble, simply because they were Aston Villa. Moreover, there was still the old belief that the board knew best and, therefore, any shortcomings must be down to the manager. In reality, of course, the simple truth is that the board were unable to cope with the realties of football in the sixties. They could not, or would not, pay the amounts necessary to bring top quality players to Villa Park, even if those players could be persuaded to join a club that was so clearly in decline. Their methods of running the club were rooted in the pre-war era when the name Aston Villa was still the greatest in world football. They seemed unwilling to appoint a big name manager, and the treatment of players was equally shoddy.

For several years none of the coaching staff were FA-qualified, although one of the players, Phil Woosnam, was the possessor of an FA coaching badge. It's hard to imagine the scenario now - the best-qualified coach at a top-flight club was one of the players. Small wonder Dick Taylor was unable to keep the club in the first division. No manager, no matter how great, would have been able to succeed in such circumstances.

8

Tommy Cummings

July 1967 - November 1968

The Villa board were scarcely in a position of strength when it came to choosing a new manager during the summer of 1967. Few top managers were prepared to take the risk of attempting to take over a club so blatantly in decline. Wolves' Ronnie Allen was mentioned as a possibility, as was Jimmy Hagan, who had recently left the Albion. Eventually the choice was narrowed down to a short-list of two names. The favourite was Willie Cunningham, who had recently resigned after a successful period at Dunfermline. However, Cunningham seemed reluctant to travel to Villa Park to speak to the board, and so the eventual successful candidate was Tommy Cummings, manager of third division Mansfield Town. There was some concern that Cummings had little experience as a manager, his only success having been to get Mansfield promoted from the fourth division four seasons earlier, although he had also shown another, more unexpected, talent during his time with the Nottinghamshire club. "They were knocking part of the ground down and one of my jobs was to help them pull the stand down. They hadn't any money and I was having to pull the stand down with the ground staff so they could put this new one up that they had from Haydock racecourse. I'd get home and I'd be filthy dirty, like I'd just got out of the pit"

Born in Co. Durham in 1929, Cummings was a member of the Burnley side that had won the league title in 1960 and reached the FA Cup final two seasons later, as well as having been England B skipper and making several appearances for the Football League at centre half. He had also succeeded Jimmy Hill as chairman of the Professional Footballers Association, a post he relinquished upon being appointed player-manager at Mansfield Town in 1963.

Cummings later spoke of how he came to be appointed the Villa's sixth manager since the war. "I was at the League Secretaries & Managers Association do in London when Bob Lord asked me if I wanted the Villa job. He must have known somebody at the Villa. Of course I said yes, they were a big club.

"I was on holiday in Devon when I got a telegram asking me to come up to Villa Park. I drove back up, and it was a fair run, and it was all over the press when I got there. When the interview was finished they didn't say there and then, but they asked me to leave for a bit and I got offered the job. They took me, a groundsman or somebody, over the other side of the ground to get out, but there was still a crowd of reporters waiting for me when I got out."

At the time of his appointment the 38-year old Cummings confessed that getting the Villa job was "A tremendous thrill". He added that, "What has happened at Villa Park in the past is no concern of mine. I have a tremendous task ahead of me." These words were echoed by Dennis Shaw, who warned in the Evening Mail, "Do not attempt to restore the old image. Let the old glory and the feuding live only in the history books".

Cummings had no doubt about the task ahead: "I spoke to Joe Mercer, he told me a bit about the job and how Villa were a good side, a good club. I was looking forward to it. Villa was a big club and I'd been with Burnley who were a big club, so I had a bit of a lead in that we'd always played a good style. A lot of people copied us at Burnley and that was how I wanted to play at Villa."

Dismissing the claim that he was too nice a man to be a successful manager, Cummings laid down what he believed would be a three-point plan for Villa's revival: "Harmony in the dressing room, pride in the club and a tactical style to produce winners. I want everyone at Villa Park to eat, sleep and breathe football".

The club had posted a profit of £78,689 during the summer, thanks mostly to the sale of Tony Hateley the previous season and the proceeds of a successful World Cup. It had been stated that money had to be spent on players in order to prevent much of this profit from being taken in tax, and a figure of £70,000 was generally reckoned to be available to the new manager for players. This may have persuaded the bookmakers to install Villa as favourites to win the second division title. Few supporters shared their optimism.

The team lost their first two matches, and supporters were immediately critical of the new manager. When he announced that he wanted to take a good look at his new players, supporters replied that they'd been watching them for long enough and weren't impressed. Cummings spoke of the need for a five-year plan to turn things round. The wry response from the terraces was that the club could be out of the league by then.

But the manager's enthusiasm remained. It was revealed that he was travelling up to a thousand miles a week in the search for new players, and his philosophy was stated simply: "Villa are my life." Whatever his abilities as a manager, Cummings had certainly made his mark with the players, as Alan Deakin remembers. "Tommy was a players' man. We'd be at an away match and he'd always have a drink with us. He was highly regarded as a player when he came to us although we didn't know much about him as a manager, but we thought we'd give it a try and see what happened."

With the club bottom but one in the table after nine games, crowds had not surprisingly slumped as low as 13,000, although the potential at Villa Park was apparent when almost 50,000 attended the meeting with Blues. Most of those in attendance would not have been impressed with a 2-4 defeat.

Malcolm Musgrove, who had played for West Ham alongside such notables as Dave Sexton and Frank O'Farrell, each of whom later went on to manage Manchester United, was eventually appointed as assistant manager. "I needed an assistant, so I brought in Malcolm from West Ham. He was a tactics man, good on the training ground," says Cummings. Alan Deakin was equally impressed with the arrival of Musgrove. "Tommy never got involved in the training, Malcolm did all the work. He was an excellent coach, up to date; he'd have us doing short, sharp shuttle runs instead of the long distance stuff. He worked on recovery rates, which was new then. We were used to things like twenty times round the pitch and up and down the terraces until then, but with Malcolm it was sprinting and ballwork, that sort of thing. He was the first one who sat and talked before the game, with a blackboard, to point out how we were going to play against the opposition and who their players were. And he was the last to do it while I was there."

League performances did improve, even if attendances didn't. A photograph of the Witton End shortly before kick-off against Blackburn showed a few score diehards spread across the open terrace. The team eventually finished sixteenth in the second division in 1967-68 - at that time far and away the Villa's worst-ever performance. In the words of a supporter who signed himself 'Punch

Drunk', "The board are to be congratulated. They have at long last managed to get together the poorest side in living memory".

Tommy Cummings, who had been brought in to get the Villa instant promotion, remembers "I didn't think they could go straight back up when I arrived. Not there and then. Naturally I hoped I could do what Alan Brown was doing for Burnley, but it just didn't work. There wasn't the same quality of players - there were some good players, Deakin and Tindall, but Malcolm and me, we used to say that you couldn't expect to get up with the sort of players we were buying. I was sorry that I wasn't able to have got the players that I could afford."

If the team had slipped into mediocrity, events off the field were hotting up. The Shareholders Association had unveiled a shadow board, and although they had failed to win control at an EGM held in January 1968, the malcontent Villa supporters were determined that things in the boardroom would alter. The manager was natural-ly aware of the rumblings from the terraces. "It didn't affect me in the respect that they were after the players and the board. They left me alone a little bit, with all due respect. The pressure of what was going on made it hard, because no matter how good they were to me, I knew inside that they felt I hadn't got a chance. They thought, 'He'll be another one on the scrap heap before long'."

Cummings recalled the previous nine months, "A most disap-pointing season…. we have been brought face to face with reality." The average gate had fallen below 20,000 and the gloom around Villa Park was not lifted by the fact that newly-crowned league champions were Manchester City, under their manager Joe Mercer. A man the Villa directors had considered a failure was now being heralded four years later as one of the finest managers in the game.

Veteran trainer Bert Bond left the club to be replaced by Arthur Cox, who later took more of a coaching role alongside Musgrove. Indeed, both men had enormous influence on the way in which the team were playing. Brian Godfrey, who had joined from Preston North End along with Brian Greenhalgh during the disappointing 1967-68 season, recalls, "Tommy didn't have a great input into training sessions during the week, that was more the role of Malcolm Musgrove. Then Arthur Cox came along, first as a trainer and then as coach working with Malcolm." Yet the manager soon began to regret his latest appointment. "He wasn't good for me,"

Cummings says. "He was very friendly with the directors, always nattering to them, and he tried to cause a rift between me and the board. I brought him to Villa from Walsall; he was obviously ambitious and he got on. He was good at fitness training, that's what I brought him in for."

The new season started much the same as the old one had ended. Things were already looking bleak for the managerial team, as Cummings explains: "From the start of the season we thought we might be in trouble, Malcolm and I. The board were saying a few things - not serious, because they were too gentlemanly to be nasty."

What was described as the 'Depression Derby' ended in a 4-0 defeat at home to Blues. Cummings had spent a reasonably large amount of money by second division standards. Yet the team still looked in imminent danger of relegation to the third division. Cummings remained optimistic: "I am prepared to back my judgement on these players," yet he must surely have realised that the end was in sight. As he now recalls, "Things were looking bad, it was getting bad. I used to have a natter with Malcolm and he'd say, 'I think our time's near, Tom,' and I'd say, 'Looks like it'."

A single goal defeat at the hands of Preston North End on 9th November 1968 marked a watershed in the Villa's history. Supporters in the 13,374 crowd unveiled banners demanding, 'The board must go' in the Holte End. The Trinity Road season ticket holders shouted, "Resign" and hurled earthier insults towards the directors box. After the match a demonstration outside the club offices had to be broken up by mounted police.

Two days later, the board held an emergency meeting. To no-one's surprise, they felt that the blame for the club's predicament lay with the management team. Cummings and Malcolm Musgrove were dismissed. Both men took the news calmly. "It is just one of those things," said Cummings, while Musgrove asked, "What can you say when you have just been sacked?"

Yet again, the board's decision to blame a manager for their own failings met with universal condemnation, and the Evening Mail's postbag was suddenly overflowing with passionate outpourings from angry Villa supporters. "Every manager cannot be wrong," said M. Mackie. 'Real Villa Supporter' pointed out that yet again "the buck is passed neatly to the manager and his assistant." However, Brian Evans, who was prominent in the ongoing campaign to overthrow the board, pointed out that Tommy Cummings must share some of the blame, being "Wrong in defending the team when they played badly." This criticism is one that can fairly be laid at Cummings. He had never sought to criticise his players, at least not publicly, and had given the impression that he was content to let matters drift when decisive action was needed. As Brian Godfrey says, "As thing got worse, Tommy didn't really change that much. You can't always blame the manager though, the whole thing was declining and Tommy was just not dynamic enough. The players always wanted to win, but there were big problems at the club."

Cummings himself supports this view. "The club was, unfortunately, on the slide. It was sad because the directors were lovely men, but I must have been a bit soft on them. You can still be nice with people and get the job done, but they were frightened to do things. Mr Smith would ask if I wanted some money for players and he'd see that the club didn't go into debt. The directors were just too old. They couldn't really cope with the way football was changing. The money wasn't there and they weren't capable of running a top line club and realising that to do well you have to have good players. It's alright saying I bought the wrong ones, but if you only have so much money, you get what you can."

Yet the former manager concedes his own shortcomings. "I look at it in two ways. I didn't do too well for them, unfortunately, but I don't want to take all the blame. There was the money side of it. If you don't have first division money you won't get into the first division. I signed about seven players, and maybe three of them I shouldn't have bought."

As for the politicking that was increasingly a feature of Cummings' short reign at Villa Park, he is equally honest. "There was always people around, not involved in the club but for some reason they'd got round one or two of the directors and they were always pushing themselves. I'd ask about them and I'd be warned off them. Malcolm was always saying they were trying to influence things, they were talking to the directors. He was maybe a bit harder me, but we worked well. At that time I was maybe a bit too nice. I should have been a bit firmer; there's a lot of things I would have done differently. You don't have to treat people badly, but I should have been firmer."

As is usually the case when a Villa manager leaves the club, there was an inquest into how much influence the board had over his affairs. It was accepted that Cummings had enjoyed a fair, some would say unprecedented, amount of authority, even though chairman Norman Smith, who had retired from his normal employment, could be found at Villa Park most days. George Robinson, the only director who had resigned by this time, pointed out that the usual accusation of interference laid at a Villa board could not this time ring true. "The manager never had any interference over team matters. I sometimes wonder whether we put too much trust in managers," was his only comment.

However, Robinson's statement finds support from Brian Godfrey. "You needed a strong manager then, particularly as the board were so weak. They were lovely men, but they were totally unsuited to running a club like the Villa. They were too old, football was changing and they weren't up to it. You had Norman Smith, he was the Villa chairman, but he used to get the bus to Villa Park. The whole thing needed modernising but they weren't capable. It's the same for managers as it is for players. Tommy had played for Burnley when they were a good side, he'd played in the cup final for them. But he didn't have much great management experience. He needed help managing the club, but they just couldn't give it to him." It appears that, for once, the problem was that the board did not interfere enough.

Alan Deakin agrees with his former team-mate. "Tommy was out of his depth, he wasn't really management material. Things were changing and he wasn't up to it. I don't think he had enough money, he was buying players on the cheap. He signed seven players for £200,000 when other managers could have spent that on two."

The dismissal of Malcolm Musgrove was seen by some as a case of getting rid of the wrong trainer. Deakin remembers, "It was disappointing that Malcolm had to go with Tommy, he'd been very good for us on the training ground. In fact, when they were sacked, Malcolm called a meeting of the players and said it was a pity that others weren't going as well."

Despite disappointing league positions, Cummings looked back on his time with a certain satisfaction. "I can leave Villa Park secure in the knowledge that the foundations of the new Villa, in the shape of the youth scheme, have been laid, and that my eighteen months as manager has not been wasted." It is not hard to imagine Tommy

Cummings had been so fed up with the infighting and politics which had accompanied almost every day he had spent at Villa Park that he was put off football for life. Brian Godfrey puts it, "When he left, I'm not sure whether Tommy wanted to be a manager anymore. He never had another job in football."

As for the Villa, who had now sacked four managers in ten years, a familiar search was once more underway. And as a letter in the Mail from 'Two Board Holte Enders' pointed out: "Do the Aston Villa board believe that some day, somebody will succeed where Eric Houghton, Joe Mercer, Dick Taylor and now Tommy Cummings have, in the eyes of the board, all failed?"

His unhappy stint at Villa Park over, Tommy Cummings moved out of football altogether. He returned to Lancashire, his adopted home, and settled into the life of a publican. "I was tired of the travelling. My family were growing up, my wife was fed up, so I entered the pub trade and had 23 years there. I was a bit tired of football to be honest. I fancied a change. I could have gone to a couple of clubs but I never fancied it. In a way I was glad to get away from Villa. I'd had a difficult eighteen months. In some respects I wish I hadn't left Mansfield - I could still be there now."

Tommy Cummings was, and is, an honest man. He admits he was out of his depth as Villa manager, unable to reverse the decades of decline that reached their peak (or should that be trough?) during the mid-sixties. Yet in failing, Tommy Cummings paved the way for the Villa's revival. It was his dismissal that brought supporter dissatisfaction to a head and ushered in the wave of revolt that would lead to the Villa Revolution and the rebirth of the club.

Now retired, Cummings still lives in Burnley, still attends games at Turf Moor where he works for the club on match-days and is regarded, quite rightly, as a legend. He still bears no ill-will towards the club where he found himself a victim of circumstance. "I had a very fair time with the supporters in the short time I was there; they treated me fairly. Fantastic supporters, they gave me a very fair trial, if that's the right word."

9

Tommy Docherty

December 1968 - January 1970

Never in the long history of Aston Villa has there been a period to rival those few weeks in November and December of 1968, when supporters were up in arms, the board finally decided they had enough and were stepping down for the good of the club, while rival consortia vied to take control of what was still seen as one of the great names of world football. In the midst of this uncertainty, the team were also in search of a manager.

Off the field, things were coming to a head thanks primarily to the efforts of two season ticket holders from Sutton Coldfield, John Russell and Brian Evans, who took the demonstrations surrounding the Preston match a step further and organised what has gone down in history as the legendary Digbeth Civic Hall meeting. A capacity audience heard Evans, who had earlier been in communication with the board, read out a statement which was interpreted as saying that the Villa were up for sale.

This announcement had the desired effect. Several groups were interested in buying the Villa, including one from the Atlanta Chiefs football club in America, who included in their number former Villa player Phil Woosnam. However, when the dust settled, the soon-to-be familiar figure of Doug Ellis emerged as the new chairman of Aston Villa. Ellis led a seven-man consortium who, with the help of financier Pat Matthews of the Birmingham Industrial Trust, took over the club and oversaw a successful share issue which raised £200,000 and placed the Villa on a much sounder financial footing. With the club's future saved, the search for a new manager could now be concluded.

Names bandied around had once more included Jimmy Hagan and Ronnie Allen, who had left Wolves shortly after Tommy Cummings had been sacked by the Villa. Indeed, pressure on the old board had increased when it was pointed out that they had procrastinated for several weeks after sacking Cummings, whilst

Wolves had been able to replace Allen with Bill McGarry within 48 hours. Tommy Docherty had recently joined Queens Park Rangers from Rotherham, and so was ruled out of the running – which was thought a pity because Docherty's style was ideally suited to the task of awakening the sleeping giant of Aston. However, Docherty's reign at Loftus Road was to last just 28 days, and when he resigned, with the Villa job still vacant, he was immediately installed as favourite for the position. Docherty, though, hinted that he was off to Spain, to take over at the Basque club, Athletic Bilbao. This proposed move, though, was placed in doubt following the death of Bilbao president Julio Equsquiza in a car accident.

Meanwhile, in Aston, events were moving with a rapidity which would have stunned those used to the sedate, almost Victorian, methods of a board whose time was now running out. On 12th December 1968, it was revealed in the Evening Mail that a prominent local businessman was poised to take over the Villa. On the following day this was revealed to be none other than Doug Ellis, at the time still a director of Birmingham City. Mr Ellis literally walked out of the directors' box of St Andrews that evening and into Villa Park on the following Monday morning. His appointment as Villa chairman was immediately followed by the announcement that Tommy Docherty was to take charge of the team.

Docherty had already enjoyed a successful career, first as a player of no mean repute. Born in August 1928, he had won 35 caps for Scotland and played for Celtic, Preston and Arsenal, before going into management with Chelsea. It was at Stamford Bridge where the legend of the Doc was born. "We'd done well, we got promoted to the first division, got to three FA Cup semis and the final in 1967, won the League Cup, never out of the top three. Then the chairman Mr Mears died and Bill Pratt took over. We didn't see eye to eye and that was me away. We had a good young side there though - Peter Osgood, Alan Hudson, I had Terry Venables there for a while - and I knew they'd get better. Dave Sexton did well with the players I left, but it was only a matter of time."

After leaving Stamford Bridge, Docherty moved on to Rotherham and then came his brief spell at Queens Park Rangers, where he once more fell foul of the boardroom. "The chairman, Jim Gregory; he promised me money for players, and it never came through. He wouldn't take incoming phone calls in the end, the only time he was ever on the phone was when he rang somebody. I couldn't work with someone like that so I was off."

And so, on to the Villa. "I'd just walked out on QPR when someone contacted me from the Villa. I was a big friend of Pat Matthews' closest friend, Charles Tagleigh. His family were all fanatical Chelsea supporters, they'd been heartbroken when I left Chelsea, and he asked me if I was interested in coming to Villa. So the next day I was appointed manager."

The lure of the Villa was a strong one, although Docherty was no stranger to Villa Park. "I'd always known Villa were a big club. Jimmy Hogan used to talk about them all the time and I knew Eric Houghton very well. I also did my National Service at Whittington Barracks, near Lichfield, and I used to watch the Villa regularly, First game I saw down there was against the Baggies at the Hawthorns. I grew up knowing about the Villa.

"I was impressed. Nice ground at the time, great supporters, but things were going wrong. To achieve success you have to have a good club, and Villa were a great club with good support. Villa had those things going for them, but it was all just going a bit pear-shaped. The club had everything going for it to achieve greatness. Tommy Cummings couldn't unfortunately do it, so I was brought in. It was just waiting to take off."

The players certainly knew what to expect from Docherty. And if they didn't, they soon learned. Brian Godfrey recalls his arrival: "We knew his reputation, what he'd done with Chelsea especially. When he arrived we knew we'd have to be on our toes. We knew he'd get the club buzzing." And he did. "Gates doubled. The press loved him. He was articulate; a populist. He knew the importance of the media, and in turn they loved him."

"Docherty will act like a whirlwind. It will be a kill or cure treatment," was the opinion of Ron Williams, writing in the Birmingham Post. Docherty was joining the Villa on a reported £9,000 per annum salary for a move which "wedded one of soccer's most unconventional characters to what has been the most conservative club in the country," as it was described in the local press. Nobody was under any illusion the team were in deep trouble. Bottom of the second division, with fourteen points from 23 games, they appeared doomed. As Docherty said, "It's difficult for the players because they will be frightened of making mistakes. I have got to build their confidence." And for supporters, he had a simple, yet powerful, message that cut straight to the heart of just how precarious the club's position was: "The one thing I have never done is beg. But I'm begging the fans to come back now." 19,923 of them, Villa's second biggest gate of the season, responded on the Saturday before Christmas to see the first game of the new Aston Villa. The team responded with a 2-1 victory over Norwich City, which followed Docherty's honest assessment of the situation: "I don't think the crowd expect miracles. But I hope we can provide them with a team that plays to the very best of their ability".

No manager had ever buzzed around Birmingham like Tommy did in those early days. Factories, pubs, anywhere Villa supporters might have been gathered was fair game for a visit from the Doc. "I was trying to find money anywhere I could. I knew the players I wanted: I was just trying to get the money to sign them." And as the board pointed out to the businessmen of Birmingham: "An improved Villa means improved productivity."

Docherty was undoubtedly providing the kick up the backside the club needed, and the supporters loved him for it. As he recalls, "The whole place was just waiting to take off." And not just on the terraces were people taking the club to heart. Paint-ins were organised, when supporters were encouraged to come along and help renovate Villa Park. Donations to keep the club afloat were being sent from supporters, and a share issue that eventually raised over £200,000 was in the process of being organised.

Of course, Docherty was not without his critics. Carlisle manager, Bob Stokoe complained about the Villa's tactics after his side lost at home to the new-look Villa. 41,250 came to Villa Park on Boxing Day to witness Villa, including new signing Brian Tiler from Rotherham, beat Cardiff City 2-0. "Where did they all come from?" wondered Docherty afterwards. "They even cheered our mistakes".

Aston Villa were now the most talked-about club in the country. After years of decline, the club was showing its potential while the supporters, described as the best in the land not long before, were responding. Small wonder that Birmingham City and the Albion were reduced to appealing for support, such was the way in which they were being totally overshadowed by their resurgent neighbours. As for Docherty, he professed to have but one aim; "To make Aston Villa the most successful club in the game." Looking at the progress made within a few short weeks, there was not a single Villa supporter who would have argued with that statement. "Beyond my wildest dreams," was how Docherty described his first month in charge. As Willie Anderson, who had put in a transfer request in the days immediately before Docherty's arrival put it, "He is the best thing that has ever happened to Aston Villa".

Crowds continued to rise. 49,110 saw the single goal defeat at home by table-topping Derby. A goal from Dave Simmons was enough to beat the Blues in front of a Villa Park crowd of 53,584, while almost sixty thousand attended the FA Cup fourth round replay with Southampton. Villa sold 13,000 tickets for the fifth round tie at Spurs, only for the match to be called off and most of their support unable to travel to the rearranged fixture, which the Villa narrowly lost 3-2.

Docherty introduced new ideas throughout the club. He took the team training at Repton public school, whose sports facilities were far in excess of anything that a cash-strapped, second division football club could afford. He got the players spending the night before home games in a hotel at Ashby de la Zouch, in an attempt to strengthen team spirit.

By this time, though, results were almost a sideshow to the main event of the Aston Villa marketing machine. Docherty, Ellis and new commercial manger Eric Woodward were described as "the most publicity-conscious team in football." The unveiling of nursery sides in Glasgow and Birmingham was done with the kind of coverage usually reserved for record transfer deals. Over a thousand season tickets were sold in the wake of Docherty's arrival, although supporters were dismayed by a rise of up to 50% in ticket prices for the forthcoming season. Never mind; 1969-70 was to be the season Villa proved that they were indisputably back in the big time.

As Docherty put it, "The way things are going, the Villa will soon be buying St Andrews to play reserve matches there". Of course, the supporters lapped this up. For years their club had been the butt of everyone else's jokes. At long last it was back in the headlines for the right reasons. The corner had been turned and the man responsible was regarded with devotion by his adoring fans. Promotion was to be a formality en route to the top.

Villa were certainly going about things the right way. Over £200,000 was spent on players in readiness for the promotion push, including £100,000 on Luton's promising midfielder Bruce Rioch, who arrived at Villa Park in a deal which saw his brother Neil making the same journey. "They cost £110,000 and Neil was ten thousand of that. I got Chico Hamilton from Southend for £5,000 - peanuts for a player of that class."

It was easy to attract players to Villa Park. The club so obviously going places, and there was also the Docherty factor. As Neil Rioch says: "What would be the right word to describe Tommy? Extremely enthusiastic, passionate, humorous, a motivator. As a manager he arrived when the club was at a crossroads, Certainly when I joined in July '69 it was just after the big changeover at board level and Villa was full of promise. Tommy Docherty captured the imagination of supporters and the feel that here was Aston Villa coming back, and everyone else felt that as well."

There were, however, grey clouds on the horizon and they came, as ever, from the direction of the boardroom. As Docherty remembers: "I thought the club would just carry on improving, until I saw the final make up of the board. Doug was chairman, but in those days he wasn't strong enough. Nice man, Villa through and through, but at that stage he lacked experience. And there were one or two shifty characters on the board. There were a couple of them, they weren't for Doug or for the club. They were for themselves. Eric Woodward was a great man, a lovely man. And Harry Kartz was smashing as well. But you couldn't tell Doug anything at that stage, he knew it all in his own head. Maybe a bit headstrong, but that's down to inexperience. He was just so keen to please everyone – the press, the supporters, everyone who wanted to see the Villa doing well and thinking big. The Villa needed a figurehead, someone the supporters could relate to, and Doug was that. He just didn't have the experience to do the job properly"

Villa were favourites to get promoted the following season, but results were poor from the start. 32,000 attended Villa Park for the first league game, against Norwich They saw the team lose, slow-handclapped, and thus began a run of six games with a solitary point that left the team firmly trapped at the bottom of the second division. Neil Rioch points out, "We got off to a bad start and things just seemed to get worse."

Despite the seemingly rosy air of optimism around Villa Park, there were many problems which Docherty was either unable to cure. Rioch recalls, "There was a great deal of player unrest in that some were Doc's men, some were the rebels if you like, and then there were the new players. The dressing room was split in three, the likes of myself, Bruce, Chico & Pat MacMahon got on well with both the other factions, but there was a massive split between the existing players, the Docherty men and the rebels. You knew there were some who Doc liked a lot - because he always played them - and others who he didn't like because of the way he treated them. There was almost a fence down the middle with the new players straddling the fence, and it was extremely strange. I was too young to understand what was happening, but in hindsight it was badly managed – you have to say that."

Brian Godfrey was one of those who were definitely out of favour. A Tommy Cummings signing, Godfrey never saw eye to eye with the new manager. "There was definitely a split in the dressing room; he treated some players badly. I was in the team at first, along with a few others, then he brought his own men in and that was it. I remember the press call at the start of the season, he said he didn't want eight of us on the team photo, and six of us were internationals. It wasn't the best way to do it. If you were out of his plans you were an outcast. He sent us to Inverness once, to play with the youth team up there. He made it plain that if you were out, you wouldn't get back in."

Alan Deakin had seen Docherty's divisive ways from the start. "On his first day he came into the dressing room and said, 'I've heard that this place is a holiday camp. That stops now.' I always got on with him, but he had his favourites. One time me and Mick Ferguson weren't playing in a match, so we didn't hang around. Tommy fined Mick for going home but he didn't say a word to me."

As the season wore on, results were just as bad for the reserve and youth teams, yet gates for Central League fixtures regularly topped 3,000 and Midland Intermediate games drew four figure crowds. The supporters appeared in a state of denial, still wanted to believe, and as Docherty said, "We don't want excuses, we want luck".

Docherty continued making changes, bringing in the veteran Coventry City defender George Curtis (and many supporters commented ruefully about the change in circumstances which saw Villa signing reserves from Coventry), while Vic Crowe returned from America to take charge of the youth team.

As the season continued its downward path, supporters grew divided as to the manager's abilities. A. Horton of Warley summed up things in the Argus, saying of Docherty, "He is the idol of the kids behind the goal, but to the older and thinking supporters his image has faded".

And while supporters were divided, the players were no more unified. Brian Godfrey; "He was used to dealing with kids. He didn't like older, more experienced players who could see past the charisma. The players he brought in backed him and the older ones didn't appreciate that. Tommy was a short-term merchant, he could get the crowd back, kick the club up the backside and get things moving again."

Bottom of the league with seven points from sixteen games, Villa went down 0-2 at home to Watford, a match marked by supporters walking out en masse with twenty minutes remaining. This was followed by a seven hour board meeting, at the end of which more money was promised for team strengthening and Docherty's job was still safe – for the time being. Meanwhile, several vice-presidents called for yet another re-launch of the club.

Results continued to disappoint, and a 5-3 defeat against Portsmouth, coming soon after the team went out of the FA Cup in a third round replay with Charlton, saw Docherty out of a job.

Was the sack expected? Docherty remains adamant: "No. A complete shock. They were too impatient. And then they brought in Vic Crowe, who had been reserve team coach and who was working in the background against me. He was in cahoots with Bruce Rioch and Brian Tiler." It must be said here that Vic Crowe always strenuously denied this charge. "I was only the second team coach at the time and happy with the job," said Crowe some years later. Rioch also denied any involvement, and as Neil Rioch points out: "If Bruce had conspired against him, why was Tommy happy to sign him again a few years later for Derby?"

During a recording for the BBC's Forum programme the day before his dismissal, Docherty was in typically forthright mood: "The new players have not performed as well as I anticipated." He did though, emphasise, "I have complete faith and confidence in the players and my own ability."

Docherty, though, with the unquenchable optimism that has always been his trademark, remains convinced, over thirty years later, that things were not as bad as they appeared. "Results were bad but we weren't in terrible danger. The board just panicked. They thought that when I came in I would just wave a magic wand and avoid relegation, which we did, then go on to win the league the next year. But football's not like that. You've got to build things. I could imagine the boardroom, all those enemies I'd made already, poisoning Doug. I'd have kept the Villa up. I never thought there was a problem with that. The problem was in the boardroom."

Naturally, these views were not shared by the Villa Park hierarchy. A statement from the board later exonerated the players and went on to say, "This season's performances add up.... to failure. In this field there is only one price for failure." The blame was laid squarely at the feet of Docherty and his coaching methods.

Maybe the biggest problem was that things were moving too quickly. Instant success was demanded, and supporters were impatient, forgetting that there was half a century of decline to be righted. Dennis Shaw, writing in the Evening Mail, noted that Docherty "had attempted to achieve the impossible too soon".

However, Neil Rioch disagrees: "Change was definitely needed. And I've found that the most difficult thing in my career outside football is people's response to change. Most people don't respond positively and managing change is one of the most difficult things to do. It was a difficult job; I don't think Tommy would say he got 100% backing from all the players, but a lot of senior players would say that he treated them unfairly. It could have been handled better - and the proof, if anyone wants to argue, is that we got relegated. Once we got on that slippery slope, it comes back to the old cliche of once a manager loses the dressing room that's it, and that's what Tommy did. But he appeared to know he was doing this; it was almost as if he wanted to lose some players. There was one incident coming back from training; things weren't going well and Brian Godfrey was out of the side. We were on our way back from training on the coach and there was a game on that night. Tommy said everybody had to report for the match, which was standard practice. Brian asked if we would have entry to the car park and when Tommy said he had to park on the street he refused to turn up. There was almost a stand-up fight on the coach, in the aisle, both of them had to be restrained. This was how he was. I think he was clearly saying, 'You're not in my plans. I don't care about you'. Management and

senior players were at such loggerheads and as a result we were
doomed. There was no chance we could get out of trouble."

Although Docherty had come in for criticism towards the end of
his reign, the reaction to his dismissal was one of outrage. As news
spread, dozens of supporters gathered outside Villa Park, where
they chanted support for the dismissed manager. A petition was cir-
culated calling for his reinstatement, whilst the Evening Mail
reported a view of 40-1 against the sacking in letters they were
receiving. Not until Ron Atkinson's dismissal three decades later
would a Villa manager's departure cause such outrage.

Tommy Docherty may have fallen out with members of the board,
but to the club itself he bore no ill-will, Indeed, his parting shot that
"Aston Villa will play in the European Cup one day" was one of the
reasons why he remained so popular. But, surely, even he must have
been surprised with how quickly his prediction was not only
achieved, but exceeded. "I was surprised, but not that they did so
well."

As Neil Rioch put it, "His legacy was that he, and it seems strange
having got relegated, but he lifted the club. He lifted the supporters, he brought some new belief into the club. And the players wanted the club to do well. They had belief and that's what he got across;
what a big club it was and what a tradition it had, how good the supporters were. He made you want to go out and play not just for yourself but for every one of those supporters. The period after relegation was pretty much successful from then on and Docherty kick-
started it. He helped blow the cobwebs away and said, 'Let's go'."

However, Rioch still has some reservations about Docherty's
methods. "We used to train sometimes on the old car park, an
asphalt surface surrounded by four brick walls. The Doc would say
there'll be a game; one team would be the first team and his
favourites, the others would be the ones out of favour. And it was
done deliberately. He was more than happy for players to be lamp-
ing each other in training and charging each other into brick walls
and the rest. It divided the players. At the time I wasn't aware of it,
but looking back, as a manager in business would I have done the
same? No I wouldn't".

Docherty still retains a tremendous feeling of nostalgia towards
the club. "I'm still a shareholder – I sold a few and made quite a lot
of money, but I've still got some. I won't hear a bad word said about

Aston Villa. The club still means a tremendous amount to me."

Docherty, of course, had a long and chequered career post-Villa. He moved to Porto and was then manager of the Scottish national side. His time at Old Trafford, when he inherited a team in decline, has often been overlooked as he refashioned a side as good as any which represented for the club between the eras of Busby and Ferguson. True, they were relegated to the second division. But they were promoted at the first attempt (alongside the Villa) and won the FA Cup in 1977. It must also be remembered that Docherty had to do everything at Old Trafford under the watchful, some would say over-powering, eye of Sir Matt Busby, who remained at the club when maybe he should have been thanked for his services and asked to leave with dignity.

Docherty left Old Trafford within months of that FA Cup triumph in 1977, after it was revealed that he was having an affair with the wife of the team physiotherapist – an incident he now recalls with some bitterness. "I got the sack for falling in love. And look at what Martin Edwards gets up to".

He then spent two seasons with Derby and ,after a spell in Australia (which prompted one disgruntled Derby supporter to comment that he'd gone two hundred years too late), moved to Queens Park Rangers. Both these clubs were in decline at the time Docherty joined them. Indeed, as he ruefully comments, "Every club I ever joined was declining. But I don't regret going to Derby. I took a gamble in so much as their last two managers had won the league - Cloughie and Dave Mackay, and that team was coming to its end. I came in and there was no money to spend, while the players were growing old together. I should have had a warning about them because we'd beaten Derby in the 1976 FA Cup semi-final so I'd seen how they were going backwards. But they were all growing old together – McFarland, Todd, Francis Lee."

Docherty spent the 1979-80 season with QPR, then managed Preston prior to taking over at the ultimate team in trouble, joining Wolves during the reign of the infamous Bhatti brothers. As Wolves, inevitably, slid into the third division, Docherty left the club with few regrets. One last spell managing his local team Altrincham, and one of the most colourful careers in English football management was over. The Doc now makes a living on the after-dinner circuit. "More money than when I was a manager. And less hassle."

In purely footballing terms, Tommy Docherty's time at Villa Park was not particularly successful. He saved the team from relegation one season and despite spending heavily, he was largely responsible for their demise the next. We will never know whether or not Docherty would have saved the team had he not been dismissed, but in the greater scheme of things such conjecture is, perhaps, irrelevant. When Tommy Docherty arrived at Villa Park the club were in almost-terminal decline. The new board, with Doug Ellis as its figurehead, did wonders in re-financing the club and leading them into the future. But none of the work they did would have been possible without the charismatic figure of Docherty bringing in tens of thousands of supporters that had been thought lost to the club for good. Whatever the Villa have done since, it can be argued that none of it would have taken place were it not for the almost miraculous work done during the early, heady days of Tommy Docherty.

10

Vic Crowe

January 1970 - May 1974

"It's a great pity that Tommy Docherty had to go," said Pat Matthews, stating that he played no part himself in the day-to-day running of the club. And that summed up Vic Crowe's time at Villa Park. No matter that he was the Villa manager for over four years, nor that in terms of league results he was the most successful incumbent of all time. Crowe was doomed to spend his career in the shadow of his predecessor.

Writing in the Sports Argus within weeks of Docherty's dismissal, Ian Johnson spoke of "Something missing, apart from the plaque on the door of the manager's office... the air of expectancy when Docherty was around." However, Johnson went on, "The dust has not been allowed to settle", and talked of "an air of quiet authority generated by Vic Crowe." "I am faced with a problem and I look at it as a job of work rather than taking over from Tommy," said Crowe. "It was a sad day and I wondered how he was feeling. Tommy was a good man to work for and I had a lot of sympathy for him."

Vic Crowe was born in January 1932, in the Glamorgan village of Abercynon. Crowe may have been Welsh by birth, but he was a Brummie by upbringing, having lived from the age of two in Handsworth, and was as much a Villa man as anyone standing on the Holte End. A regular in the Welsh side, for whom he made 16 appearances and was in the squad for the 1958 World Cup finals in Sweden, Crowe had spent many years in the Villa half-back line. Although he may not have been an experienced manager, no player he selected would ever fail to appreciate what a signal honour it was to play for the club.

It was reported in the Daily Sketch, for whom Docherty wrote a regular column, that the former manager had offered to loan the club £5,000 interest free and work without wages for two years. Mick Wright asked for a transfer as a result of the sacking, while the rest of the squad were reported as saying they were looking forward to playing for Crowe. Neil Rioch was one of the first to appreciate the new manager. "I got on extremely well with Vic. He taught me more in one season than I'd ever learnt at Luton."

Crowe's first signing was the 28 year old Leicester City centre forward, Andy Lochhead, at a cost of £35,000 Results remained disappointing, and a late revival was not enough to save Villa from the drop. Despite a 2-0 victory at St Andrews, Villa finished the season with 29 points from 42 games, two points short of safety.

With Villa bound for the third division, Doug Ellis looked to make economies. After all, the crowds that had stuck by the Villa throughout their unsuccessful relegation battle would surely decrease in the third division. "Will the name Aston Villa mean anything in division three?" was the question posed by the media. Tommy Docherty stated, "Don't blame me. It broke my heart to leave the club." But supporters did, in part at least, blame Docherty for the worst reverse in Aston Villa's history.

During the summer, the Villa began adapting both for life in division three and for the revival that everyone connected with the club was convinced would follow. Ron Wylie returned as assistant manager and first team coach, while Frank Upton took charge of the youth side. £50,000 was taken in season ticket sales, while 6,000 supporters attended an open day at Villa Park. However, Crowe was keen to remind everyone that Aston Villa had no divine right to success. "Other clubs in the third division will not lie down for us because we are Aston Villa," he declared.

And this was to prove the case. Despite topping the league early on, Villa never looked truly capable of gaining promotion at the first attempt. Performances were inconsistent and goals hard to come by with Lochhead in particular struggling to get amongst the scorers during the early part of the season. However, the League Cup provided another story altogether.

First division Burnley were one of the opponents Villa brushed aside with ease on their way to a semi-final with Manchester United, European champions three years earlier and still including the triumvirate of Best, Law and Charlton in their ranks. The first leg at Old Trafford was an opportunity for Villa supporters to forget their league placing for a while and remember that this was the type of stage on which the club belonged. A 1-1 draw was just reward for a performance that transcended the gap between the clubs' league places. It also set the scene for one of the greatest nights in Villa Park's history.

62,500 packed into the ground on 23rd December 1970. The facts are that United scored first, with Andy Lochhead forcing an equaliser and Pat MacMahon sending Villa on their way to Wembley with a late header. The story of the night was far greater. "A night of almost hysterical rejoicing" was how it was described in the Evening Mail, while supporters and players remain convinced of one thing. If ever such a monumental feat as reversing decades of decline can be pinpointed to one specific occasion, then this was it. The Docherty era was, undoubtedly, the time when Villa stopped going backwards. The beating of Manchester United sent out a message to the rest of the world that the Villa were on their way back. Doug Ellis and the rest of the board were beside themselves with joy. Crowe took his success in a more studious, but equally pleased, fashion. "Quiet, but not shy" was how Crowe described himself, while others preferred more lavish praise. Dennis Shaw wrote in the Evening Mail of the flourishing partnership between manager and his assistant. "There isn't a partnership quite like it. Both men have such a regard for Villa the job is a labour of love".

Anyone, though, who mistook Crowe's retiring nature as a sign of weakness was sadly mistaken. Shaw recalled the night at Leicester when Villa had a goal disallowed when a linesman because to realise that the ball had crossed the line and bounced back into play after rebounding from a stanchion at the back of the goal net. "A certain door almost kicked off the hinges of a certain directors' box" was Shaw's recollection of a night that was to have a fatal consequence for Villa's battle against the drop.

And Crowe would have been the first to acknowledge the part that Ron Wylie played in their partnership. Brian Little, at the time a promising youngster, remembers the way in which he was introduced to the first-team squad: "Ron was an excellent coach, great with me on the training ground. Training with the first team, it was all ball work, dribbling and being brave with the ball. Ron brought a lot out of me.

After the drama of the semi, the final against Spurs could have been an anticlimax. Villa raised their game once more, but were out of luck and found the London side just too strong and experienced during the latter stages of a final the Villa could have won before two late Martin Chivers goals took the cup to White Hart Lane. Andy Lochhead had a shot that could have altered matters cleared off the line by Steve Perryman, but despite the result, Villa had proved that they could match the best, given the right circumstances. At the end of the game, they received from their supporters an ovation the like of which Wembley had never experienced.

Cup run over, the team found returning to league competition less successful. With Lochhead failing to score in 22 games after his semi-final heroics, Villa ended the season in fourth place. Supporters, naturally, accused the team of inconsistency and of not trying in the 'ordinary' matches. However, Crowe would later say things had been much worse than were first thought: "No-one who was not at Villa at the time can understand how bad things were. Problems could not be put right and the biggest obstacle was time."

Captain Brian Godfrey has the answer to anyone who thought that Crowe allowed the team to treat any match with less than total effort. "Those big League Cup games, he treated them exactly the same as any other match. He would have made a great poker player, the way he kept us on our toes. We could win 4-0 one week and he'd have us in for training the next day; then lose the week after and we'd have the day off. Then the next time we lost he'd have us in again. You never knew what was happening. The game before Wembley was away at Tranmere and he made it clear that anyone who didn't give 100% wouldn't be in the team for the final. And he made it especially clear to me that he expected me to fly into the first tackle."

The summer of 1971 saw Villa making further advances. Bristol Rovers winger, Ray Graydon, arrived in a swap deal with the popular skipper. Crowe was determined, though, that nothing would get in the way of his plans. "Whatever decisions I make are in the best interests of Aston Villa, whether or not they are popular."

Off the field, the Trinity Road enclosure was seated, while the club's search for a training ground ended with the construction of modern facilities at Bodymoor Heath, near Tamworth. These developments were financed by a club record profit of £84,452, boosted by the Wembley run and an average gate of 26,687, the highest outside the first division.

Villa started the new season in the same inconsistent manner as they had ended the previous one. Top after nine games, they then went on a run of one victory in four games, including a 3-0 defeat away at newly-promoted Bournemouth. Supporters were critical of the team, and of Crowe in particular. "Fans were humiliated as Villa were outclassed by Bournemouth," said Disgusted, of Bournville.

A single goal defeat at fourth division Southend in the FA Cup first round caused another outpouring of anger. E. Jackson held that "Another low has been reached," while the thought that "They will soon be telling us how they plan to win the fourth division" was the prediction from 'Disgusted', who by now had moved to Rubery.

Things improved dramatically from this low spot, however. Jim Cumbes, a £35,000 signing from the Albion, was Crowe's answer to Villa's goalkeeping weakness. Cumbes had little chance to show his abilities on his debut, as Villa beat Oldham 6-0 at Boundary Park. Shortly before their new keeper's arrival, Villa had beaten Notts County in front of a crowd of 37,462. Yet this amazing attendance was soon eclipsed by the volume of people who began to flock to Villa Park as the team's bandwagon began to roll. A third division record attendance of 48,110 witnessed the 2-1 victory against Bournemouth. Yet even this crowd was overshadowed by the arrival of Santos, with Pele in their ranks, for a friendly nine days later. A crowd of 54,437 paid club record receipts in excess of £35,000 to witness a 2-1 victory for the Villa in a game where the world's greatest player became the latest legend to tread the Villa Park turf.

Such resources were, indeed, beyond the reach of any other club in the division, and Villa were able to buy players not only to get them out of the third, but also to prepare for greater battles to come. Centre-half, Chris Nicholl was signed from Luton for £90,000, while Ian Ross joined from Liverpool for £70,000. Nicholl was not the only Villa player who suffered from the weight of expectation in the Villa Park air. "If Vic wasn't happy, you knew about it. But he was very supportive. It took me a year to get used to the size of the club, the vastness of Villa Park overwhelmed me. Vic helped me enormously to settle into the job and gain the confidence to run out in front of 40,000 people." Yet for all the club's size, Crowe was determined to keep feet on the ground, developing a way of dealing with those who said, no doubt meaning well, that the Villa did not belong in such lowly company. On one occasion, it was reported that Crowe grabbed a copy of the league table, thrust it under one supporter's nose and shouted, "What does that tell you?"

The season ended at Villa Park on 29th April, when another

crowd of over forty thousand saw Torquay defeated 5-1, Brian Little scoring on his full debut. Villa finished the season with a club record 70 points and 85 goals, the most they had scored since 1961. An added bonus saw the FA Youth Cup arrive at Villa Park, as the youth side saw off Albion and Blues en route to a two-legged final against Liverpool, which they won 5-2 on aggregate.

Yet amidst the celebrations, there was a realisation that Villa should never have been in this position at all. "The most humiliating two seasons in the club's honour-strewn history," was the verdict of veteran local reporter, Tom Duckworth, while Harry Parkes was even more forthright. "It was like Muhammed Ali winning the Boys Brigade championship," the Villa legend stated.

Praise was directed at Crowe and his assitant. They were a double act in the Clough and Taylor mould and complemented each other perfectly. Jim Cumbes pays tribute to the way in which their differing personalities brought success to the club. "Vic was a thorough coach rather than a manager in the conventional sense. He often passed a lot of the work with the first team to Ron Wylie, but he was very astute and he could read the game very well. His half-time team talks got to our weaknesses and more often than not they were put right. Wylie was more forceful. Vic was quiet but analytical. He never raised his voice, but he was very much straight to the point. At half-time in that Bournemouth game we were one down, but after the team talk he said, 'You know lads, if you lose today it isn't the end of the world.' And that did the trick. It settled us right away and we won 2-1, but I never heard another manager say anything like that during my career."

The summer of 1972 saw the next round of skirmishing in the war that characterised the Aston Villa boardroom during the sixties and seventies. The rest of the board, tired of Doug Ellis's seeming hogging of the limelight, passed a vote of no confidence in the chairman, and he was replaced by Jim Hartley. Crowe passed little comment on the situation, observing, "It is our duty to serve the club and not specific individuals," but there was no doubt that the situation did not help preparations for the forthcoming season.

Accusations and counter-accusations flew, an EGM was held, and when the dust settled Ellis was back in the chair, his old foes Hartley and Harry Parkes departed from the scene and with new directors Allan Smith and Eric Houghton on the board Ellis's position was strengthened. Within four years, the new regime that had been swept in during the heady days of December 1968 had all, with one exception, left Villa Park.

Villa were top of the second division after ten games, with Leeds manager Don Revie hailing them "The most exciting team I have seen all season" after a 1-1 draw in the League Cup at Villa Park. However, all was not well. Despite holding down a regular place in the top four, the team were plainly not good enough for promotion and supporters began to air their discontent. The cry "Crowe must go" rang out around Villa Park following a 0-3 reverse at the hands of table-topping Burnley, while a short-lived petition to remove the managerial duo surfaced as the season progressed and crowds dipped to pre-Docherty levels. Villa eventually finished third in the table, but were a long way off promoted sides. This was, of course, the season before three clubs were promoted, but it has to be said that the Villa side of 1972-73 would have needed substantially strengthening to have stayed in the first division had they gone up. Jim Cumbes, though, believes that the boardroom wranglings of the previous summer played their part. "If it hadn't been for that, I'm convinced we'd have gone straight through the divisions; but we went from a situation where everyone was pulling together, to one where the board were divided and there was a lot of politics. The first game, up at Preston, there was only Doug Ellis travelling with us on the team coach, while the rest of the board went by car. Before that, they had always travelled together with us. "

The summer of 1973 saw a rights issue, which did not raise as much as expected, while Andy Lochhead departed to Oldham for £20,000, his place in Villa folklore assured. Sammy Morgan joined as a prospective replacement for the same amount from Port Vale, and Trevor Hockey arrived from Norwich for £14,000.

The season started brightly, but the side was hampered by a lack of goals and poor away form. However, they were still on the fringes of the promotion chase when, midway through the season, it was announced that there was just £65,000 available for new signings. Crowe put a brave face on things: "With support and understanding we can achieve anything," was his response, but there was no doubt that from this moment on, any promotion challenge was doomed. Form slumped, although there was a brief moment of glory when beating Arsenal in an FA Cup fourth round replay at Villa Park in front of 47,821. Defeat in the following round at the hands of Burnley led to the departure of Bruce Rioch to Derby County for £200,000. Rioch's departure was inevitable; here was one of the finest midfield players in the country and it said everything about the Villa's stature, and Vic Crowe's management ability, that such a player was happy to stay in the lower divisions for so long. Rioch went on to win the league championship with Derby and captain Scotland, but his departure was still seen as another reason why the Villa revival was running out of steam. And as ever, the manger bore the brunt of the criticism. As the team slumped to seventeenth place in the table, just three points off the relegation places, Crowe was variously described by fans as "the master of excuses" and castigated for "inexperienced management and lack of ideas". What was not mentioned was why it was that, after two share issues and several years when Villa's income had been the envy of every club outside the first division, there was so little money available.

A brief revival saw Villa climb the table, but they eventually finished the season in fourteenth position, with 41 points. In the words of the Argus's Ian Johnson, "a very ordinary second division club". As the season ended, Crowe refused to consider the position of manager of Wales, stating, "My ambitions lie with Aston Villa." This show of loyalty was as commendable as it was ill-advised. The following day, he and Ron Wylie were dismissed. Sir William Dugdale, a member of the board at the time, now says of Crowe's departure, "Vic Crowe was, I felt, rather hard done by. He was not a great seller of himself and didn't make things as easy as he could have done. He was a poor communicator to the board and I got the impression that he resented being given what was well-meaning advice."

That Crowe could, unwittingly, be his own worst enemy is a theory supported by Neil Rioch. "Vic was a quiet man, he was never going to sing his own praises. He'd rather let the team and the results do his talking, and by and large they did. Certainly in my experience, when I talk to supporters now, the part Vic played has been largely forgotten or not appreciated properly by a lot of people, because he was quiet, because he wasn't on the back pages all the time. But he did an enormous job in taking what we had; relegation and a dressing room split, all those problems. To take us out of the third, to Wembley was magnificent. His work in the transfer market was superb; the development of the youth system, which began with Tommy, no doubt, was progressed by Vic Crowe. I put that almost on a par with Manchester United in the nineties."

Chris Nicholl was another who was disappointed to see his manager depart. "It was obvious that Mr Ellis's ambition was overtaking everything and there was no hanging around, he wanted it all now. He wasn't happy with the third or second division and he was getting a bit impatient, maybe he thought the momentum had stopped a little bit. Most of us were Vic's players; when your manager is sacked you must take your share of the responsibility, so I thought it was partly my fault".

Crowe was, naturally, upset at his sacking. In a lengthy interview with the Evening Mail, he stated: "The foundations we leave behind are ideal... we leave Aston Villa in a far healthier state than it was when we took over". Crowe, the epitome of a life-long Villa servant, acknowledged, "There is no other club I shall get so much pleasure and satisfaction from, that club has virtually been my life." Ironically, Crowe's two sons became Villa shareholders on the day their father ceased to be the club's manager.

Someone else with reason to regret the timing of the manager's departure was Brian Little. The player who was destined to be the finest graduate from the Youth Cup winning side of 1972 was in the process of being offered a new contract, when he suddenly found out that the man with whom he was negotiating terms was no longer in the club's employment: "When Vic got the sack I didn't know what would happen, so I asked him what I should do and, even though he's just lost his job, he spent a lot of time helping me. That was the kind of man Vic was."

Supporter reaction was mixed but the Birmingham Post's Randall Northam had probably the best take on the situation: "Crowe and Wylie were not sacked because they failed, they went because they did not succeed in the fashion Aston Villa have come to expect".

After he left the club he loved, Vic Crowe did not remain in football for long. He moved back to the USA, where he managed Portland Timbers in the emerging North American Soccer League from 1975-76 and again from 1980-82. Many years later, he re-emerged for a spell with Bilston Town in the Southern League. But he never seemed to have his heart in football after leaving the Villa. Until recently, Crowe was still a season ticket holder in the Trinity Road stand, where he was always willing to pass the time of day with supporters, many of whom took the opportunity to apologise for the way in which he had been treated by their number.

If he was ever a boxing man, Vic Crowe would certainly empathise with Larry Holmes. One of the greatest heavyweights of all time, Holmes was unlucky to be world champion during the period between Muhammed Ali and Mike Tyson. Sandwiched between two of the best-known fighters in history, Holmes has been overlooked. Similarly, Crowe's place in history has been down-played. He took over from a populist, instrumental in saving the club and was succeeded by the most successful manager in the Villa's history. Jim Cumbes is of the opinion that, "He wasn't a big name, and maybe he suffered a bit from the hangover of Tommy Docherty, who'd been the great white hope and had been seen as the rebirth of the Villa. Maybe there was a bit of resentment that Vic had been his number two and the Villa hadn't brought in another big name to replace Docherty. Vic wasn't particularly charismatic, he wasn't a hogger of the limelight but he was claret and blue through and through. Managing Villa was the love of his life"

And Vic Crowe can be proud of his managerial achievements. Indeed, on the basis of results in league games, he was the most suc-cessful Villa manager of all. He brought stability to the club, presided over a successful period and left the team in much better shape than he found them. Furthermore, his team contained a large number of players who would go on to have successful managerial careers of their own. Brian Little, Chris Nicholl, Bruce Rioch and Ray Graydon were just some of those influenced by Crowe's mana-gerial style. Nicholl remembers: "It's a tribute to the kind of char-acters Vic wanted in his team that so many of them became man-agers. He definitely influenced us as managers, he was into psy-chology, but in an understated way - a raised eyebrow, rarely a slanging match; he didn't go for confrontation. Ron was the upfront, in your face guy, so it worked well. But you knew who was the boss."

11

Ron Saunders

June 1974 - February 1982

A formidable array of candidates lined up in the race to succeed Vic Crowe. Sir Alf Ramsey, recently departed from the England job, was interested, as were such luminaries as the Queens Park Rangers boss, Gordon Jago. But far ahead of the rest of the field was Brian Clough, in exile at third division Brighton after walking out on Derby County the previous season.

Clough made no secret of his desire for the job. "I don't think I could get Aston Villa into the first division, I know I could," was his opening gambit. Supporters made no secret of their wishes: an Evening Mail poll found that 93% wanted Clough, with Ramsey in a far-distant second place on 4%. But Clough's demands that Villa had to prove themselves to him would be his downfall, if, indeed, he ever did want the job. After all, it is difficult to imagine him lasting long in the same room as Doug Ellis, never mind at the same club. With Clough out of contention, former Manchester City boss, Ron Saunders entered the running and by the time an announcement was made, the identity of the new manager was no great surprise.

Vic Crowe had said his successor would "think it's Christmas". Saunders concurred. "The potential here is screaming out to be tapped," he said, although he did point out that, "My priorities are to entertain the public and to win matches - in that order." Dennis Shaw wrote in the Evening Mail that the new manager "has to find a short cut to the top of division one" and warned his first job was to win over fans, without whom the team could not hope to succeed.

Saunders was born in Birkenhead in November 1932. He started his playing career with Everton, for whom he made just three full appearances before moving to non-league Tonbridge. Saunders spent three years with the Southern League club before playing the 1957-58 season with Gillingham, for whom he scored 20 goals in 49 games. This form earned him a move to first division Portsmouth, where he became one of the Fratton Park club's most prolific-ever goalscorers. Saunders played 258 games for Portsmouth, scoring 157 goals before winding down his playing career, first with Watford and then Charlton Athletic.

His managerial career began in 1967 at Yeovil, moving on two years later to Oxford United, in doing so becoming the first manager to move directly from a non-league club to the second division. So determined was Saunders to get the Oxford job that he had cut the plaster from his leg the night before he was interviewed as he believed the fact that he had a broken foot might have gone against him. Saunders kept Oxford in the second division before moving to Norwich City, where he was to have his first falling out with a dictatorial chairman. Saunders had four successful seasons in Norfolk, winning the second division in 1971-72 and taking the club to a League Cup final appearance in the following year. However, the next season saw Saunders fall out with new chairman Arthur South and move on when offered the chance to manage Manchester City.

Saunders' time at Maine Road was stormy, unhappy and, above all, brief. Appointed in November 1973, he was sacked on Good Friday, 12th April 1974. In that short period he had taken City to a League Cup final appearance, once more finishing on the losing side, and also managed to upset much of the City playing staff. Many of the more experienced players demanded the dismissal of Saunders and chairman Peter Swales agreed. Saunders found himself out of work at the time the Villa were looking for a new manager. Such timing was either coincidence, or fate.

Married with four children, Saunders was Villa's sixth manager in ten years and was appointed on a contract worth a reported £10,000 per annum. He came with a reputation for being a strict disciplinarian, although defensively claiming "I am not a hard man, I am a gentleman." He admitted his honesty sometimes made him unpopular, and regarded football as a vocation "just like the priesthood".

It has to be said, though, that supporters were not entirely happy with the appointment. It was reckoned that Villa had gone for second best, especially as Clough had moved to Leeds a month after Saunders' arrival at Villa Park (and woe betide anyone who pointed out that second division Villa were hardly the same draw as the league champions - Villa supporters of the period had an assurance of their club's place in the greater scheme of things). The new manager's claim that results would be more important than performance also found disfavour with supporters expecting things to be done properly.

As for the players, they looked forward to the new arrival with interest. Chris Nicholl recalls, "He'd come from Manchester City and we knew the rumours that the players had got him the sack. And that excused him all his hyper-suspicion. I got the feeling that he was suspicious of everything and everyone." Neil Rioch was one who soon came to realise what would be Saunders' greatest strength: "One thing he was hard and fast on immediately was how he want-ed the game played, particularly from the back. He got people organised. He took away the players' flexibility and made things more rigid in terms of the pattern of play. It was extremely well-organised. Ron at first worked very quickly and very hard with defenders on how 'this is how you're going to play, this is your job'. Even when we got possession.

"I played right back against Sheffield Wednesday, and rolled the ball inside to Chris Nicholl, about twenty yards away with no-one near him. At half time Ron called me for everything: 'You do not pass it inside to your centre half. In my team you don't do it'. "

Saunders' first signing was Frank Carrodus, a £90,000 capture from his former club, Manchester City, in a deal which came about as a result of Saunders' discussing compensation with his former chairman, Peter Swales. The hard-working Carrodus was to epito-mise Saunders' approach to football.

During the first week of the 1974-75 season, a minor development took place that attracted little attention in the local press. Local businessman, Ronald Bendall loaned the club £23,000, which was then converted into shares. However, Mr Bendall stated he had no intention of becoming a member of the board and returned to the obscurity of his accountancy practice. Midfielder, Leighton Phillips joined from Cardiff for £70,000 and the team made a reasonable start to the season. By the end of October they were in fourth place in the table, six points behind leaders Manchester United with four-teen games played. Moreover, Villa were top goalscorers in the sec-ond division. Saunders was named Manager of the Month for October, and things were looking good.

However, a disappointing run of form saw Villa in seventh place in the table at the halfway point. Supporters were beginning to show signs of unrest - just 15,840 witnessed the 4-0 defeat of York City at

Villa Park. The League Cup, though, as it has on many occasions in the Villa's history, proved a lifeline. Hartlepool were beaten in a fourth round replay, Brian Little scoring a hat-trick on his 21st birthday. Chester City of the fourth division proved more difficult semi-final opposition than might have been anticipated; after a 2-2 draw at Sealand Road, Villa let a two goal advantage slip at home before running out 5-4 aggregate winners to give the team another Wembley appearance. In the week before the final, runaway leaders Manchester United were beaten 2-0 at Villa Park in front of a crowd of almost fifty thousand, a win which saw Villa move into fourth place in the table a point from the promotion spots. Of less apparent significance was the news that Ron Bendall, now the club's biggest shareholder, was again invited to join the board and this time accepted the offer.

Typical of Saunders, he spent the time before the final talking of "blend and balance", stressing that "when you pay big money for first division players you buy that club's problems." The final itself, against Saunders' former club Norwich City, was a poor game, won by a single goal scored by Ray Graydon when his penalty was saved but fell fortuitously for the rebound. This game took place during a league run that saw 32 points from 18 games, promotion eventually being sealed with a 4-0 win at Sheffield Wednesday on a night of high emotion when Villa supporters made up some three-quarters of the 24,000 crowd. The final match of the season at Villa Park saw a capacity crowd of 57,266 witness a 2-0 victory that killed off Sunderland's promotion hopes. At the end of the match, as thousands spilled on to the pitch to acclaim the Messiah who had taken them to the promised land, Saunders made a speech to his adoring public. "The greatest moment of my footballing life."

Villa finished the season in second place in the league, with 58 points. They had scored 110 goals in all matches and to round matters off, Brian Little became the first Villa player to make an England appearance since Gerry Hitchens in 1961 when appearing against Wales in the Home Internationals. Villa were back in the first division, and the man who had made it all possible was Ron Saunders. Voted Manager of the Year, Saunders pointed out at the awards dinner that twelve months previously he had been unemployed. "It is a sobering thought", he said, "to think that the dividing line between success and failure is so thin."

Supporters worshipped Saunders, who had known from his first days at Villa Park that things were different at this club. "I got the feeling that they wanted to be involved in everything," he said years later. "At some clubs the fans are distant, but at Villa they always let you know where they were".

For the following season, Saunders was content to give the squad who had served him so well in wining promotion the chance to prove themselves. However, it soon became obvious that the team would struggle in the higher division, and so Saunders made several purchases. Goalkeeper John Burridge joined from Blackpool for £90,000 and he was quickly followed by two new signings, both of whom broke the club's transfer record. Nineteen-year old forward Andy Gray arrived from Dundee United for £110,000, in a deal which saw his new manager incur the wrath of the local press when he flatly denied that the transfer was imminent less than 24 hours before it was confirmed. Gray was followed by Coventry City's Dennis Mortimer, who cost £175,000 when he arrived at Villa Park shortly before Christmas 1975. Mortimer remembers how Saunders gave him little say in the matter: "I'd heard about him at Coventry from David Cross, who had played for him at Norwich and he told me what I might expect. I wasn't too sure though, I just knew I had to go - Coventry needed the money. He met me at Stonebridge Island and drove to Villa Park. We had a chat on the way and he highlighted things about his plans, not in huge detail but he just assumed that I'd sign. There was no thinking about it, as far as he was concerned I was going to sign and that was it."

Villa's form during the 1975-76 season was inconsistent. They lost just two games at home, yet failed to win on their travels. Relegation never looked a real danger, and in finishing sixteenth Villa never really looked capable of anything other than a mid-table position. Yet Saunders was showing signs of making his mark on Villa. Players who had served the club well during the revival of the early seventies were allowed to leave; most went with mutual good wishes, although the way in which Charlie Aitken was pushed out of the club, being told half an hour before the transfer deadline that he was being given a free transfer, undoubtedly showed Saunders at his most inconsiderate. Indeed, it was becoming apparent that anyone who didn't conform to Saunders' standards, or who was dropped from the first team, may as well have not existed. Neil Rioch saw how the situation was developing. "He always liked to come into the dressing room and make a crack about certain players, belittle them slightly, and that was his style. He appeared to get a kick from that, but there were some pretty smart players around: Jim Cumbes, Pat MacMahon, intelligent guys, who could give it back better. And they would come back and top him." Chris Nicholl also recalls what could happen to players who crossed the manager: "He'd get the keepers, especially Jim Cumbes, and he'd get a bag of balls, hitting them on the volley from seven or eight yards away. It was almost a deliberate session to establish who was the dominating factor. And that had to be Ron Saunders. Then Ron would say 'You're all over there', all the squad was split up and Sammy Morgan, who'd been fantastic for the Villa and had helped me so much, he was singled out one time and stuck with the reserves; 'You're over there with the shit,' Ron shouted at him. He was letting you know that if you weren't in the first team you were nothing; but it got the message across to everybody. It became known that if you were out you had to perform to get back."

And Jim Cumbes, who plainly didn't get on with Saunders, concedes, "We had a healthy respect for one another. He put me through my paces; there were all those times when he'd have the players and himself firing drop kicks at me from two yards out, but at the end of it he'd always say 'Well done'. Cumbes eventually left Villa to join up with Vic Crowe at Portland Timbers in the USA, after seeing a side of Saunders that rarely became public. "John Gidman got injured in that firework accident at my house. A firework went astray and as bad luck had it, it hit Giddy full in the eye. I was expecting Ron to blast off at me but he said, 'Don't worry, accidents happen'. Then, in the second leg of the semi-final with Chester, I spilled a corner that led to their equaliser. Brian Little got the winner, and as I was in the shower after the match Ron came over. Same again, I thought I was for it, but instead he handed me a glass of champagne with the words 'It happens to all of us'. I got the feeling that he would have always been there if he was needed. In fact, I'd say he wanted to be needed."

1975-76 was a time when the Villa felt their way back into the first division. The following season, though, they performed in a way that was beyond the wildest dreams of supporters. Andy Gray ran riot through defences; the team's 4-3-3 formation, Gray linking up with John Deehan and Brian Little, was a counter to anyone who claimed that Saunders was a dour manager whose teams played similar football. The 5-1 win over Liverpool is still regarded as the greatest Villa performance since the war; the League Cup was won after a three-game rollercoaster, when Saunders' team had to call on their last reserves of fitness to overcome Everton, thanks to a Brian Little winner, with seconds remaining of a second replay. The team ended the season in fourth place, Villa's highest league position since the thirties. But it could have been even better, as Dennis Mortimer explains. "If we'd had no replays we'd have won the league. That run-in after the three finals, we dropped points against teams we should have beaten. We just had too many games to play after that."

Other Villa sides may have had more success, but the team Ron Saunders put together in this period is regarded by those who saw it was the most attractive in living memory. Chris Nicholl, though, says that those who thought it was built on a philosophy of free-flowing total football are mistaken. "We knew our jobs, knew what the team was about and what we had to do. My job was to win the ball and give it to John Gidman or Frank Carrodus. If I played a square ball you could be sure that after the game he'd tell me about it. His coaching sessions were very specifically targeted to winning the ball. We may have looked an attacking team but everything was in fact built on winning the ball and countering."

And just as the team's style was becoming clear, so too was the Saunders method of managing at the top level. Dennis Mortimer, who had by now become as good a central midfielder as any in the league, says "Ron kept us going, he kept us fit, but he wasn't a great coach in the Wenger, Houllier mould. They have a great coaching brain, he was just a very straightforward, pragmatic man. Everything was practical, everything was done for a purpose. He instilled the thought of getting on with it, no moaning, just get on with it and you performed to your best because if you didn't, you weren't in the side."

The next three seasons were less notable. Good as the class of '77 had been, Saunders could see their limitations. Chris Nicholl left, and in his place came Ken McNaught. The newcomer, a record signing at £200,000 from Everton, took some time to win over the crowd, who could not understand why such a popular captain had been moved on. Nicholl himself has a couple of theories: "My contract was up and I had a long discussion with him. All the arguments were in my favour, but I realise now I'd reached about thirty. He had a thing about older players, because when you reach 30/31 there was a thing going at the time, Shankly believed it as well, that by that age they used to get rid because you knew the game too well, which some managers don't like. I'm fighting for a rise, maybe it was in his mind to get rid and that was an excuse. So he just kept saying no. Another thing was that we often played golf together and he always beat me, but one day that summer I won for the first time. Two weeks later I was sold. That did enough, pushed him over the edge in a quirky sort of way."

And it has often been said that Saunders preferred to work with younger, less experienced players who were less likely to cause him problems or to question his authority. Obviously, the problems he encountered at Manchester City remained burned into the Saunders psyche long after he had departed Maine Road.

League finishes of eighth, eighth and seventh might have indicated that the Villa had gone as far as they could, and there were rumblings that Saunders had reached his limit as well. However, it can be seen in hindsight that he was having to contend with numerous problems off the field. In August 1977, Saunders was approached to take over at Everton, who offered to make him the best-paid manager in the league. Saunders declined this offer, saying, "I've worked hard to achieve what I have and I will have to work even harder in the future." Over the next couple of years he was to find that his hardest battles came off the field.

At the beginning of the following season, Saunders found himself once more in demand, this time from both Leeds and the Saudi Arabian national side. The wrangles that followed led to the departures of Alan Smith, Harry Cressman and chairman Sir William Dugdale from the Villa board. However, it transpired that the departure of the three directors was less to do with Saunders and more to do with boardroom politics. Sir William recalls, "Ron wanted a better contract after we won the League Cup. He said that he'd been offered a job in Saudi Arabia on the sort of money that we could never have been able to afford. I told him to accept, called his bluff if you like, and the matter ended. Ron Bendall then attempted to vote Alan Smith off the board and replace him with his own son,

Don. In the end I resigned when Bendall ruled that he would get rid of Alan Smith. Once we'd gone, Ron got his new contract after all. I think Ron Bendall did that to show that he was now in charge."

Villa finished the 1978-79 season in eighth place with 46 points, an identical record to the previous year. Saunders could look on a season of horrendous injuries as the reason why the team had seemingly stagnated. He could also say that the club's youth policy was once more bringing forth a crop of promising youngsters and the future looked bright. However, he still had work to do before he could claim to be the unquestionably dominant force at Villa Park.

Even before the start of the 1979-80 season, the Sports Argus was asking, "What is going on at Villa Park?" Players were asking to leave the club, and much of the blame for this discontent was directed at Ron Saunders. Dennis Mortimer recalls: "Andy Gray and John Gidman wanted to get away. Ron wanted them out because they made it clear they didn't want to stay. Money was a big factor in the game and Ron kept the wage structure down to a level the club could sustain, but there were big bonuses, which is how the game should be. He gave you the incentive to do well, but some players thought they could get more money somewhere else. Ron was bringing players in who didn't fit in with his system, Tommy Craig for example, so we lost our way a bit."

Andy Gray had indeed fallen out with Saunders in a big way. Their feud had its origins in the PFA Awards Dinner which took place on the evening after the League Cup Final in 1977. Gray had won both the Player and Young Player of the Year trophies, but, with the replay scheduled to take place three days later, Saunders refused him permission to attend the ceremony. Relations were further strained in the run-up to the UEFA Cup quarter-final the following season, when Saunders claimed that Gray had been feigning injury in order to miss the second leg in Barcelona. Gray later claimed Saunders was wrong, and his story is backed up by long-time friend Neil Rioch. "Andy played so often with injuries when he shouldn't have been playing that to say such a thing was an insult to one of the most exciting and courageous forwards I've ever seen. It's the worst thing that you can say to a player - you don't want to carry out your profession."

Gray and Gidman eventually moved in the autumn of 1979, shortly after the departure of John Gregory, who claimed that he had

been pushed out by Saunders. Their departures led to another of
the boardroom battles for which Villa Park had become notorious
during the seventies. This time the outcome was unusual. Doug
Ellis, who had made no secret of his desire to return to the chair-
manship he had been forced to relinquish shortly after the club's
return to the first division in 1975, called for an EGM at which he
intended to get rid of the Bendalls and their ally Harry Kartz.
Saunders had equally made no secret of his feelings towards Ellis
almost from his first day at Villa Park, as Dennis Mortimer recalls;
"On the day I signed he told me to be aware of Ellis".

The boardroom battle consequently became a battle between the
two largest personalities at Villa Park. Dennis Mortimer remembers
the time: "Ron Saunders wanted Ellis out and everything worked
out well for him. He was a very persuasive person, very charismatic, and when you spoke to him, his demeanour was of never smiling
but when you knew him he wasn't like that at all. Ron knew that
working with stars wasn't for him. He needed to work with people
who weren't stars, who were good, reliable, hard workers. He relied
on good management to be successful."

And on the other hand, the self-styled Mr Aston Villa, a man for
whom limelight has, over the years, appeared to be as vital as oxy-
gen. As Mortimer puts it; "If you look at the time since, there have
been the type of players who have obviously been Ellis-type players;
Six, Collymore, David Ginola, the type who have ability but don't fit
in with the team or the philosophy of the manager."

Ellis's bid for power failed and he resigned from the board. He
had been unable to overcome the size of the Bendall shareholding
and although, in a scenario reminiscent of Tommy Docherty's dismissal a decade previous, he had the support of the majority of
small shareholders, the rank and file Villa fans had been solidly
behind the manager. Whether by accident or design, the club was
now built in Ron Saunders' image. He had a squad of players who
owed him total loyalty, a board he could work with and supporters
who worshipped him. Accident, or design? Dennis Mortimer has no
doubt. "Ellis used their disagreement with Gray and Gidman for his
own ends. If Ron had gone they'd have stayed, Ellis would have broken the wage structure and he'd have had a manager who would
bring in the street-entertainer type of players, whereas Ron was
about making a team."

Saunders may have claimed to have taken no interest in what was going on in the boardroom - later saying, "I only have vague memories of that time. I went to work, grafted and then went home." However, there is little doubt that he spent much of this time using his considerable influence to swing a significant amount of shareholders against Ellis and made the point at the subsequent AGM that Ellis's protests at the way the club was being run was a slur on his own abilities. With his off-field battles won, Saunders could now set about putting together the third team of his reign. The Villa Park youth production line was in full swing, players such as Gordon Cowans, Gary Shaw and Colin Gibson becoming first team regulars. Midfield had been a problem. Part of the money raised by Gidman and Gray was spent on Des Bremner, who slotted alongside Mortimer and Cowans as though born to the role. Up front, David Geddis was yet another record signing. However, as has often proved the case at Villa Park, a record fee was no guarantee of success. Dennis Mortimer, by now club captain, remembers: "Geddis had his assets but he was different from what we were used to. He was a runner, he needed the ball over the top to run on to, but we were used to hitting target men, Andy and John Deehan, which wasn't David's style. We lost our direction a bit."

Geddis was obviously not the answer, so as 1979-80 ended with Villa finishing in seventh place and once more missing out on European qualification, a record fee of £500,000 was spent on a similar type of player to Gray, the experienced 28-year old Peter Withe from Newcastle United. The 1980-81 season was ready to begin.

As the season got underway, Villa were not expected to do anything other than make up the numbers in the first division title race. Inside Villa Park, though, the feeling was quite different. As Dennis Mortimer explains, "I always knew, from the pre-season, I knew it when we kicked off against Leeds. On that day we were fantastic, and from then on I knew we would win the league. We had a maturity about us. We had young players but there was a maturity that was needed to be successful. And we just went on and on, result after result. We played Ipswich in the first month of the season, they were full of internationals and we absolutely battered them. We lost 1-0 but we played them off the park. We were playing some absolutely fantastic stuff."

As the season wore on, Villa overcame the occasional setback with total professionalism. Liverpool and later Ipswich might have got the acclaim, but Villa kept on picking up results, going top of the table in October after defeating Brighton 4-1 and rarely being out of the top two from then on. Eventually, after the defeat of Liverpool at Villa Park, the title challenge began to be taken seriously, and with some justification. Dennis Mortimer, whose goal that afternoon remains the defining moment of the season, recalls, "The Liverpool game was the one. The one team you needed to get out the way was Liverpool and I felt before that, win this one and that would put them out of the equation. And we won, and the feeling after was that we'd won the league. Ron was difficult to gauge. He never changed, no histrionics, never threw things round the dressing room or lost his temper at half-time. But for all him being a hard man, there was never ever any confrontation. Game by game he'd say to me 'Just do what you do well, keep on doing it. Not a problem'- and that was it."

The defeat of Liverpool left Villa top of the table with 36 points from 26 games, a point ahead of Ipswich, who had two games in hand. But everyone at Villa Park knew who would top the table at the end of the season. As Saunders says: "I felt very strongly for most of the season that we would be league champions."

For all they were being written off by the press, Villa kept winning. It is well-known that they used just fourteen players in the first team that season, tribute both to their incredible fitness and also to Saunders' philosophy of keeping faith with his players. As Allan Evans, signed as a striker and converted to a top-class central defender, recalls: "Once Ron felt he had the players he thought could do it, he was confident. He got that team together and showed total confidence in them."

One player reputed to have his difficulties with Saunders was Tony Morley. Contradictorily, the player stresses that nothing could have been further from the truth. "He was a great bloke, we got on really well in everything bar one respect. He thought I was rubbish and I thought I was good. But he used things like that to get the best of the team. He'd go round the dressing room and he'd have a go at me, at Sid and Gary Shaw. He'd tell me that he'd have the apprentices on the bench counting how many tackles I made, which wasn't many, or how many passes Sid hit that went wrong. The other players he'd praise up but he knew how to get the best out of all of us."

The Villa team of the era was notable for its lack of international recognition. None of the players during the championship-winning season made an appearance for their country, and although this was a scandalous omission, it had its origins in Saunders' all-encompassing desire for success. Tony Morley, who was to play for England some time later, recalls an incident as the title race reached its climax: "We'd just lost 2-1 at Spurs and Gary Shaw and I were due to pay for England B the week after. We're coming off the pitch and Sunders asked us if we were injured - told us, almost. Then after the match he announced that we'd both been injured during the match, so that was it for the England B team."

That Saunders had no great love of the media had been obvious throughout his Villa career. The local press respected him, the nationals preferred to ignore him. The feeling was mutual, as Jim Cumbes had seen years earlier, "He didn't get on with the press, mainly because he wanted to control everything. He didn't endear himself to them, there was always that stone face in his interviews." As the season progressed, the media had to concede something was going badly wrong in their world. And how Saunders must have enjoyed having the upper hand. Gary Shaw recalls; "He did an excellent job with the TV and his attitude towards our rivals. He looked at people who were knocking us and he was quietly confident all the time, his manner shown in the players."

Never was Saunders' character more in evidence than the night when Ipswich, for the second time that season, were played off the park by Villa but somehow won the match. Their 2-1 victory at Villa Park appeared to end Villa's title hopes. Saunders walked into the subsequent press conference and asked of the assembled media pack: "Do any of you want to bet against us?" There were, of course, no takers. "Thank you for your confidence, gentlemen," was the manager's exit-line. "I can still remember watching that and it still sends a shiver down my spine," is the verdict from Allan Evans.

And subsequently it was Ipswich, not Villa, who cracked. Bobby Robson's team lost four of their last five games to hand Villa the league title, despite a last match defeat at Highbury which gave the world at large one last chance to cast aspersions on Villa's title-winning credentials. But in the words of Dennis Mortimer, "There's nothing in the rules that says you have to win your last game to be champions". And with 60 points from 42 matches, four more than Ipswich, Villa were, indeed, worthy champions, Saunders' reward coming by way of a second Manager of the Year trophy.

The following season was, at least in terms of league performance, one of anti-climax. Other than that it was as dramatic a season as any club has ever known. The departure of Ron Saunders from Villa Park is one of the greatest mysteries of modern football. On the surface, things were running smoothly, despite the team's moderate league form. Then on 5th March 1982, the Evening Mail broke a story that Saunders' roll-over contract was to be scrapped and replaced by an ordinary three year deal. Ron Bendall, by this time chairman of the club, pointed out that economies had to be made, with Saunders ominously replying that "the odds would appear to be against" his long-held ambition of finishing his career at Villa Park. Saunders claimed that the terms of his contract, believed to be unique in football, helped provide stability for the club and that with it's scrapping he was worse off than he had been four seasons previous. Three days later, Saunders collapsed during training and drove out of Bodymoor Heath reportedly suffering from flu.

That evening, the news broke that Ron Saunders had resigned as manager of Aston Villa. To the rest of football it was a bombshell. To his players the news was totally unexpected. Allan Evans recalls: "We knew there were a lot of problems going on, but he didn't tell us what was happening."

The true story of Saunders' departure has never been made public, and it probably never will be. If he had ever felt the need to tell anyone, Dennis Mortimer would have been the obvious choice, yet as Saunders' captain says, "He spoke to me the night before he resigned and said, 'There's a battle going on, but I am not leaving this football club.' You can imagine my amazement when he resigned the next day. He never told me why and I've never spoken to him about it. One day I might get the opportunity, but I would imagine he's put it behind him and will never revisit it." Like Evans, Mortimer has his own theory about what went on. "I've heard one or two stories; his autonomy was being taken away from him, stuff like that, but nothing definite." The subsequent story that Saunders' contract had not been as lucrative as was first thought would bear out the theory that its scrapping, and the manager's subsequent departure, was more for political than for financial reasons. Harry Kartz, who had recently stood down as chairman in favour of Bendall, later revealed the new incumbent had, a few weeks after taking the chair, stated that he intended to goad Saunders into resigning. Although Bendall apparently changed his mind shortly afterwards, Kartz remained convinced the two men would not be able to work together for much longer.

On the following day, Saunders stated that, "The fans have been fantastic to me and I am sad to be leaving them. I am not bitter. I am paid to manage Villa, not to be a puppet or office boy". In the days that followed Saunders' resignation, claim and counter-claim bounced back and forth between club and former manager. The board issued a statement saying that, "He has always had complete control of the playing side. Difficulties arose when the manager wanted complete control." They also claimed that Saunders had been guilty of broadcasting confidential club information to the press, a reference to an interview Saunders had given shortly before resigning, in which he had said that he was being forced to sell players before he could buy others. This statement, Saunders claimed, was "completely misleading." He had no ambition to become managing director, a role which it had been reported he had craved, and had told the press of the difficulty in buying players merely to keep supporters informed of the situation at Villa Park.

Ron Bendall later said that on the evening Saunders resigned, the two men had had a telephone conversation, which ended with Saunders, in the words of Bendall, "ranting and raving and claiming I was undermining his management". Saunders then apparently informed secretary Steve Stride of his resignation.

Supporter reaction to the news was, not surprisingly, angry. The day after the news broke Villa played a league match at home to Southampton. Four fans ran on to the pitch before the game holding aloft a banner calling for the resignation of Bendall, and Saunders' reinstatement. There was continual chanting throughout the match, a 1-1 draw, and a demonstration outside the main entrance afterwards. Fans wrote to the local newspapers with the air of those who had seen it all before. Yet the groundswell of opinion was to suffer from yet another surprise move.

On the following Monday, Blues sacked manager Jim Smith. Saunders was immediately installed as favourite for the vacancy, despite saying that he intended to have time away from football. Within days it was announced that Saunders was, indeed, to become manager of Birmingham City, and with this move, he immediately lost much of the sympathy of the Villa fans. It is worth wondering what would have happened had Saunders not moved across the city with such haste. Might he have returned to Villa Park on a wave of popular support? Bendall said that there was no question of Saunders' re-instatement, but stranger things have happened. Such as the manager of the league champions resigning his job on a point of principle and joining their bitterest rivals the following week.

At St Andrews, Saunders found himself in immediate conflict with several highly-paid members of the playing staff. Colin Todd, Archie Gemmill and in particular the flamboyant Frank Worthington soon found themselves surplus to requirements and in their place came the sort of hard-working professionals Saunders found easier to handle, many recruited from the ranks of the Villa reserve team. Under Saunders, Blues were relegated in 1983-84 and promoted again the following season amidst a welter of controversy surrounding the off-the-field activities of both players and support-ers, culminating in a riot at St Andrews on the final day of the 1984-85 season in which a Leeds supporters was killed. Saunders became involved in anti-violence community projects, but seemed increas-ingly alienated from football. In January 1986, with Blues facing certain relegation from the first division once more, he resigned after FA Cup defeat at home to non-league Altrincham.

Saunders completed a hat-trick when taking over as manager of West Bromwich Albion. Bottom of the first division, he was helpless to prevent his new club from slipping into the second alongside Birmingham. Tony Morley, who played under Saunders at all three local clubs, remembers of the time, "He'd lost it. When he was at Villa the five-a-sides in training were really competitive things, with hardly any goals being scored. By the time he got to the Albion he'd have matches that used to finish 11-9. Things like that made me realise that he couldn't do it any more. He wasn't as fierce, the dis-cipline had gone, the players weren't frightened of him any more."

Results were poor the following season, and with Albion stuck in mid-table, Saunders was dismissed in September 1987. It was an ignominious end to a magnificent managerial career, and one that has never received the recognition it deserved. Indeed, from the day Ron Saunders left Villa Park he simply ceased to exist, certain-ly as far as the club's hierarchy were concerned. His car park space was hastily painted over and it is to the Villa's eternal shame that no permanent public record marks Saunders' achievements. But perhaps he prefers it that way. Saunders has made no public comments about his time at the Villa, and declines invitations to club functions, bar an appearance at Tony Barton's memorial match in 1994. Making a nostalgic return to Villa Park to manage the European Cup-winning side in a warm-up to the main game, he received a standing ovation as he made his way pitch-side for the last time. If the club wish to play down the Saunders era, for whatever reason, the feeling appears to be mutual. As Dennis Mortimer comments, "From the day he walked out he made no attempt to contact any of us, certainly not me. I think the next time I spoke to him was when he was at West Brom. I was at Brighton, we played at the Hawthorns, and I'd never seen him look so ill. He looked pale, drawn. I just thought 'the game's getting to you'. Things hadn't worked out at Birmingham or at West Brom, and for Ron to be there was just, well, you don't do that."

Saunders was a deeply complex character. His time at Manchester City had made him thoroughly mistrustful, yet he rarely went out of his way to endear himself with those around him. Roy MacLaren, for example, worked with Saunders for years, but in the words of Neil Rioch, "He treated Roy abominably. He was a bully. Chester in the League Cup semi-final in 1975, we were having a team meeting at Bodymoor and he said 'This team have got to know where they are. I want them full of anxiety, stress, apprehension. I want those dressing rooms spick and span, I want them full of flowers, I want them to realise just what they've come to.' Roy was smiling and he said, 'I don't know what you're laughing at Roy, you're fetching the flowers.' And off he sent him."

Yet for his faults, Saunders was an expert motivator. He got the best out of players he didn't get on with, such as Tony Morley and Andy Gray. And yet, Saunders never gave the impression that football to him was anything other than a job. He may have once described the role of a football manager as akin to the vocation of the priesthood, but Saunders was firmly of the attitude that once the day's work was done, football was out of his mind. "I went to work, did my job and went home" was how he described a typical working day. And as Allan Evans says, "He didn't like watching football, he didn't want to be part of the scene. I got the impression he never cared about anyone else but the team he was in charge of." Chris

Nicholl confirms this view: "You never saw him at games - never at reserves, never at other games. He was never into the coaching scene, wasn't with the Lilleshall crowd. He just didn't get on with people. He knew what he wanted as a manager but that didn't include getting on with anyone he didn't have to."

Saunders certainly didn't like to mix with football people. The Midlands had its share of charismatic managers during Saunders' time at Villa yet he was never part of the crowd. As Jim Cumbes recalls, "He gave the impression that he didn't like football." Which begs the question – what would he have been like if he HAD liked the game?

He didn't get on with the press, yet Martin Swain, a junior reporter on the Evening Mail during Saunders' time at St Andrews, says, "It wasn't happening for him at Blues, so half the time I was with him and half the time I was pitched against him. But I would still never have a complaint about him. He dealt with me fairly, saw me for the young whippersnapper I was and gave me some great stories. Others might have thought he was a bastard, but I have nothing but respect for him."

His public persona, that of a hard man who suffered fools badly and broached no criticism was in part true. Saunders demanded hard work and loyalty, and anyone who crossed him was frozen out of his personal and professional life forever, yet he was also capable of tremendous kindness. He ensured that players' families were looked after and his Soccer-Care charity and work with the unemployed were pioneering examples of football working in the community. He also made it clear that everything at Villa Park was done for the ultimate benefit of the fans, with whom he shared an empathy such as no other Villa manager has ever achieved. And yet, despite his self-description as a Villa supporter himself, he twice joined their bitterest and oldest rivals. Such a paradox typified of the man.

He may not have been the most easy-going, nor with his players the most popular, football manager ever. But that, along with every other facet of his character, is irrelevant. Ron Saunders was the most successful manager Aston Villa have ever employed. Nothing else matters.

12

Tony Barton

February 1982 - June 1984

On the day that Ron Saunders resigned, Tony Barton was away from home on a scouting mission. This was a common occurrence, with Barton regularly being despatched to watch opponents or check up on promising young players - often, he believed, as a way of being reminded by Saunders who was in charge. This night, though, ended differently. Tony's widow Rosina remembers: "I got a phone call that evening from Mr Bendall, trying to get hold of Tony. He was off watching a game and when he came in, he'd heard the news and he phoned Mr Bendall, who told him he wanted Tony in charge for the next game." At this point the team were fifteenth in the league, with 25 points from 23 games, six away from the relegation places. They were also in the quarter-finals of the European Cup.

Born in Sutton, Surrey, in 1937, Barton had been an England schoolboy international, playing on the wing in the same team as the legendary Duncan Edwards. Barton's professional career began at Fulham, then spent two years with Nottingham Forest. He moved in 1961 to Portsmouth, for whom he played 184 games, scoring 34 goals, until cartilage problems forced him out of the game at the age of 29. Barton then took a job as chief scout for the club and became assistant manager when Ian St John took the manager's job in 1974. In the following year Barton moved to Villa to work under Ron Saunders. This was not the first time the two men had worked together; they had been in the same Portsmouth side, and had even been neighbours for a time.

As Saunders' assistant, Barton gained a reputation for being the best talent-spotter in the game, recommending most of the championship-winning squad and reputedly eulogising to Saunders about a young player at Chester by the name of Ian Rush during Saunders' final days at Villa Park. However, the relationship between Barton and Saunders was never an entirely happy one, with the manager often making it plain that he would be happy to see his assistant move from Villa Park.

Of course, Saunders would be the one to leave, although he may have initially thought that his departure might be a temporary one. Barton later said that, "Ron contacted me to say he thought he would be reinstated after a few days." However, the manager's assistant - he was always careful to emphasise that this was his title, rather than the more customary one of assistant manager - took the caretaker job when it was offered to him by Ron Bendall, and Saunders moved to St Andrews. This unprecedented transfer across the city helped Barton as, overnight, it quelled a growing current of protest at Saunders' departure. Had he remained on the sidelines, there would undoubtedly have been a split between those who wanted Saunders to return (4,000 of whom still signed a petition calling for his reinstatement at Barton's first game in charge, a 1-1 draw at home to Southampton) and those wanting to get behind the new manager. With Saunders now having committed the ultimate act of treason, the overwhelming feeling amongst Villa supporters was to rally behind the new man.

In taking the job on a temporary basis, Barton staked his claim for the position to be made permanent. "I think I could prove capable," he said, and events confirmed this. Despite going down to Spurs in an FA Cup fifth round tie the following Saturday, Barton soon settled into the job. That his side beat the Blues the following week thanks to a Peter Withe goal, with Ron Saunders watching from the directors' box prior to being appointed manager at St Andrews, was a great help to Barton.

In all, a spell of fifteen points from nine games, plus victory over Dynamo Kiev in the European Cup quarter final, saw Barton being given the job on a permanent basis on 1st April, with Roy MacLaren named as his assistant. In making the appointment, Ron Bendall spoke of the "old family atmosphere throughout the club" since Barton had taken charge. The manager, for his part, conceded that, "The team virtually picks itself. They have been taught good habits and will not lose them easily." Such modesty was to prove both Barton's forte and, perhaps, his undoing. Tony Morley remembers, "We had a bit of a problem adjusting to Tony being in charge. He'd always been around the place, friendly, approachable. Now he was the boss, and for some of the older players, especially, that took a bit of getting used to."

Leon Hickman, at the time the Evening Mail's chief football writer, says, "The appointment was typical of Ron Bendall. He gave the job to Tony because he didn't know anything else about football and he got lucky." Barton certainly made the most of his chairman's lack of footballing knowledge, setting about taking his place in history. Anderlecht came to Villa Park for the European Cup semi-final intent on stifling Villa's creativity. They succeeded in part, with the home side restricted to a single goal from Tony Morley, whose performances throughout the campaign were nothing short of world class. In the return leg Villa had to deal with the experienced Belgian team as well as the unwelcome distractions of violence off the field and a brief pitch invasion. Not only did they cope successfully, they did so with a game plan that showed the ingenuity of their manager. Anderlecht were scarcely able to move out of their own half, whilst the fast-moving Villa forward line counter-attacked with regularity. That they were unable to add to their first leg lead was down to bad luck and a referee who disallowed what appeared to be a perfectly good Peter Withe goal for offside.

There is little that hasn't been written countless times about the European Cup Final of 26th May 1982. The events of the previous two seasons had seen the team adopt a siege mentality, Allan Evans remembers, "No-one gave us a chance in the league. Saunders didn't give a damn about what people thought, and after Ron had gone, with Tony in charge we started thinking that way as well. We didn't give a damn that we were outsiders, that nobody gave us a chance. We thought we'll show them, and it gave us that impetus to go and do it."

As for the manager, he was probably the calmest man in Birmingham as the day approached. Rosina Barton remembers, "Tony was very laid back in the run up to the final. I was a different matter though. I wish I could do it now, but I lost about a stone before the game. The week before, I was a wreck."

Barton's chief achievement of the day was to keep news of Jimmy Rimmer's injury hidden. Or so it appeared. However, modest as ever, Barton played down his part in the subterfuge, "Everyone thought I'd done a marvellous job in keeping Jimmy's injury quiet. In fact, he'd told us it had cleared up and I was as surprised as anyone when he came off." Rimmer's replacement, Nigel Spink, had little time for nerves. Barton recalled that, "As Nigel was about to run on he looked at me and smiled 'My mum won't half be pleased'."

And so after leading his team to the European Cup, Barton was entitled to reflect in the glory of his achievement. However, even on this momentous occasion, he was realistic. As Martin Swain, reporting on the final for the Evening Mail, says, "Like everybody else, I was totally knocked out and I can't remember the first question; something like 'where's it going to go from here?' His answer was 'The only thing I know for sure is I'll get the sack'. It was as if he knew what was around the corner, that even with this incredible success, he would forever be thought of as the junior partner in the firm. And it really took me back that on a day like that, he would be thinking in such a way."

Barton knew that his triumph would be attributed to 'Saunders' team'. He accepted this, and yet the greatest tribute that can be paid to him was that he had the strength of character to appreciate that things were best left unchanged. Martin Swain continues, "He realised that he had to let them get on with it, he'd pick the team and sort out training, but that was his greatest gift – he knew what to do and what to leave alone." Gary Shaw agrees, "We hardly saw Tony at Bodymoor before he got the job. But when he was appointed he just kept things ticking over, which takes a lot of character. He was never going to change things dramatically, he was clever enough to assess the squad, maybe see one or two changes for the future. He was a great scout; that was his game. He knew what had to be done and what had to be left alone."

And Dennis Mortimer, the rock upon whom Barton relied in the run-up to Rotterdam, points out that "We went about the semi- and the final in the same way as we did with every match. There was no special attention paid to detail, it was typical of the way Ron Saunders went about things. Neither he nor Tony ever burdened us with the opposition, they never needed to tell us about any special qualities the other team might have. Ron's attitude was that he had quality in his team and he had to make sure everyone gave 100%. Tony was the same."

The European Cup won, Barton now set about managing the team in his own way. Villa started the 1982-83 season respectably, moving to third place in the league with ten wins from fourteen matches and progressing through the first two rounds of the European Cup with ease. Then in December 1982 came the news that Ron Bendall was selling his controlling interest in the club and, after a period of confusion, the man left in charge was none other than Doug Ellis, last seen leaving Villa Park under a cloud three years earlier. Harry Kartz, by now the longest-surviving board member, watched proceedings with concern. He said of Bendall, "The old man was ill, I think he was going senile. He wouldn't sell to me or (fellow director) Trevor Gill because we'd brought the police in to investigate the problems concerning the North Stand. Harry Parkes might have got the club and I'll never know why he called in accountants and solicitors to handle the sale. He should have bought swiftly and without fuss – the shares were amazing value. Once Ellis knew Bendall was selling there was only going to be one winner. They were a strange family; Bendall sold cheaply to a man he despised."

Barton said nothing in public about the change of regime, but privately his feelings were well-known. Indeed, he was heard to remark that Villa were in trouble from the time Ellis returned.

The manager's future was equally unstable. "His days were numbered as soon as Ellis took over. Unless, of course, he won the title," is the opinion of Martin Swain. Players of the time were equally sure that things had changed for the worse. "When he handed the first team sheet over to Ellis, Ellis said "I see you've got Dennis Mortimer in the team," recalls the captain of that great side.

Tony Morley says of the change of ownership, "The mood of the club changed entirely. We'd always had a happy dressing room, everybody was laughing and joking, we all used to love going in to train. Once Ellis came back it was as though Tony had a shadow hanging over him all the time and that came over to the players."

A 3-0 defeat at St Andrews on Boxing Day led to Jimmy Rimmer being dropped from the team and inconvenience for the Barton household. As Rosina Barton recalls, "Our phone number was always listed in the directory, but after that match we got so much stick, people phoning up at all hours, that we changed the number and went ex-directory. Even then Tony didn't want to, but he realised it was affecting the family." It is impossible to imagine any top manager now being listed in the phone book, much less the manager of the European Champions, but Barton remained as approachable as possible. "The press were always ringing up and he'd always speak to them or ring back. I used to love talking to them and they thought it was wonderful that they could ring a house like this, where they were so welcome. But that was Tony's way - he couldn't see why he shouldn't be decent to everyone."

Ellis moved into Villa Park determined to cut costs in any manner possible. Villa finished sixth in the league in 1982-83, qualifying for the UEFA Cup. They had won the European Super Cup after a 4-2 aggregate victory over Barcelona that has gone down in Villa Park folklore due to the brutal tactics of the Spaniards, while the European Cup was relinquished following a defeat at the quarter-final stage by Juventus. Losing to the Italian giants, a team packed with world-class players, was no disgrace, but in hindsight it was to herald the end of an era.

The team may have been breaking up, but Barton was still able to attract quality replacements. Highly-regarded young forward, Paul Rideout joined the Villa from Swindon Town during the summer of 1983, as did Everton midfielder, Steve McMahon. Both players were signed in the face of stiff competition from league champions Liverpool. "Tony sold the Villa to me," McMahon later said. "Villa was a fantastic club but he was so humble, such a nice man. He was a football man, knowledgeable, people wanted to work for him."

Barton was also bringing players through the youth system. Paul Birch, who had played in the second leg of the hard-fought win against Barcelona, recalls Barton's attitude towards his younger players. "He was brilliant for the youngsters. He had total confidence in the ability of anyone he brought into the side."

Unfortunately, Barton's hopes of rebuilding the team were dealt a double blow when, over the course of a few weeks, Gordon Cowans broke his leg during a pre-season tournament in Barcelona, then Gary Shaw suffered the first in a series of injuries that effectively finished his career. "Like Liverpool losing Dalglish and Souness," was how Barton later described this double blow, and this team never recovered.

The 1983-84 season was one of disappointment. Villa finished tenth in the league, and went out of the Milk Cup in a semi-final with Everton. As the season wore on, Barton's job was increasingly in jeopardy – Ellis saying before the Milk Cup quarter-final at Norwich that the club "will not accept consistent failure". Gates were down, just over thirteen thousand watching the penultimate home match of the season, against Notts County. And forever in the background was the spectre of Doug Ellis, whose obsession with cutting costs was equalled only by his desire to play an active part in every aspect of the club's running. It later transpired that Ellis had attempted to sell Gary Shaw to Barcelona without Barton's blessing, while Barton told the story of how reserve goalkeeper, Mervyn Day had been in the manager's office one afternoon when the chairman arrived and complained that he had no-one to collect some business contacts from Birmingham airport. Pointing to the player, Ellis declared, "He can fetch them".

There is little doubt that Barton and Ellis clashed regularly. Rosina Barton remembers, "There were so many little things, they were happening all the time. There was one occasion when Tony was playing golf on his day off and someone came up to him and told him that Doug wanted to see him right away. Of course, Tony thought that it must be something important so he left the golf course and drove over to Villa Park. When he got into the chairman's office all Doug said was, 'Have there been any enquiries for players today?' He knew full well that there hadn't, he just wanted to show Tony that he was in charge and everybody had to jump for him."

Barton was always open with the players, far more so than Ron Saunders had ever been, and they were quick to realise that all was not well between manager and chairman. Tony Morley, whose move to West Brom saw yet another part of the European Cup-winning team leave Villa Park prematurely, also bears witness to the conflict between manager and chairman. "I'm sure that Tony didn't want to sell me, but Ellis seemed determined to get rid of any player he could sell for a decent price." And Morley has another theory as to why Barton was unable to exert as great a pressure on Ellis as he would have liked. "Managers in those days weren't as secure financially as they were later on. Tony couldn't afford to lose his job, and he couldn't walk out in the way Saunders did, knowing that he'd walk into another job straight away. That's why, for instance, Saunders was able to stop Ellis from coming into the dressing room but Tony never could."

Despite a poor league place when compared to the successes of recent years, there was room for optimism at the end of the 1983-84 season. Barton had made some excellent signings and several young players were coming through the ranks, most notably the future England internationals Tony Dorigo and Tony Daley. A post-season tour of Italy had seen several young players making their mark and hopes were high that the team would do well in the future. "Next year I expect Villa to win a trophy" was Barton's verdict, while Harry Kartz was so optimistic about what he had seen on the Italian tour he made a large bet that Villa would win the league title the following season. However, such optimism was not shared by Doug Ellis.

In the middle of June, over a month after the end of the season, and some weeks after the board had expressed confidence in the manager, Barton was sacked. Although Ellis stated that the decision was a unanimous one, it was obvious whose vote had been significant. Harry Kartz later said of the time that Barton's fate was sealed: "The decision was already cut and dried, so there was no point in voting against. Ellis could have given Tony a bit longer, though. Another twelve months might have made all the difference".

Rosina Barton recalls the fateful day. "We'd just come back off holiday, when Tony's secretary Debbie rang me in floods of tears and said I should talk to Tony, who was at Villa Park. He came on the phone and said 'He's sacked me'. It was a total shock to us all. Steve McMahon and Alan Curbishley turned up on the doorstep at nine o'clock the next morning, and they stayed with us all day. Our son Gary was getting married the Saturday after, and his reception was due to take place in the McGregor Suite at Villa Park. He offered to cancel it, but Tony was having none of that. He insisted that we went there, and we did. Doug apparently complained later that he hadn't been invited."

The reaction to Barton's dismissal was one of fury. Leon Hickman called the decision "untimely and disgraceful" in the Evening Mail. Two thirds of supporters who contacted the local media were against, while Steve McMahon reacted to the news by asking for a transfer. Gary Shaw says of the sacking "Tony's record was good, not really a sackable one. He'd bought Rideout, McMahon, Curbishley, so he was looking to change things round but his relationship with the chairman wasn't the best." Indeed, it was later revealed that Luton manager' David Pleat, a former colleague of Barton's, had been offered the job before Barton's dismissal but refused to countenance such a move against his old friend.

Barton's great problem was to improve on what had gone before. The players were getting older, while the opposition were getting wiser – they were learning the importance of stopping Tony Morley, how important it was to close-mark Gordon Cowans. The manager not only had to cope with this, he had to do it without the kind of money available that there should have been to replace European Cup winners. Indeed, as one member of that side said, "We should have been going in for the likes of Ray Wilkins and Paul Mariner. Alan Curbishley suited the chairman's wallet better."

Since the day Barton left the Villa there has, of course, been a theory that his dismissal was down to Doug Ellis's desire to get rid of all traces of the success the club enjoyed while he was in exile. Alan Evans says, "I don't know whether Ellis wanted to get rid of the successful team. I know the stories but I don't really care about them. With what we'd won, standards were high and finishing tenth after what had gone before would have been a good enough excuse if you wanted to get rid of a manager."

Dennis Mortimer puts things more bluntly. "The players didn't talk to Ellis, and it was a real strain to him that on the away trips he had to keep his distance. He's always wanted to be loved and while we were there he couldn't have any affinity with the players, he couldn't get in with them at all. He wanted to be accepted and to do that he had to break up the loyalty of the players to the manager. That's part of the reason why he got rid of Tony."

The sacking of Barton signalled the end of the glorious era that had begun when Ron Saunders had been appointed in 1974. Successful clubs need stability above all else, and with Saunders and then Barton in charge, a dynasty was beginning to take shape. As Tony Morley says of the playing side, "Every Villa team of that era, from the first team to the schoolboys, played in the same way. The same formation, the same style. Only a handful of other clubs in the country could have said that and they were the other successful ones." Both managers had done their best work with a chairman who stayed firmly in the background, allowing them to get on with the job and running the club as they saw fit. This is invariably the case at all successful clubs. However, since the appointment of Jimmy McMullan half a century earlier, Villa managers had often appeared to be engaged in a constant struggle to keep the influence of the board to a minimum. Over the years there had seemed an assumption on the part of Villa directors that they knew better than the manager – a reaction, perhaps, to the fact that the club's glory days occurred when the board were all-powerful.

While Saunders and Barton were in charge, and while success kept coming, the board's interference was minimised. This particularly suited Ron Bendall; he had no interest in football, indeed, he had missed much of the European Cup final, and was content to keep a distant eye on affairs from his home in the tax haven of the Isle of Man. Once Doug Ellis returned, though, things were very different. Barton's dismissal – and it is difficult to argue with the theory that Ellis had had his eye on replacing the manager with a more compliant figure from day one, and did so at the first available opportunity – caused the balance of Villa Park power to shift unquestionably from the manager's office to that of the chairman. Its location has rarely been in doubt since.

For his part, Ellis claimed that, "Aston Villa is bigger than any individual. At the present moment Villa seems dead and I don't like the status quo." Ellis cited poor away form (the club had won just seven away matches in two seasons) and a 25% drop in season ticket sales as reasons to get rid of Barton. However, the truth was far more complex. Chairman and manager had clashed over the cost-cutting measures implemented since Ellis had returned to the club. Some of these were essential, with debts mounting and attendances throughout football rapidly declining. Others, such as the scrapping of overnight stays at some away games and the tour of Italy at the end of the 1983-84 season, were seen as petty irritants that got in the way of the team's well-being. Ellis was growing increasingly irritated by Barton's laid-back style, which the chairman, who has always thrived on confrontation, took for a sign of weakness. It was noticeable that the club appeared unconcerned by the increasingly bitter comments made about Barton by BRMB Radio's Tony Butler, making no attempts to defend the manager or impose sanctions against the radio station.

Ellis also wanted the numbers of the playing squad reduced and Roy McLaren replaced as Barton's assistant by his own long-time friend, Ron Wylie. Barton refused to countenance these measures and his job became increasingly difficult. As he said upon leaving the club, "I love the Villa, but in the end I hated going to work in the mornings."

The players were sympathetic to Barton. Steve McMahon believes that, "Shaw and Cowans' injuries had a massive effect, they were the shining stars. We had the nucleus of a good side but those injuries killed the team. I never felt things were slipping away; with Shaw and Cowans back we would have had the nucleus of a good team. Tony shouldn't have gone"

Leon Hickman gives another slant to the story. "Villa had become a home team. Good as they were, they'd become a soft touch in away games. Here was where Tony's inexperience showed – and it has to be remembered that for all his achievements in Europe, Tony had never been a manager until 1982. He needed people he could rely on to help him but, of course, had he asked Doug Ellis for advice then Ellis would have taken that as a sign Tony wasn't up to the job."

A month after leaving the Villa, Barton was appointed manager of fourth division Northampton Town, but soon realised that moving down the divisions was a big mistake. As he later said: "They showed me plans for a new ground, but they didn't say that they were twenty years old. They didn't even own the land". And shortly afterwards, Barton suffered a heart attack. Rosina Barton remembers of the time, "It was partly brought on by the stress of football, no question. While he was recovering in Good Hope hospital, one of our sons said the words 'Doug Ellis' and the heart monitor went shooting up. All the nurses came rushing in."

Leaving Northampton after a season in charge, Barton spent three years at Southampton as assistant to Chris Nicholl, until they disagreed over playing style. "I wanted to play football, he preferred the long ball game," was Barton's recollection.

Then came a short spell scouting for Birmingham City before a return to Portsmouth, first as chief scout and then as caretaker manager. Barton had been promised the job on a permanent basis if he kept Portsmouth in the second division but, despite avoiding relegation, found himself once more out of work when the job was given to Jim Smith. Barton was then approached to work for multiple sclerosis charity ARMS, as head of their Football Against MS fund raising campaign in 1992. However, this role was short-lived and the charity folded shortly before Barton's death in August 1993, at the age of 56.

The way in which Tony Barton was treated by Aston Villa was nothing short of disgraceful. Requests for a testimonial match were turned down and the only help he was given was a benefit lunch organised by the Shareholders Association. Even after Barton's death, the club's attitude scarcely changed. News of his passing drew a brief comment from secretary Steve Stride and silence from the boardroom. A long-overdue benefit match took place at Villa Park shortly before Christmas 1994. Virtually ignored by the club, the game attracted a small attendance and from that day on there has been no public recognition of the part played by Tony Barton in the history of Aston Villa. It is difficult not to agree with those who say that such an attitude is part of the club's attempt to pretend that the glories that took place while Doug Ellis was otherwise engaged never happened.

Barton was often criticised for being just too nice. Allan Evans partly agrees with this. "The only bad thing you could say was that he was too nice to be a manager. We knew him well, he'd always been there and you felt comfortable around Tony. And that was probably his problem as manager."

Steve MacMahon disagrees. "You don't have to be a ranter and a raver and a big shouter. Sometimes you need to be firm, but like most managers he talked to you. A little word here and there and you respected him."

Barton's record of finishing sixth and tenth in his two full seasons at Villa Park was solid, if unspectacular. That he achieved such a feat against a background of cost-cutting and boardroom interference adds to his credit, as does the fact that it took six seasons and three managers before the club bettered those placings. But the league tables of the period, and subsequent developments, can only portray a fraction of the impact Tony Barton made on the club. He managed Aston Villa on the night of their greatest achievement. Barton's place in history is secure for all time.

13

Graham Turner

July 1984 - September 1986

As ever, there was a strong list of candidates for the vacant Villa manager's job during the summer of 1984. Keith Burkenshaw, who had surprisingly resigned after leading Spurs to the UEFA Cup a few weeks earlier, was amongst the frontrunners, as was John Toshack of Sporting Lisbon. Toshack was reported to have turned down the job and, after a period of uncertainty, Graham Turner of Shrewsbury Town was the surprise choice to fill one of the biggest jobs in football.

Although it had taken over a month to fill the vacancy, Doug Ellis was adamant that Turner was his first choice from the beginning. Turner tells of how his appointment came about. "It started as a phone call from Doug at the end of the season, to see if I was interested in a goalkeeper. My comment was, 'I see you're looking for a manager, any point in applying?" I met him, had a second interview with the rest of the board and there were one or two areas I wasn't happy with – the terms of the contract, not the money but one or two other things, such the timing of tours abroad and buying and selling of players. I was asked whether I would take that contract if it were offered - he was shrewd enough not to offer it, but there was one there. I said no, and a month later, while I was on holiday, I had a call from him asking to get together and talk again."

Turner was astute enough to know that taking over at Villa Park was far from a dream scenario. "There were certain aspects of the contract, a few people had warned me about the Villa job, one or two had distanced themselves from it, but at that age it's an opportunity you couldn't turn down. It wasn't an ideal scenario, but I went with it warts and all."

Turner had been born in Ellesmere Port in October 1947 and had spent an unremarkable playing career in the lower divisions first with Wrexham, then Chester City and finally Shrewsbury Town, where he had enjoyed a successful six years as player-manager. At the age of 36, Turner was the youngest manager in the Villa's history. He was awarded a five-year contract worth £30,000 per annum, and which specified that the manager would have full control of playing and transfer matters. Obviously, the new boss had taken heed of the warnings that came with the job.

Concern was raised about Turner's lack of top-level experience, but supporters seemed pleased with the appointment. The new manager certainly seemed ambitious enough, stating that, "Managing Villa isn't the fulfilment of my ambitions. My ambition is to have the first division trophy on my desk".

Reaction from the players was mixed. Steve McMahon, who had been close to Tony Barton, recalls that, "The first reaction was 'Who's Graham Turner?' It was a baffling signing. The supporters wanted a big name, as fans at all big clubs do. It didn't go down very well. I don't think Graham knew what he was letting himself in for."

Allan Evans had equal reservations. "There was a question mark from the start, from the media and from others in football – is he ready for this, is the job that big a jump? Having come in, and not having played top level, that's always a problem. Did we disrespect him? I didn't. I accepted that here was a guy with great potential, otherwise he wouldn't have been given the job, who had to come in and do things his own way. The question was, were they his own ways?"

Turner made the best possible start. His first two matches produced six points and a top of the table place. However, just when things seemed easy for the new man, disaster struck. Dennis Mortimer remembers the time that Turner decided changes had to be made. "We went to Newcastle top of the league, and they beat us 3-0. Then on the Tuesday we played Forest. They were one up at half time, Ian Bowyer had scored a thirty-yarder in injury time, and then after half-time they scored three in fifteen minutes. For the first time ever I was subbed without being injured. Maybe he'd decided I was finished, but the next day we had a meeting and that was when me and Des Bremner were told we could leave. Some time between the end of the match and the next morning we were surplus to requirements, and I remember thinking 'You've made a big mistake there, Graham'. I think he was determined to put his best side out at first, then after that game maybe he came under a bit of pressure and he had to bring in some new players."

For the manager to publicly criticise two such great servants of the club was wrong. His later comments, "The likes of Des and Dennis have gone at this level. It would be in the best interests of them and the club if they left quickly," compounded the insult.

Within weeks of Turner's arrival there were problems in the Villa dressing room. Much of this was down to Turner's inexperience. Steve McMahon says of the time, "He couldn't come to terms with such a massive club. It was big headlines when he criticised a lot of players – calling them fancy dans and all that, and he named names. It was a bit naive and he learned from it, realising he should have done things privately. He didn't realise how the press covered the club. And some players couldn't believe that Graham Turner from Shrewsbury was actually tearing a strip off them. So he started on the wrong foot and once you do that it's difficult to get it back."

Turner had castigated the players for a lack of desire and the high wages they were earning, despite the fact that average earnings amongst the Villa players had actually gone down since Tony Barton's managerial spell. Ian Johnson praised Turner's honesty in the Sports Argus but doubted his wisdom. Several players were asking for transfers at this time, although Steve McMahon believes that this was less due to Turner than it may have appeared. "Some players had wanted to leave for some time. They wanted a change and Graham arriving was the excuse."

However, for one player at least, the arrival of Graham Turner had been a positive move. Paul Birch was just beginning to break into the side. His view is, "For the younger players it was refreshing that a younger manager had come in and we could associate with him. Some managers are stuck in their ways but he came in and he was very pleasant to work with."

However many players wanted to leave, there was one, at least, who was keen to join the club. Didier Six had been a part of the French squad which won the 1984 European Championship. For the Villa to sign him on loan for the rest of the 1984-85 season was a coup both for the club and for a manager supposedly unable to handle big names. Turner recalls how the transfer unfolded: "We got a phone call offering his services; organised a match against Tranmere to see how he fitted in. He looked fit, so we put him straight in against Manchester United. It was the best game of my two years. Full house; Didier was terrific. A great match."

Indeed, it looked as though a new era was dawning. Inspired by Six's wing play, Villa beat United 3-0, and the new signing came off after 70 minutes to a standing ovation. Unfortunately, Six could not live up to his magnificent start and in total made just thirteen appearances for the Villa, scoring twice. Turner rues: "Why didn't he fit in, I just don't know. I wouldn't have said he was too good for the team, but he was Cantona without the flair. For long periods of the game he'd do nothing, then he'd be wonderful. You knew that you would have to carry him for long periods - he wouldn't track back, but just occasionally there were bits of magic. In fairness to him it was the wrong time to come here."

The rest of the season passed by in a blur of mediocrity. Villa were in the bottom six at the halfway mark of the league programme, but improved form after Christmas saw them finish in tenth place. That this was the same position deemed unacceptable for Tony Barton was an irony not lost on the fans who, nevertheless, generally remained supportive of the manager. Turner had set about dismantling the side he inherited - the European Cup-winning side had virtually all departed within twelve months of his appointment - but was still unable to shake off the outside perception that his was a puppet management, with the real power being displayed in the Chairman's office. Turner, however, denies that Doug Ellis played a disproportionate part in running the club at this time: "I had an office at Bodymoor. I was told he wanted one there before I arrived. That would have been a massive mistake but it never looked like happening. His contact with players was limited; they would eat at Bodymoor, train there and they wouldn't see much of him. He'd pop into the dressing room before the match to wish them luck, which is a done thing with chairmen, but I didn't find interference from anyone on the board a great problem. Doug's got an ego, and he never would share the driving from any match we went to watch, but I didn't have a problem with him."

It can, though, be said that while Turner was getting rid of players, it was difficult to persuade Ellis to finance replacements of equal stature. "Doug was always penny-pinching; there were three targets I wanted – Ipswich wanted £800,000 for Terry Butcher and I also wanted Alan Smith at Leicester and Richard Gough at Dundee United, but that kind of money wasn't available. Yet it was a big club and they should have been spending big."

During the summer of 1985 Dennis Mortimer and Peter Withe left on free transfers, while Gordon Cowans, fully recovered from his broken leg, joined Bari alongside Paul Rideout for a combined fee of £850,000. It appeared as if every Villa player had his price, a feeling confirmed when Steve McMahon, the type of player around whom Turner wanted to build his side, moved to Liverpool for £325,000. He says of his time at Villa with Turner: "He couldn't understand the big wages, that was his problem. The players were internationals, European Cup winners. Maybe one or two of them were past it but there's a way to do things. What they'd done for the club was absolutely fantastic and what you say in that situation is 'thanks and goodbye'. Graham will have learnt a lot from that."

And Allan Evans, by now team captain, says of the period, "When you've had a successful side, people don't want it to break up. But it can't go on for ever and it has to come to an end sometime. I thought it did come too quickly, but players were getting older, we'd been successful but the players couldn't last for ever and we had to get players in to take their place."

The 1985-86 season started reasonably, but the air of decline was obvious. Attendances were down, money was tight throughout football and nowhere was the general gloom surrounding the game felt any keener than at Villa Park. McMahon had been replaced by Nottingham Forest's Steve Hodge, but with gates barely scraping into five figures there was little chance of the kind of arrivals who would take Villa back to the top.

Andy Gray had returned to the club where he had first made his name, while Simon Stainrod had signed from Sheffield Wednesday. Central defender Paul Elliott cost £400,000 from Luton Town, a strange signing as he was recovering from a broken leg and had been kept out of the Luton side by Steve Foster, sold by Villa the previous season for just £70,000. Whilst the new arrivals were decent players, none were at this stage of their careers the kind around which a championship-challenging team could be built. Villa were twelfth in the league after ten games, at a time when Doug Ellis announced that the club were heading for a £400,000 loss over the course of the season with a break-even attendance of 21,500, which they never looked like attaining. This was doubtless one of the reasons why Colin Gibson was sold to Manchester United for £275,000. The first team squad, with an average age in the early twenties, was the youngest in the club's history. Such reliance on youth was to have a fatal effect on the team's progress.

As the season progressed, the team's fortunes slipped and by New Year's Day, discontent was plain. A single goal defeat at home to Manchester City left Villa sliding inexorably towards the relegation places, and the crowd was placing the blame firmly on Graham Turner. The manager was doing himself no favours with his handling of the situation. Paul Birch remembers the time, "He would take defeat badly. If he looks back, I'm sure he'll realise that's one of the things you learn as a manager. The last thing the players want to see is the manager coming in after you've lost and he's down. You look to him to say, 'Okay, we got beat. Now let's learn from it and improve on what we did wrong'. In any walk of life, if you see your boss unhappy it's got to have an effect on you."

The departure of youth team coach, Brian Little, who claimed that Turner had failed to back him in an argument with chief scout, Don Dorman, was another blow to the manager's popularity amongst the fans. Nobody at this time could be seen to disagree with Brian Little and remain unscathed.

However, a glimmer of hope presented itself in the cups. The FA Cup third round tie against Portsmouth saw Villa on their way out of the competition until an injury-time equaliser from Paul Birch set up a 3-2 win in the replay at Villa Park. Similarly, an unexpected 2-1 victory in a Milk Cup quarter-final replay at Highbury handed Turner a lifeline when defeat could have seen him losing his job. He remembers the time well: "Barry Davies asked me that at Highbury – would you have got the sack if you'd lost? And I said no. There's no good worrying, you've always got to believe that it won't happen. And I didn't think that before Arsenal, just as when we lost to Oxford in the semis. When Andy Gray signed he said, 'I'm a lucky mascot, I always win something as soon as I join a club'. We avoided Liverpool in the semi, they got beaten by QPR and we got Oxford. We should have beaten them, but they got an early goal. Andy and Mark Walters had good chances at their place but nothing went right for us."

And so it proved. Oxford United, newly-arrived in the first division and boasting players of the quality of John Aldridge and Ray Houghton, followed a 2-2 draw at Villa Park with a 2-1 win at the Manor Ground and went on to win the trophy, beating QPR in the final. Following a disgraceful performance in the FA Cup against Millwall, when Villa were defeated in a replay after being outplayed over two games by a side struggling against relegation to the third division, things looked grim. However, Turner was able to re-sign two former Villa midfielders, Steve Hunt from Albion and Andy Blair from Sheffield Wednesday. Against a backdrop of supporter unrest, and despite relegation at one point seeming inevitable, Villa took nine points from six games, beating fellow strugglers Ipswich and Leicester. Safety was finally assured with two games remaining.

During the following summer, Turner made several signings who looked as though they would strengthen the side. Garry Thompson joined from Sheffield Wednesday for £450,000, while Aberdeen's Neale Cooper was a £350,000 purchase. Also arriving was Arsenal's highly-promising defender, Martin Keown, for whom Turner paid £120,000 in unorthodox circumstances. "Keown: that was a terrific bit of business. I saw him play twice, against Man United and Liverpool. He marked Hughes and Rush out of the game; he had pace and tenacity and this was just a 19 year old. He's matured into a great player, but we were on an end of season tour and I saw in the paper that there were about five young lads at Arsenal whose contracts had expired. George Graham had just arrived; I nipped in, found out where Martin lived and knocked on his door, getting him before Arsenal knew what was happening."

With Ron Wylie promoted to first team coach, in place of Malcolm Beard, hopes were high that the struggle of the previous season would not be repeated. Turner had certainly learnt one lesson. "One of my early problems was that I didn't change the backroom staff. Whatever their attributes, you need to bring your own men in." However, the season turned out to be the worst since relegation to the third division almost twenty years previous.

The team took just three points from the first four league games, with Steve Hodge, player of the year the previous season, taking advantage of a trip away on England duty to hand in a transfer request. His timing was disgraceful; his comments about the club made matters worse. Turner retains a sense of betrayal to this day: "He'd gone to the World Cup, and maybe someone had a word with him while he was over there. We know he'd been brought up with Cloughie, to play in their disciplined style but he was always a wide left player. It wasn't until we gave him more freedom that he won his first cap. He might have stayed at Forest and never blossomed or gone to the World Cup. And look how he reacted"

The situation at Villa Park was reaching crisis point. And when that happens, the end is never far off. Villa travelled to the City Ground, Nottingham, never the easiest of places for a struggling team. They went down 6-0, and far from turning on manager and players, the Villa fans seemed to be laughing at them. Turner must have known the inevitable outcome of a disastrous day, on which the reserves also lost 7-0, to Manchester United. "The result was devastating, obviously. Doug came down and, to be fair, he said, 'Come on, let's have a drink in the boardroom.' I said I was off to face the press and I didn't see Doug until the following morning. 10 o'clock and I got a call to say there was a board meeting at his house and would I go round. It doesn't take a genius to work out after a 6-0 defeat and you're bottom of the league. One of the kids asked 'Where you off to dad? Why've you put a collar and tie on?' I thought well, I'm going smart, I'm going in style and my reply was 'I'm off to get the sack'." At this point the team was bottom-but-one in the table, with three points from six games. Relegation already seemed inevitable, as did Turner's dismissal.

"Doug was waiting and ,to be fair to him, we went into the garden. The rest of the board were inside, he wanted to tell me before I faced them. I appreciated that. It would have been easy to have just walked straight in and hit me with the full board meeting and wallop! - you're sacked. I didn't need telling, I knew what the meeting was about. You can't disguise those results." There was a sense of irony about the timing. It was a five goal defeat at the beginning of Turner's reign that led him to believe that change had to be made, and quickly. And a six-goal defeat by Forest led Doug Ellis to believe that it was now the manager who had to be changed.

And so it happened. Graham Turner became the latest victim of Doug Ellis's desire for success. The chairman was full of praise for Turner: "I have never worked with anyone who has such honesty and integrity," he stated. But redeeming though these qualities may be, they don't win football matches.

On paper, Turner's record was a poor one. He had taken a side that needed rebuilding, but still contained many fine players, and turned it into a team doomed to relegation. However, as is often the case, there were mitigating factors.

Turner was faced with an ageing team and, for whatever reason, the money was not available for quality replacements. The likes of Dennis Mortimer and Peter Withe are not easily replaced, and certainly not under the budgetary constraints placed by Doug Ellis at the time. Turner was also unlucky when Neale Cooper, a top-class player in Scotland, suffered a pre-season injury that meant he was unable to play for the manager who signed him.

But the truth is that Graham Turner was out of his depth at Villa Park and the gap between Shrewsbury and Aston Villa too great to bridge, a point that he himself readily acknowledges. "Although we were only just off the pace at Shrewsbury, we'd finished eighth in the second division, the clubs weren't that far apart in league positions but in terms of size and expectations, the jump was a massive one. You don't think it at the time, and the circumstances didn't lead me to believe it, but with age you look back and the jump was too big." And if those circumstances didn't make the job difficult enough, the timing of Turner's appointment was a further handicap. "They'd won the European Cup. Part of that side had already moved on. Shaw and Cowans were badly injured, and others such as Peter Withe were coming to the end. They'd been brilliant but they were coming to the end of their top quality shelf life. That's not being detrimental, but it was a side breaking up, a very popular side, and it was an awful time to go in because it was a hatchet job that had to be done. Maybe we should have kept a few of the older players, but I left the nucleus of a good, young squad. Maybe a new manager wants all his own players but there were some good players there and it was a shame that the likes of Tony Dorigo and Mark Walters were allowed to leave."

Whether he was acting under orders or not, Turner undoubtedly changed things round at Villa Park too quickly. Paul Birch makes the point: "It would have helped the youngsters if he'd kept the experienced players on. I was lucky enough to watch and learn from Des, Dennis, Gordon, they were good with the kids and they wanted to help us. I learnt under a great set of players but they weren't around for the next set of youngsters."

And Martin Swain, who has seen Turner's career unfold while covering Midlands football, by this time with the Wolverhampton Express & Star, sums up the period. "His big problem, and this cuts to the heart of the Villa's problem, was the paranoia Ellis brings on

managers. Villa were signing someone and we couldn't get hold of
Graham. So we ended up calling Doug, asked him about this story
and Doug said, 'Yes, that's true.' Graham rang up and went ape at
me, saying it was typical, and how could he run the club when the
press go running to the chairman all the time. Graham didn't have
the experience and the wisdom to take hold of a club of Villa's size.
Doug would have run rings round him, and I'm sure Graham would
agree. The whole period was a silly folly that did Graham Turner no
good. He proved himself to be entirely competent at Wolves but
Villa was a bad appointment for him. Nothing against Graham, but
how was he supposed to go into the dressing room with Mortimer,
Withe, European champions and internationals all over the place?
How stupid is it that to expect a young manager whose highest playing level was the second division, to go in and take hold of that
dressing room?"

Turner moved to Wolves, where he did a magnificent job in turning round a club that had seemed on the verge of going out of the
league altogether. Successive promotions took them from the fourth
division to the second, with the bonus of the Sherpa Van Trophy. Yet
Turner was unable to take the final step back to the top flight and
was eventually sacked in 1994, despite being virtually single-hand-
edly responsible for keeping the club in business a few years earlier. Paul Birch, who signed for Turner during his time at Wolves,
says, "He was more relaxed, much more self-assured. He'd learnt
how to cope with results; he'd probably found his level."

Turner then joined Hereford, where he became manager and later
chairman. In control of an ambitious Football Conference side, he is
able to look back at his time at Villa with total honesty. When asked
if he regrets taking the Villa job when he did, he replied; "If I could
turn the clock back to Shrewsbury, there were other jobs that had
cropped up, and the success I'd had meant that there would always
be interest from other clubs. I've always thought that the answer
would have been the same, I'd have gone to Villa. But as you get
older and wiser, you do think that maybe I should have turned it
down, had three or four years at the sort of club who were between
Shrewsbury and Villa. If, say, I'd gone to Wolves first, then to Villa,
maybe things would have been better. But you don't get offered jobs
like the Villa very often."

14

Billy McNeill

September 1986 - May 1987

Any manager who was interested in the Villa job would have been excused for taking a look at the situation at Villa Park and immediately changing his mind. The team played one game under caretaker manager Ron Wylie, losing at home 4-1 to Norwich City to go bottom of the table. Steve Hodge, who had been critical of the club when asking for a transfer, played badly and received non-stop abuse from the crowd throughout the game. The team looked demoralised and destined for the second division. Small wonder the list of candidates appeared to consist of one man - Ron Atkinson - and that he turned the job down with seemingly little thought. The days following the Norwich game saw Atkinson's Mancunian counterpart, Billy McNeill linked with the position. Manchester City chairman, Peter Swales refused Villa permission to talk to McNeill, whose response was to resign from his job at Maine Road and promptly be installed as Villa's third manager in as many seasons.

On the surface, McNeill's decision to leave Maine Road was a strange one. City were fifteenth in the first division and, although there were rumours that McNeill's job was in jeopardy, things seemed placid enough at Maine Road. Football writer Kevin McCarra, who had followed McNeill's career from his playing days, remembers: "He did okay at City. They were on the verge of bankruptcy, but he brought in some decent players for very little. I think he regarded Villa as a step up. They were a bigger club, they had better players and, despite their league position, Billy thought they had more to offer him."

McNeill certainly had the pedigree to take on the Villa job. Born in 1946 in Bellshill, Lanarkshire, he played his local junior side, Blantyre Victoria, before transferring to Celtic for the princely sum of £250. At Parkhead he became one of the greatest Scottish footballers of all time, captain of Celtic when they won the European Cup in 1967 and winner of nine Scottish league titles. He made 29 international appearances and was awarded the MBE in 1976.

McNeill's managerial career had been scarcely less successful, encompassing time at Clyde and Aberdeen, prior to taking over at Celtic. Here he won a further three league crowns during the period 1978-83, before leaving Parkhead to take charge at Manchester City following an argument with Celtic chairman Desmond White over the sale of Charlie Nicholas to Arsenal. Although his period in Manchester had subsequently seen less success than he had been used to, McNeill had certainly made the team capable of the mid-table position in the first division which, at that time, was as much as the Maine Road club could have hoped for.

The reason why McNeill joined the Villa can be guessed at from an interview he gave on his arrival, when he talked of Villa's new signings, hinting he wanted some of them for Manchester City but had been unable to afford them. McNeill was under no illusions as to the size of the task he faced at Villa. "When a big club hits a slide it can be difficult to correct. I anticipate a difficult job but I am confident I can do what's required." He also stated, perhaps with hindsight, somewhat ominously that, "Discipline is important, but I am not a schoolteacher. Discipline is an adult thing." Doug Ellis talked of the need for "a dominant figurehead to breathe confidence back" into a playing squad that chairman and new manager were both sure were good enough to avoid relegation. But Ellis hinted that there was no money available for new signings

Such optimism certainly did not seem misplaced as Villa responded with just one defeat in a ten game run that lifted the team out of the bottom six and into the fourth round of the Littlewoods Cup. Garry Thompson spoke of "a completely new feel" to the club and, briefly, Villa Park seemed in the throes of recovery. However, it was not to last. Villa beat Leicester 2-0 at Villa Park on 1st November 1986. Their next victory was on Boxing Day, when substitute, Paul Birch inspired a 2-0 victory over Charlton. They had also gone out of the Littlewoods Cup at Southampton, a game that saw Martin Keown and Gary Williams sent off. The Charlton victory was followed by a winless run of 12 league games, during which just five points were gained. By the time Coventry were beaten 1-0 at Villa Park on March 28th, relegation was inevitable.

During this period the players, many of them senior professionals, had grown increasingly frustrated with McNeill's perceived lack of interest in the job. Club captain Allan Evans had been at odds with McNeill almost from day one. "I didn't like the guy. I can understand why he now gives the attitude that Villa don't exist to him, as they didn't while he was there. When he arrived, although I was never a Celtic supporter, I respected him as a legendary Scottish footballer. I thought he'd had a bad time at Man City and as a Scotsman I should really get on with this guy. But I didn't get on with him at all."

Gary Shaw saw things differently. "I found him okay to get on with. I was in the reserves, scoring a few, and he did play me a few times. I found him decent enough. He tried to help me, he offered me the chance to go on loan, but it was with John Bond and St Andrews so I turned that one down sharpish. But I got on with him, I found him a decent bloke." However, Shaw does agree that, in one respect at least, McNeill was lacking as a manager. "I was disappointed with his training, it was just five-a-side, nothing really worked on to alleviate the problems. We did the same things every day: a bit of shadow play and mainly five-a-side. Ron Wylie was okay, but all McNeill wanted to do was play five-a-side. He had a sinking ship on his hands but he didn't change it round."

Paul Birch has similar memories, although he at least found McNeill's tenure lucrative in one respect. "I used to get one or two things. I'd been selling perfume, the first week at Bodymoor I was walking through the corridor and I'd heard he was a disciplinarian; as I was coming past his office he pulled me in and I thought I was for it. Instead, he was asking me how much it was and could I get him some. I can't remember him being there every day training. He wasn't the hands-on manager I thought he would have been. Being a Scot, I thought he would have been a great motivator, but he was never a great motivator or tactician. He didn't lead as well as he should have done."

McNeill's time at Villa Park saw little transfer activity. Steve Hodge joined Spurs for £650,000 while Everton's young striker, Warren Aspinall cost £300,000. McNeill may have been frustrated by the lack of money available - he spoke during the season of having to sell before he could buy "and even then all the money won't be available" and this inability to improve the playing strength may have been at the heart of McNeill's perceived indifference to the Villa's plight. Kevin McCarra certainly thinks so: "Billy soon realised that the job was different from how it had been sold to him - there wasn't much money available for players and he just didn't get on with Doug Ellis from day one." It has to be said, though, that Ellis had hinted from the start that Graham Turner's buying spree the previous summer had left nothing in the transfer kitty for his successor. And in any case, surely no manager has ever been appointed by Doug Ellis expecting to spend freely on new players.

It is hard to pick out one particular lowspot of McNeill's reign, but the league defeat away at Southampton is a strong candidate. Three down after twenty minutes, Villa eventually lost 5-0. Martin Swain was covering the match and remembers: "I've heard Villa fans over the years say that they're watching the worst Villa team ever, but Southampton away in 1987 is still the most outrageously incompetent Villa performance I've ever seen. I followed the team coach out and Steve Hunt was on the back seat, saw me and signalled a noose round his neck, pulling it."

The match at Southampton was also a watershed in the fast-declining relationship between manager and team captain. Allan Evans recalls: "I had a bad game, awful. I always held my hands up when I played badly, but after that game he went overboard in his attack on me. I didn't say anything afterwards because I thought it was wrong to say it in public so I left things until Monday morning and I saw him in his office. He blamed me for virtually every goal in that game, and one was an own goal from Paul Elliott, so you could hardly blame me for everything. Things got a bit heated. He accused me of not caring about the club, after ten years of playing my heart out for Villa, and Ron Wylie had to keep me away from him. I've never, ever, been like that with any manager before or after. Billy McNeill got that out of me."

As the season progressed towards its inevitable conclusion, rumours grew that McNeill intended to leave Villa Park. "The last thing on my mind is to quit. My only interest is getting this club out of trouble." But he was unable to perform this feat nor, in truth, did he ever look like doing so. The relegation that seemed inevitable for months was finally confirmed when Villa lost their final home game to Sheffield Wednesday and other results went against them. The result of a board meeting four days later was equally inevitable. A brusque statement was issued, lacking the usual words of encouragement for the departing manager. Instead, the board stated that under the terms of his contract McNeill would be unable to comment on his dismissal and it would therefore be unfair of them to say anything. Leon Hickman, commenting in the Sports Argus, said: "The team are not even good on paper," while pointing out that McNeill appeared, "Slow to find real commitment to the Villa cause until it was too late," adding, "His heart may have been elsewhere" - the view of many who were involved with McNeill during his time at Villa Park.

McNeill's reign at Villa Park lasted just 43 games and 228 days. In pure statistical terms he was the worst manager in the club's history and it is difficult to summon up much sympathy for him. His parting shot that "the club has been in decline for five years" may have been true, but only for a brief period did McNeill look capable of reversing that decline. He certainly never showed any great commitment to the club. He failed to move into the area, showed no interest in speaking to supporters clubs, and never appeared as though his heart was in the job. For a man renowned throughout football as a great competitor, this was a fatal flaw. Kevin McCarra remembers, "There was the shot on TV of him during one game, flicking pebbles off the top of the dug-out. He just didn't look interested. He had to have a feel for the club he was managing - he had to have some emotional attachment. Because of the problems he had with Doug Ellis, because he felt misled when he was offered the job, he never had that feeling for Villa. That was his main problem."

McNeill certainly failed to have any sort of working relationship with his chairman. Martin Swain offers first-hand evidence of how manager regarded chairman. "During that relegation run-in our editor organised a session with McNeill, Ellis and two reporters. There we were, the four of us, and Villa were going down so it was real crisis question time. You could see the contempt McNeill had for Ellis; for him as a person but also for putting him through this grilling. You could see how uneasy the alliance was and how it subsequently ended was no surprise."

In McNeill's defence he was unlucky with injuries. The absence of Neale Cooper was a real blow, while it was becoming inevitable that Gary Shaw's top-flight career was over. And there were other, obviously deep-lying, problems eating away at the very fabric of the club. The five-year period culminating in McNeill's was a period of decline unparalleled in English football history. It needed a man-

ager who had the desire to rebuild every aspect of the club from top
to bottom in order to turn things round. Billy McNeill was unable,
or unwilling, to even begin to engineer this major overhaul.

McNeill's subsequent appointment as Celtic manager did,
inevitably, lead to the theory that he had always intended to return
to the scene of his greatest triumphs. Allan Evans has no doubts
that, for McNeill, Villa Park was just a brief stopping-off point on
the way back to Glasgow. "Absolutely. And who do you blame for
that situation? There's only one guy. You have to question why he
was ever brought to the club."

McNeill enjoyed a brief moment of glory as Celtic celebrated
their centenary in 1988 by winning the Scottish Premier League
and SFA Cup double. However, unable to cope with the amounts of
money being spent by Graeme Souness at Rangers, Celtic entered a
period of decline that included McNeill's dismissal in the summer
of 1991. After leaving the club for whom he will chiefly be remembered, McNeill drifted out of football on a permanent basis. He
spent some time as director of football at Hibernian, then owned a
bar in Glasgow for some years before settling into semi-retirement.
McNeill stood for the Scottish Pensioners Forum in the 2003
Assembly elections. He works in the media as well as for Celtic on
matchdays in a public relations capacity.

In terms of results, Billy McNeill was by far the poorest manager
in the club's history. However, he arrived at the culmination of five
years of decline unprecedented in English football history. No team
has ever fallen from the summit as fast as the Villa did. The players
were certainly good enough to keep the team up, yet when McNeill
was appointed they were bottom of the league, a position they rarely
looking like improving upon. In hindsight, relegation was
inevitable, yet McNeill certainly had enough time, and a good
enough squad, to have made a better fist of the job than he did.

Whether he was a victim of circumstances at Villa Park, or
whether he just wasn't capable of doing the job well enough, is open
to debate. What is more easily answered is the fact that Billy
McNeill never seemed to regard the job as manager of Aston Villa
as anything more than a temporary assignment. He certainly
appears to have wiped his brief time in Birmingham from his memory. With that sort of attitude, failure was inevitable.

15

Graham Taylor

May 1987 - May 1990

With the 1986-87 season over and Villa relegated, the way was clear for a new manager to make a fresh start. Dave Bassett, newly resigned from Wimbledon, appeared to be the clear favourite while also in the running were Derby's Arthur Cox and a host of former Villa players including Dennis Mortimer, Peter Withe and Bruce Rioch. Of the latter three, only Rioch, with previous experience at Middlesbrough, was a realistic contender.

The news that broke on the afternoon of 18th May 1987, though, was nothing short of a bombshell. Doug Ellis had pulled off what was described as the footballing coup of the year in persuading Watford manager Graham Taylor to leave Vicarage Road in order to take over one of the hottest seats in the game.

Taylor was 42 years old, married with two children. He had begun his playing career as a full-back with Grimsby, with whom he had spent six years before moving to Lincoln City in 1968. Injury cut short his career but a timely vacancy at Lincoln led to Taylor becoming, at the age of 28, one of the youngest managers in Football League history. His spell in charge of Lincoln had seen the club win the fourth division title with a record points total before Taylor was offered the job at Watford, then also in the fourth division, in 1977. Shortly before taking over at Vicarage Road he had been offered the manager's position at first division West Bromwich Albion. Here, Taylor's independent streak came to the fore, when he was informed by an Albion director that he should give his right arm for such an opportunity. "I don't give my right arm to anyone," was the reply and Taylor promptly chose to move to a club three divisions lower.

His time at Watford became the stuff of legend. Taylor took the team from the fourth division to runners-up in the first, with UEFA Cup qualification and a place in the FA Cup final as bonuses. Equally importantly, he played a leading part in Watford's pioneering role as a club who saw its role in the local community. Taylor once took part in the London Marathon to raise funds for Watford's community scheme and refused to allow a roof to be put on the dugouts at Vicarage Road, claiming that if supporters had to get wet so would he. Watford's youth policy flourished under Taylor, bringing forth John Barnes, Luther Blissett and Nigel Callaghan. Although criticised for playing a long-ball game Taylor was unrepentant, once pointing out that his team's style was only mentioned once they started beating teams from the top of the first division.

His appointment as Villa's fifteenth manager was heralded as a masterstroke for a chairman who was coming under increased fire, both for the club's performances and for his own decision to pay himself an annual salary of £40,000. Leon Hickman, who had never shied from criticising the Villa chairman, wrote in the Argus that Ellis had, "...staged a magnificent coup. Taylor is as capable of scaling the footballing rock face as anyone in the game. No manager in football has a better overall reputation."

Astonishing though the capture of Taylor was, it owed everything to Doug Ellis being, for once, in the right place at the right time. Taylor describes how the situation arose: "I'd kept in touch with Dick Taylor, who always said that it was one of his ambitions to see me as Villa manager. He rang me when Billy McNeill got the sack and asked if I fancied the job. Doug hadn't mentioned me at all, but Dick phoned him and said I was interested. Dick deserves all the credit." For Taylor, the timing of his old friend's call was perfect. "I'd been ten years at Watford. In five we'd gone through the divisions then we'd had five where we were never out of the top twelve in the first division. But I felt that things had gone as far as they could. For example, we'd played Plymouth at Villa Park in the 1984 FA Cup semi-final and sold out 19,000 tickets within days. Three years later, we played at Villa in the semi-final against Spurs but couldn't sell the same number of tickets. I couldn't see Watford ever winning the championship, they would either stay where they were or go back down, and some of my enthusiasm was going.

"I drove up to see Doug with my wife and I could see all the reasons why not to take the job. But my ambition overcame them. It would be wrong to say that I wasn't thinking of the England job, people had been talking about it for years. I knew I had to be seen to be able to manage a big club, but I wasn't prepared to tout myself around the first division. Here was a club who'd been relegated, sacked their manager and because of the chairman it was seen as a club that was unmanageable. It was a massive risk, I could have anything I wanted at Watford, yet they were never going to be able to achieve anything like Villa could."

Ellis realised that if Taylor were to join Villa then the relationship between manager and chairman would have to be redefined along drastically altered lines to those Ellis was used to. He may not have been entirely happy with the idea of seeing his influence reduced. But the Villa chairman also knew that appointing Taylor would galvanise a club in danger of sliding out of control. Graham Taylor was offered the job of managing Aston Villa, accepted, and set about a task that turned out to be larger than anyone could have imagined.

Taylor hit Villa Park with a force unseen since the arrival of Tommy Docherty almost twenty years earlier. On his first day at the club, the new manager made the first of many memorable statements. "The whole of the club needs restructuring. The youth policy is not good enough, the scouting system is not good enough, the football team is a shambles and I have come to sort it out." Taylor also showed great sympathy for the Villa supporters. "How can I ask them to be patient when Villa were European Champions five years ago?" he pointed out, adding, "It will be hard work, but the job will be done."

Supporters, of course, loved this talk. "At last, Doug Ellis appears to have got the right man," wrote S. Phillips to the Evening Mail. Players were equally impressed. Club captain Allan Evans, who had seen the club fall from the heights to a point where things were almost out of control, was one of the first to see how Taylor would operate. "We'll never know how bad it could have got but it was on the cards. The club was so low, no one had any confidence in the board or in the club at all. We were wondering what would happen next. When Graham got the job, my reaction was one of waiting to see what might happen. Right away he got every individual player in and he had a list on a board of every player's name and appointment times in his office. From that first one-to-one chat with him, I knew he was the right man. And his organisation was different class. He turned the club from the shambles that we'd had into something that was totally organised."

Taylor was also keen to impress that the players' responsibilities extended a lot further than playing matters. There were reports that

Taylor was turning up in places where he was least expected, show-ing an almost telepathic knowledge of his players' social lives. Paul Birch recalls, "One of his quotes was: 'If your life's right off the pitch, your football's right on the pitch.' He looked into the back-ground of all the players and everything about the club. He seemed to know everything about everyone."

Within days of arriving at Villa Park, Taylor had not only spoken to the playing staff and galvanised the fans. Paul Elliott and Tony Dorigo left for almost a million pounds between them and were replaced by Steve Sims, a £50,000 capture from Watford and free transfer, David Hunt from Notts County. Taylor was making sure everyone at the club knew just what was required to gain promotion when he pointed out that the new arrivals "may not be the best play-ers in the world but they do not lack honesty and whole-hearted commitment." It was this effort that would become a trademark of the sides Graham Taylor fielded. Gary Shaw remembers, "The training was so much harder, pre-season was torture. I had some achilles problems, and I really suffered. Pre-season was even hard-er than under Ron Saunders, Graham kept us at it for much longer. He worked on free kicks, set-pieces, running. He wanted to get the last drop out of everyone."

So determined was Taylor to ensure he kept abreast of the entire club he stayed behind when the players embarked on a tour of Jamaica, delegating the responsibility of being in charge of the tour-ing players to his newly-appointed assistant Steve Harrison, who he had previously worked with at Watford. Here was yet another exam-ple of Taylor's philosophy, namely that he saw himself as being in control of more than just the first team.

Taylor had inherited a situation where, as he later explained, of a first-team squad of 23 professionals, fifteen were either injured, wanting to move or had contracts that were running out. Speaking at the club's AGM, which, as expected, was one of the more acrimo-nious gatherings of the year, Taylor outlined both his managerial philosophy and the problems that he was already facing at Villa Park. "People know things before I have finished speaking," he stat-ed. And in a clear warning to Doug Ellis, he spelt out the way in which he expected to operate. "Don't clip my wings, because if you do you are wasting money, wasting your time and you will give yourself a heart attack." None of Ellis's previous appointees had ever spoken to him like this. But then again, none had been in such a position of strength on their arrival. Taylor had the support of the fans and knew that, should he leave Villa Park, his reputation was such that finding another high-profile job would not prove difficult. For Ellis, though, the loss of such a well-respected manager may well have been one departure too many. He needed Taylor to stay, and to succeed.

Before the first ball had been kicked, the remaining players were beginning to feel the benefit of having Graham Taylor in charge. Allan Evans recalls, "From my point of view, the first thing he did was to buy a couple of centre halves to replace me, and he didn't hide the fact. That was the kick up the butt I needed because I'd got a bit stale and maybe I should have left by then to get myself going. But with Graham and Steve it gave me the impetus to start again and I had two more great seasons with Graham."

Taylor got off to a bad start on the pitch, the team gaining a single point from the first three matches. However, things gradually improved on the back of superb away form, and with thirteen games gone stood sixth in the table with twenty points. By this stage Taylor was able to state, "The job has only just begun, but we are gradually starting to take shape." However, off the field all was not well. Taylor had come from a club where he was in effect master of all he surveyed, and where harmony reigned to such an extent that the longest AGM he had known had lasted twelve minutes. He soon found Villa Park to be a different battle scene altogether. Martin Swain recalls, "A few weeks into the job, the poison he encountered, the politics, the cliques, the chairman's sycophants, he'd never encountered these things before. It was a big eye opener as to how a club could be so fractured, just how self-serving players could be. He had to take all that on."

Of his problems with Ellis, Taylor recalls, "Coming to Villa after Watford was like stepping into the real world. At Watford I could have the final say on every appointment, and I think I'm at my best when I'm in complete charge. I was manager of the club rather than just the team, and I had to bring a bit of that to Villa. The situation needed it."

"The first board meeting I attended was in September - and I'd been appointed in May. We hadn't got off to the best of starts and I had a massive row with the chairman at this meeting. The media

had got hold of the story that I wasn't happy with what I was finding, Doug wasn't happy at this and decided to take me to task over
it. At the time the board consisted of him, his doctor, his solicitor
and his son. I told him that we weren't compatible and if he didn't
like it then he should sack me. Of course, I knew he couldn't afford
to do that. We agreed that I wouldn't attend another board meeting
but that every other Friday afternoon Doug and I would meet in his
office to discuss what was appropriate. I would dictate everything to
my secretary, Doug would read what she had written and changed
what need to be changed and sign it. From then on our relationship
was excellent."

The manager was reported to have already written his letter of
resignation. Indeed, the letter stayed, awaiting signature, in his
desk at Villa Park throughout Taylor's time as manager. Ellis's attitude was typical of the way he has operated throughout his time as
Villa chairman. He may not deliberately interfere in the football
side of the club, but he just can't help it. A frustrated footballer himself, Ellis, to be kind, can be said to let his enthusiasm run away with
itself. For Graham Taylor, struggling to rebuild a club that had
almost been brought to its knees prior to his arrival, this nearly
became one problem too many. However, Taylor learnt to use Ellis's
self-proclaimed football knowledge to good effect. "If I wanted to
sign any players I would talk to Doug and I'd talk in a manner; say
we were weak in the left-back spot as an example, I'd sit with Doug
and start talking about left-backs and ask him what he thought.
Sooner or later, I could manipulate him so that he'd mention the
player I was after. And once he mentioned him, I'd chip in and say
what a good shout it was, and I knew I'd get the player because Ellis
could say he'd recommended him - as long as they came good."

Taylor remained at Villa Park, and left his players in no doubt as
to who was in charge. Paul Birch remembers: "Ellis used to come
into the dressing room fifteen minutes before the game to wish
everybody all the best. I remember Graham was doing a team talk
and he knew what was going to happen so he stood right by the door.
As Ellis opened the door and stuck his head round, Taylor slammed
it and just said 'I'm doing my team talk, keep out.' And Ellis never
came back. That was the first time we thought we'd got a manager
who will do it his way." And Birch is in no doubt that Taylor's
threats to quit were entirely serious. "I'm sure that if he said he was

going to walk out, he would have meant it. He knew exactly what he wanted and if the board wouldn't give it to him, he wouldn't hit his head against a brick wall. He wouldn't have stayed."

Whatever the arguments off the field, Villa's form continued to improve, despite the departure of Mark Walters to Rangers. Walters was one of the few shining stars of Villa's decline throughout the eighties, but had been unsettled for some time and a fee of £615,000 proved adequate compensation for a player who never subsequently fulfilled the promise he showed as a teenager.

The team went top of the table on New Year's Day when beating Hull City 5-0 and promotion seemed a certainty. One minor setback occurred when Steve Harrison left to take the job as Watford manager, succeeding Dave Bassett, who had been sacked after six months and replaced by another of Taylor's previous assistants, John Ward. Also arriving at this time was Crewe Alexandra forward, David Platt, whose £200,000 transfer fee Taylor regarded as high.

With promotion there for the taking, Villa began to stumble, and went into the last two games of the season needing maximum points. A Bank Holiday game at home to fellow-challengers Bradford City, played in a frenzied Villa Park atmosphere, was won by a single goal from David Platt. The final game of the season, away at Swindon, ended goalless but results elsewhere meant that Villa had gained automatic promotion. Taylor was carried shoulder-high around the County Ground by supporters who believed that here was the man to take Villa back to the top. Taylor, meanwhile, played down his achievement, turning down the offer of a civic reception, as he believed that, "Finishing second is nothing to celebrate."

The following season was always going to be one of struggle. In hindsight, it could be argued that Villa had gained promotion too early and that the club had not been ready for an immediate return to the top flight. The team made a good start, three defeats of Birmingham City in the Littlewoods and Simod Cups boosting supporter morale if not actually proving much in the greater scheme of things, and stood tenth in the table after 14 matches.

Much of this success was due to the form of Alan McInally, whose transfer fee of £225,000 from Celtic the previous summer was now looking a bargain despite reservations at the time of his signing. McInally's part in the promotion season had been limited due to injury, but he scored nineteen goals in as many games as Villa found their first few months back in the top flight easier than anticipated. However, a slump in McInally's goalscoring form was mirrored by the Villa's performances after Christmas. A 0-4 defeat at Nottingham Forest was described by Taylor as, "The most disgraceful and inept performance I have known in seventeen years of management" and for the first time, the manager had to cope with supporter disquiet.

It was at around this time that the team went on a tour of Trinidad and Tobago, spotting a bonus in one game they played, in the shape of Dwight Yorke. "The first time I saw him play I was frightened in case anyone else had seen him. I couldn't believe that nobody else had noticed this player. So I didn't mention him to anyone, even Doug, just in case word got out. And despite what Doug might say about persuading me to sign Dwight, he never said a word about Dwight to me"

With three games to go Villa may have seemed safe enough, in thirteenth position in the league, but their 39 points was just four away from the relegation spot. Two successive defeats saw them drop just one place, but they were now a solitary point away from the bottom three. Supporters were split on whether or not Taylor should take the blame for the team's slump. While some called for the manager's head, others pointed out the strides forward that the team had taken under his command. Taylor certainly came in for criticism for the signings he made during the season, spending £450,000 on his old Watford player, Nigel Callaghan from Derby, and on the same day breaking the club's transfer record for Bradford City's giant forward, Ian Ormondroyd. Taylor says of these deals, "I should never have signed Nigel. I fell into the trap of assuming what I had before from him he could do again and it never worked. Ormondroyd, though, we beat Arsenal for his signature. They really fancied him."

After a nerve-wracking finale to the season, Villa's first division place was ensured when West Ham failed to win their final two games, played after Villa had concluded their own fixtures. The fact that the team had come so close to relegation did not inspire confidence for the following season. Neither did the sales of Martin Keown to Everton for £650,000 and Alan McInally to Bayern Munich for £1.1 million. Taylor says of McInally's transfer, "He'd been tapped up for months. There was an agent working for him, trying to get him a move, and also working for Bayern Munich, trying to sign him. Then the same agent came to us and tried to get us to use him to sell McInally. He'd have been paid by all three sides." While Keown's loss was an undoubted blow, albeit one that Taylor would have found difficult to prevent, the decision to sell McInally was proved correct. The Scottish international striker started his time in the Bundesliga well, but injury and loss of form soon saw a return to Scotland and premature retirement.

The money received for these two players enabled Taylor to make two significant developments in the Villa's modern history. Keown's replacement, Paul McGrath, was signed from Manchester United for £425,000. Not only did he become by common consent Villa's greatest post-war player, McGrath was also responsible for smashing the club's wage structure. Taylor had long argued that the Villa needed to pay top money to attract quality players. Now, McGrath's reported £3,000 per week showed that the lesson had been heeded.

At the start of the 1989-90 season, Taylor remarked, "I am not passing comment on what I expect. I will just be doing my job to the best of my ability." During the club's AGM, Taylor had stated that, "We were never good enough last season. We had to fight and scrap to get out of the second division and we had to fight and scrap to stay in the first."

The season started off much as the previous one had ended. Villa were seventeenth after seven games, following a 1-3 defeat at home to Queen's Park Rangers, a result made worse by the hat-trick scored by the club's old Birmingham City hate-figure, Trevor Francis. Taylor's job was on the line, gates were down and those supporters who were still backing the manager were certainly quiet about it. Villa's next game was at home to Derby County. Defeat here would have meant that Taylor's job would have been in jeopardy, yet Paul Birch remembers that whatever worries the manager might have had weren't allowed to affect the players: "He didn't show his off-field emotions, he was 100% focused on the job in hand. Any worries, he kept them back." Villa beat Derby 1-0, thanks to a goal from David Platt and a hatful of chances missed by Derby's Dean Saunders. It may have appeared a reprieve for Taylor but, if so, it was certainly one that he accepted eagerly.

Five months later, Villa were top of the league. Forty-six points came from eighteen games, including a Boxing Day 3-0 victory at home to Manchester United and a 2-0 win at Spurs that were as good as anything seen during the championship winning season nine years previous. Taylor claimed that he stumbled across the formula for success by pure chance. Paul McGrath was injured early on and in his place the central defensive pairing of Derek Mountfield and Danish international Kent Nielsen did so well that neither could be dropped, with the result that Taylor played all three as a central defensive unit that became the best in the country. Ian Olney, by now a regular fixture in the side, remembers that Taylor's story was unnecessarily modest. "We were due to play Wimbledon and they played a lot of long balls into channels. Graham said that the best way to counter this was to play with three central defenders so that their forwards had less room and it worked. We won. The defence did well and we stuck with that team from then on." Taylor for his part was also confident. "We beat Wimbledon and that was when I thought 'We've got something here'. When I saw them at Plough Lane I knew there was a team in the making there."

The formation adopted by Taylor was unorthodox in the extreme. The three-man defence allowed wing-backs to push up, with David Platt and Gordon Cowans in central midfield. Platt became an England regular, while Cowans was unlucky not to join his colleague in the England party for the following summer's World Cup finals. Up front Ian Olney was a lone target man, with six foot four inch Ian Ormondroyd the unlikeliest winger in football and Tony Daley playing a free role that caused havoc amongst opposition defences as he scored some of the most spectacular goals Villa fans had seen for years. As with his time at Watford, Taylor had adapted his tactics to suit the players at his disposal to good effect. "We played Olney, very good at holding the ball up, Daley with licence to run with the ball and Ormndroyd as almost an old-fashioned inside-left. We played Arsenal, for example, and Tony Adams and Lee Dixon couldn't work out who should be marking him."

Villa ran out of steam in the final stages of the season, which was hardly surprising for a team who had been unfancied throughout the year. Looking back, the turning point appears to have been the signing of Tony Cascarino. Bought by Taylor as the final piece of the jigsaw, Cascarino failed to make an impact in the title run-in, scoring just twice in ten matches and crucially upsetting the balance of the side. When Cascarino signed, the team were top of the league with 55 points from 28 games, two points clear of Liverpool who had a game in hand.

Taylor tells the story of how the deal came about. "The last week in February we were challenging Liverpool for the title. Doug suddenly tells me I've got £1 million to spend. This is what annoyed me immensely; it was three weeks before the transfer deadline and now I've got this money, which as it came out was going to have to be paid in corporation tax anyway. I'd got a settled group of lads, but one or two were starting to show a bit of nerves and I had no forward cover so I went for Teddy Sheringham. I spoke to John Docherty, Teddy's manager at Millwall, and he didn't want to sell Sheringham but he said he might sell Cascarino. I wasn't so sure about Tony, but we needed cover so I told Doug what the situation was. Doug spoke to Reg Burr, the Millwall chairman, and then told me that there was now £1.4 million to spend. There's 12 days left to the deadline, we've got an FA Cup quarter-final coming up and now we've got this money to spend. So Doug goes to Reg Burr, fails to get Sheringham, and asked me what I valued Cascarino at. I said about £750,000 and Doug promptly pays Millwall £1.4 million. In one respect he can say that the money stayed in the game, but since then it's always been me who signed Cascarino for that amount. But of course, it was him who signed Dwight Yorke."

Taylor's tactics may have been unorthodox, but they took a side been tipped for relegation into runners-up spot in the league, nine points behind champions Liverpool. The thousands of Villa supporters who flocked to the last game of the season, a 3-3 draw away at Everton, refused to leave Goodison Park until the manger returned to the pitch for one final goodbye. "Doug came into the dressing room after the match and told me that I had to go back onto the pitch because nobody would leave the ground until I did."

And goodbye, it was. Taylor's performance at Villa Park had made him the hottest property in management. With Bobby Robson a near-certainty to be leaving the England job after the forthcoming World Cup finals, Taylor was almost as certain to take over the national side. This proved the case, with Robson handing over after England reached the semi-finals thanks to goals from David Platt, converted by Taylor from a fourth division forward into an international midfielder.

A brief bit of haggling over compensation aside - it was later revealed that the FA paid Villa £225,000 for Taylor's services, the first time an English club had received money in this way - Taylor acceded to the England job with little fuss. Indeed, it was as though he had been expecting the call as a matter of course. His final words to the Villa players were prophetic ones: "Don't throw the last three years down the drain."

It's worth wondering now whether or not Graham Taylor wishes he could turn the clock back to the time when he was offered the England manager's job, and if so, would he have accepted? "I could never say I wish I hadn't taken it because few people ever achieve their ambitions." While the job of managing the national side must surely be the peak of every manager's career, it is debatable whether the treatment Taylor received at the hands of the media was worth the honour.

He would always have faced a difficult job, in many ways mirroring that of his successor at Villa Park. Bobby Robson had got the England team playing above themselves during Italia '90, and the side would need extensive re-building if Robson's achievements were to be emulated. Taylor made a decent enough start, with twelve matches unbeaten at the beginning of his reign and qualifying for the 1992 European Championships with few problems, going into the finals with a record of one defeat in 21 games. However, a poor showing in the finals in Sweden, where Taylor was pilloried for taking off Gary Lineker, in his final international, led to the manager being criticised in the press.

From then on, the treatment Taylor was dealt by the media grew ever more disgraceful. He resigned from the job when it became mathematically impossible to qualify for the 1994 World Cup finals. Taylor's record as England manager was as good as that of his successors, yet none suffered as much abuse. Taylor remained a respected figure with his players, as Steve McMahon recalls, "He was respected by the squad because he'd served his apprenticeship. He'd done it at club level, he'd worked his time. The players welcomed him. We got on great with him, we were all fine with him." Yet Taylor was, and remains, vilified in the eyes of the nation's gutter press. "I went into the championships with twenty years of success as a manager; from Lincoln to Watford, then to Villa and one defeat in two years as England manager. People just remember that bit of my career from Sweden onwards."

After leaving the England job, Taylor moved to Wolves. Paul Birch, by now a Wolves player, welcomed the opportunity of working for his old manager once more. "He hadn't changed, he was still much the same as when he was at Villa. Graham was still focused on the job he wanted to do. He was the best manager I played for; he got the best out of his players."

Taylor took Wolves to the first division play-offs in 1994-95, but fell out of favour with the supporters the following summer when Molineux legend Steve Bull was linked with a transfer to Coventry. "I asked Steve after we failed to get promotion if he wanted to move to the Premiership. He said that he would, provided he didn't have to move house, which meant a Midlands club. I knew that Ron Atkinson at Coventry was interested and the board agreed that Steve could have the opportunity. Steve went to speak to Ron, who couldn't believe the money Steve was on - he said Steve earned more than he did. So the deal broke down, and where I felt let down was that the board let me be hung out to dry when all I'd done was give Steve the chance to get into the Premiership and they'd agreed."

The supporters moved against Taylor and, following a poor start to the new season, he resigned as Wolves manager. It is now generally thought that Taylor took the Wolves job too soon, while memories of his England time were still fresh in the public mind, and was forced out prematurely. Paul Birch is in agreement: "He definitely left Wolves too early, but there was the trouble with Bull, and the fans turned against Graham. It didn't help when that came out. That's what did for him. You should never have one player bigger than the club, but back then Bully was everything at Wolves."

Realistically, there was only one place in football that Taylor could move back to, and Vicarage Road welcomed him with open arms. At first as director of football, then back in his old job as manager, Taylor once more set about revitalising Watford. He took them from the second division to the Premier League in successive seasons, but found the gap too great to bridge second time round and Watford were relegated at the end of the 1999-2000 season with a record low Premiership points total. The following season, unable to take Watford back to the top flight, Taylor announced that he was retiring from full-time football. It was, or so it seemed at the time, the end of one of English football's noblest managerial careers.

Critics of Graham Taylor will jibe that he never won a major trophy during his career. This may be true but, as Martin Swain points out, "There were only about three seasons when he was managing a club capable of doing anything – a couple of years at Watford and his final season with Villa." And whatever his record on the field, Graham Taylor's legacy is probably best felt off the pitch. Journalist and broadcaster Chris Green, who interviewed Taylor for his book about football management, The Sack Race, points out that "Watford under Taylor appointed the first chaplain at an English club, and that started off a lot of work about morality and ethics in the game. Even now, much of the work undertaken by Football in the Community was first developed by Graham Taylor."

As for his time at Villa, it is fair to say that Taylor performed wonders. He took a dispirited club that was heading for the rocks, turned it round and encouraged it to face the future with confidence. If he had done nothing else, he would have been revered for three signings. David Platt developed into one of the finest midfielders in Europe and his eventual sale helped finance a team that almost won the title. Dwight Yorke became Villa's most consistent goalscorer of the nineties, his eventual sale for a club record fee again helping a future Villa manager to build a new. And the third of this triumvirate, Paul McGrath, will be remembered for as long as an Aston Villa team play football.

Taylor did all this, and more. What he would have done had he turned down the England job is open to conjecture. There are those who would say that for whatever reason, 1989-90's runners-up position was as good as it was going to get. The experiences of Taylor's successors certainly shows that Villa find it easier to lose title chases than to win them. It could equally be said that the league champions of the next two years, Arsenal and Leeds, were no better than Taylor's Villa, and that with the right backing his side could have gone on to win the title. Taylor does say, though, "We'd have had to change things round. Sides would have worked out how to play against us."

Whatever the opinion, even those who for some reason still found fault with his managerial record would have to admit to what was Graham Taylor's finest Villa Park achievement. He remains the only Villa manager who can claim, without argument, to have bested Doug Ellis.

16

Josef Venglos

July 1990 - May 1991

The summer of 1990 saw Doug Ellis yet again looking for a manager. While the Villa hot seat looked an attractive proposition, with Europe in the offing and some of the most talented players in the country in the side, candidates showed a marked reluctance to want to take over where the new England manager had left off. Fancied contender such as Bristol Rovers' Gerry Francis and perennial favourite Ron Atkinson (who had been Taylor's recommendation for the job) gradually ruled themselves out. Eventually, a press conference was held and with the words, "Hands up if you know this man," the newest, and most unlikely, manager in the club's history was unveiled

Josef Venglos had enjoyed an illustrious career in football before his arrival at Villa Park. As a player he had spent thirteen years with Slovan Bratislava, captaining them to the Czech league title, before becoming a coach. He took the Czech Under-23 side to the European Championships in 1973, following this up with a win in the European Championships three years later, when his side beat West Germany on penalties in the final. Venglos had also worked as a club coach, managing Slovan to the Czech title before moving on to Sporting Lisbon, where he replaced Malcolm Allison. After a spell in Malaysia, Venglos returned to boss the Czech national side for the 1990 World Cup, qualifying from a strong group that included hosts Italy to reach the quarter finals before losing to eventual winners West Germany.

Venglos recalls the moment when he was first approached to take over at Villa Park. "I was lecturing in Malta for FIFA after the World Cup, when I received a phone call to say that Aston Villa wanted me to be their manager. I liked British football, I liked the great attitude, it was very attractive football played over there. I was very keen and it was very important to adapt myself to the style of Villa. They are a great club, strong history, great players. It was for me a great privilege and I thought that I could adapt Villa's style to my beliefs of more combinations in the play, passing and so on."

At the time of his appointment, Venglos was 54 years old. The press made great play of the fact that he was a doctor of philosophy, a lecturer at Bratislava University and spoke four languages fluently. Experienced football writer Brian Glanville described him as "a cultured man with a university background," whilst Venglos's old friend Don Howe said that the new arrival was, "a bold and courageous step". Howe's words may well have been diplomatically phrased, for many football people who publicly congratulated Villa for this move were no doubt privately relieved that they were not the ones to be taking it.

For their part, the Villa players were hardly overjoyed at the thought of being involved in one of English football's most pioneering experiments. Ian Olney remembers, "We were on a pre-season tour of Sweden. We'd got used to the idea of a big name, someone like Ron Atkinson, so when John Ward said it was going to be Jo Venglos, we felt a bit flat. None of us had heard of him."

Venglos started off reasonably, Villa settling into a mid-table position and Venglos winning the Manager of the Month award for October, a time during which Villa were unbeaten and pulled off a remarkable 2-0 victory in the home leg of their UEFA Cup second round against Inter. However, this was the high spot of the season. Already, the playing squad were able to see that problems lay ahead. Paul Birch remembers the culture shock that greeted him and his colleagues when they arrived for their first training session under the new manager. "He got us running the length of the pitch without breathing. He thought that was good aerobically but all the lads were laughing to each other. I don't think the players respected him as much as they should have done. He was more laid back than Graham Taylor, quieter, he wasn't as much of a disciplinarian. He was used to the continental style, he thought that players would be self-disciplined, but that wasn't the case."

Results declined following Villa's 3-0 defeat in the return leg against Inter and supporters started to criticise Venglos's inability to alter Villa's style of play from that of Graham Taylor. The manager's response to this criticism was to say "I didn't come here to make change, it is my duty to add something." His plans were also dealt a blow by the continued loss through injury of Ivo Stas. Signed from Villa's UEFA Cup first round opponents Banik Ostrava, Stas was a highly-rated midfielder who Venglos thought would have been a bonus to the Villa side. "I wanted a libero to surprise the opposition. We had Stas checked out and he seemed to be the one. He had medicals here and at home. He signed and then in his first training session he sprinted and snapped his achilles. I am sure he could have been a big player. He was skilful, he could head and he could read the game. It has been said that Stas was already injured when he joined us. But he was fit when he signed."

Seeking to add experience to his coaching staff, Venglos appointed the legendary figure of Peter Withe as assistant manager in place of John Ward. At the time, Venglos said of Withe, "I read about him in a book," a statement for which he was much criticised. Later, though, Venglos said of the appointment, "I thought that he could act as the link between me and the players, get them to understand what I was trying to do better. He was a top player and we got on well. I had the chance to bring my own staff but I decided it was better to have an assistant who knew the club."

After Christmas, Villa's decline gathered momentum with frightening speed. With 26 games gone they were fourth from bottom of the league, just two points clear of the relegation zone. While home form had been good, the first Villa Park defeat not coming in the league until March, the team was in trouble. Battling for their first division lives, the Villa players were finding out that their manager was not the best choice for such a fight. Paul Birch recalls, "He was such a nice bloke, but he took the blame too much, he didn't make the players feel guilty about losing. It was an easy get-out for us."

Ian Olney was finding the season difficult on a personal level. "I'd got into the England under-21s the previous year, but now I was in and out of the team and I was finding it hard. Graham Taylor had changed the Villa from top to bottom and the whole club still had Graham's identity stamped on it. Jo was introducing techniques that were ahead of their time, and the players never really respected him for that. When you look back you'll see that our best results towards the end of the season were when Tony Cascarino was out of the side and we were playing the old Taylor style"

At around this time, Birch was sold to Wolves for £400,000, while Coventry City striker David Speedie was lined up to join the Villa, only for the transfer to fall down over personal terms. Villa did, however, make two signings: Watford forward, Gary Penrice for £1million and the young Scunthorpe full-back, Neil Cox for £400,000.

Venglos was already the subject of hysterical press reporting. This reached its height following a 5-1 home defeat at the hands of Manchester City. The Evening Mail, which had been so supportive of the manager a few months earlier, screamed, "FOR GOD'S SAKE GO DOCTOR JO". The team, they said, "are bad and getting worse" while Venglos was criticised for his "inexperience in English football, a foreign tongue and totally different social background." This attack, disgraceful though it may have been, had the effect of galvanising public sympathy for the Villa manager. Supporters and club officials alike condemned the newspaper's reporting, while Venglos himself takes a more philosophical view of his treatment. "As a coach and manager you have to be able to receive bad treatment, untrue things, but you have to control yourself. I was alright with the press, I was polite. I had so many letters and presents from people who said that they appreciated me and told me not to worry about the press. 'Don't worry, they do this to all managers,' many people said."

Further worry was heaped upon Venglos with the uncertainty surrounding David Platt. The previous summer's World Cup finals had confirmed the Villa captain as one of the brightest stars in European football, and with his performances in claret and blue one of the few successes of a disappointing season, it was inevitable Platt would attract attention from the biggest names on the continent. A move to Bari was mooted, then cancelled as Platt changed his mind about joining a lowly rated Serie A club, Rather than seeing this as evidence that Platt would stay at Villa Park, it was generally felt that he was waiting for a bigger name to step in. Whatever the intention, it could not have helped Venglos for his star player to be so unsettled.

Villa eventually avoided relegation more by luck than judgement. Their final position of seventeenth was seven points clear of the two relegation places, although as Venglos says of the season, "We had a better team than the results showed. They had almost won the championship the year before and sometimes three or four results can make all the difference."

By now, though, it was apparent Venglos's time at Villa Park was drawing to a close – indeed, there had been speculation for several weeks as to who would be his successor. It was a surprise to no-one that the first board meeting after the season ended resulted in the announcement that Jo Venglos was to become the club's Director of European Scouting and the club would be looking for a new manager. "I am very, very sad," Doug Ellis said, and for once the words of regret seemed genuine. "He is one of football's gentlemen. It's been done mutually. He hasn't been sacked and he hasn't resigned."

Venglos's new role was not taken seriously, and he was never to appear at Villa Park in an official capacity for the club again. He does, though, retain fond memories of his time in Birmingham. "I can say that I am still an Aston Villa supporter. I look for their results, I keep in touch with the players and staff."

Reaction to the departure of Jo Venglos was muted. Most supporters had seemed genuinely fond of the softly-spoken Slovakian and were disappointed that his tenure had not been a successful one. Louis Marks wrote that, "The attitude of English players and their capabilities are peculiar only to this country", while Peter Vos described Venglos as "truly, an innocent abroad".

"A sad outcome for an imaginative appointment," proclaimed the Birmingham Post's leader column, while their football reporter Michael Lawrenson wrote of how Venglos had stamped surprisingly little authority on the club. "He came with a reputation as one of the world's top coaches and left with Villa vainly attempting to play in the same way as under Graham Taylor. Venglos's legacy? You can't say it is good or bad. It just doesn't exist." There had certainly been a year of stagnation at Villa Park, and the general consensus from press and fans alike was that Doug Ellis shared the blame every bit as much as the departing manager. Venglos was, after all, the chairman's appointment.

Venglos himself remains sanguine about his departure. "If I had stayed a second year it would have been better, but I thought maybe it would be better Villa had a British manager."

Venglos joined the Turkish giants, Fenerbache, with whom he had a respectable time, leading them to runners-up in both the league and cup. Then came political changes in Slovakia, and Venglos was asked to return home to coach the national side of the new republic. He then spent two years in Oman, before returning to Britain in 1998 to manage Celtic. "There were problems at Celtic at the time, but I didn't really get involved. Some coaches like to know all about the club, but I didn't want to get involved with that. The problem was that Celtic had not much money to spend, much less than Rangers. I bought Ludo Morovik, and I was criticised because he only cost £300,000. Then he made his debut against Rangers; he scored two and made two as we won 5-1. I went into the press conference and said 'Don't apologise, you can see Uncle Jo has a good nose for a player. Thank you'."

Venglos's time at Celtic saw yet more upheavals at a club who over the years can rival even the Villa for boardroom politics, and he left after a season. There was time for a spell in Japan, managing Ichihara in the J-League, before Venglos stood down from management. He is now chairman of the UEFA Technical Development Committee, a Technical Advisor to FIFA, and president of UEFD, the European coaches group.

His period as Villa manager was, it has to be said, an unsuccessful one. A team that had finished runners-up in the league the previous season struggled to avoid relegation and for much of the time there was no method in the play. More worryingly, as the season progressed it appeared as though things were going out of control and no-one was able to assert their authority. As Martin Swain, who reported on the Villa throughout the season, says, "I never saw anything from Villa that season that had the stamp of Dr Jo on it at all. I saw a disjointed team kept up by two world class players, David Platt and Paul McGrath."

There is no doubt that Venglos allowed the players too much freedom, and that the trust he placed in them was often abused. "You have to be elastic. You can't change players' habits, especially when you are a foreigner, saying 'Don't do that.' But it was a learning process and you can't do that straight away."

The language barrier was also cited as a problem, though, Venglos believes that this was not as great as it was perceived: "I speak several languages, but sometimes special things, not slang but the informal things, the language of football, are important and that caused a problem. From the beginning it took time to adapt, and when I had to prepare press conferences things did not always get communicated properly. But I had no real problems. Maybe it was not Oxford English, but I coped."

And it would, of course, be impossible to mention the problems Venglos faced without making special reference to Doug Ellis.

When it was announced that Ellis was to appoint a foreign manager, it was taken as read that the chairman would relish the prospect of working with someone who was used to a hands-on president. "Doug's got his club back," was the verdict of one player when the news broke.

However, Venglos insists that his new employer did not cause him any great problems. "I worked well with him, I am not complaining. He did not interfere; he told me 'don't be afraid to spend money.' When I came from Eastern Europe we were used to coaching, but not experienced in dealing with transfers and I think what he said was true." Paul Birch, though, recalls the circumstances surrounding his transfer to Wolves. "When I was sold, I was told by Ellis that a fee had been agreed and that Wolves wanted to speak to me. I mentioned it to Venglos and I could tell that he didn't know anything about it." And Doug Ellis himself said. 'I don't think Jo realised the difference between the Eastern bloc and the West, where money rules the roost."

It is now accepted that Josef Venglos arrived in Britain too soon. His methods, which appeared strange to the English game at the time, are now accepted as normal in the Premiership. As he explains; "When I read Dwight Yorke's memoirs he was saying that I helped him; things we did at Villa, other clubs were doing seven or eight years later. I was trying to add methodology from Central Europe with more scientific research for preparation for players. Football is a simple game but preparation is very important." And looking back on games was also a part of the Venglos philosophy. "I would always analyse the game when it was over, on video, while I could still remember it, and work on what went on. Maybe sometimes it's better in England, if you've lost, to just forget about the match and concentrate on the next one."

Equally, there is no doubt that Venglos would have found things much easier had he joined an English club some years later. "There were no foreign players, and I was a foreign coach. I should have come to England later, when I could have brought players to adapt to the English style. The managers who came after me - Wenger, Vialli, Tigane, they were able to bring players with them and build a team round them."

Venglos certainly came into English football at a time of great change. The national game was starting to accept that, perhaps, it could learn something from the continentals after all, although the die-hards were still adamant that the English way was the best. Venglos became unwittingly caught up in the arguments between the modernisers and the traditionalists, and his failings were high-lighted by those who clung to the notion that English football had nothing to learn from the continent.

Whether Venglos could have been a success in English football at a later date is open to question. While his methods were revolution-ary, he can be accused of being too much of a theoretician to have survived in the cut-throat world of English football. Yet, for Venglos at least, it was not entirely a wasted time. Martin Swain believes, "He wasn't as daft as he wanted us to think, his English wasn't half as bad as he made out. I've since had someone who worked closely with him say Villa were something to put on his CV and what we saw of him backs up that theory. Jo was a lovely man: urbane, polite, well-travelled, but up to working in the muck and nettles of English football? I don't think so."

It is ironic that Doctor Josef Venglos, one of the least-regarded managers in the club's history, at least by Villa supporters, is held in such wide regard elsewhere. When the Champions League final took place at Old Trafford in May 2003, UEFA took the opportuni-ty to hold meetings of the technical committee whose members form the elite of football managership. Alex Ferguson, Rinus Michels, Giovanni Trappatoni, all were in attendance. And chairing the meet-ing was a man who had been hounded out of English football as an ignominious failure.

Paul Birch gives the last word on Jo Venglos's time at Villa Park. "If he'd come a few years later he might have done better because by then the ideas of European living, especially preparation, was better accepted. He made it easier for the likes of Wenger and Houlier, though. English football was always going to go the European way and Jo was the start of it."

17

Ron Atkinson

May 1991 - November 1994

Ron Atkinson's image has been described as that of "a big man weighed down with 24 carat jewellery and afloat on a tide of Bollinger." Which is exactly how Ron wants the world to see him. But underneath the swagger lies someone who can shun the limelight as often as he'll enjoy it, and whose seeming ambition to invent an entire new language disguises a deep and abiding love of football. Ron loves the game as it should be played: with style, with passion and with skill.

Born in Liverpool, in 1939, Atkinson's family moved to Birmingham when Ron was a youngster. His playing career began with BSA Tools in the Birmingham Works League, and he was also on the Villa's books as an amateur. Dennis Jackson knew Ron at the time: "He wasn't the most athletic player in the world, because he wasn't full-time so he only trained a couple of times a week, but he was one of the most enthusiastic. He loved playing football. I always got on with him, his enthusiasm shone through and it always has. I must have played a hundred games for the reserves with him and according to Ron he was man of the match in at least ninety-nine of them. But you couldn't dislike him, he was always such a likeable character. And thank God he never used to sing in those days."

Atkinson joined Headington United in 1959. The club changed their name to Oxford United the following year and with Ron as captain went from the Southern League to Division Two. His first job in management was at Whitney Town in 1971, then after a short time Atkinson joined Kettering Town, where he achieved promotion to the Premier Division of the Southern League in his first season. After three years at Kettering, he became Cambridge United's manager in 1974. United won the fourth division title in 1977 and this success attracted the attention of West Bromwich Albion. Ron moved to the Hawthorns in January 1978 and well remembers the time when he first made his name. "They were great times, exciting times. I had a great bunch of lads, we still get together now. They've got a great history at Albion and we had some top class players. We'd finished third, then fourth the year Villa won the league and there was the match of the Batson backpass. If we'd won that one we'd have been a couple of points off the top and we just might have been able to steam through."

Under Atkinson, Albion were consistently good enough to qualify for Europe without ever quite threatening the elite. The team that featured the Three Degrees - Batson, Regis and Cunningham - at times played scintillating football but invariably froze on the big occasion. When the opportunity arose to join Manchester United in the summer of 1981, Atkinson left the Hawthorns amidst much acrimony. "Albion had a better team than United when I moved. But I wouldn't have thought anybody would turn United down. If I had one regret: I took Robson and Moses and I would love to have taken eight or nine others and we'd have definitely won the league. If things had been different I might have stayed at the Albion, I'd have liked a couple more years there. If we'd have stuck together we may have won something."

Atkinson's five season stint at Old Trafford were as good as any United manager during the eighties could have hoped for, with two FA Cup final victories and regular places in Europe. But like every other incumbent in the Old Trafford hotseat, he found the twin shadows of Liverpool's domination and Matt Busby's legacy too great and was sacked as the team struggled during the start of the 1986-87 season.

Atkinson returned to the Hawthorns in September 1988, where he found a dispirited Albion now languishing in the second division. Working with little money, he made several astute purchases that helped steady the club until, little more than twelve months after his arrival, Ron yet again left the Albion in controversial circumstances. This time the opportunity that was too good to turn down was the chance of joining Atletico Madrid - and their unpredictable president, Jesus Gil. Ron describes his 96 days in Spain as "a footballing experience: four years in four months. Brilliant." Despite a healthy league position and a place in the quarter-finals of the Spanish Cup, Atkinson fell foul of the labyrinthine mind of Jesus Gil, and after being sacked from the Spanish club he joined Sheffield Wednesday a month later.

Atkinson's time at Sheffield was initially unsuccessful, with the club suffering relegation from the first division at the end of his first full season. It was at this point Graham Taylor recommended Atkinson to be his successor at Villa Park, although Ron turned the job down, as he had done on previous occasions. "I was sounded out about the Villa job when I was at Man United. I met Doug when Tony Barton left, then again when Billy McNeill left, towards the end of the 1986-87 season when I'd just left United. That would have been a good time. I spoke to Doug but out of the blue Graham Taylor took the job. I was thinking about going abroad at the time, the Atletico job was in the wind and I wouldn't have missed that for the world. Then, when I was at Sheffield, Graham spoke to me and said that I would be the ideal man to take the job on.

"But at Sheffield we'd just been relegated, which was a weird one. We had forty points with six matches left, we could have gone fifth, but we got beaten 4-2 by Spurs in an absolute classic. We came off the pitch on the last day and we just couldn't believe we'd been relegated. Under no circumstances could I leave then. In fact, I went to a supporters club meeting within an hour of being relegated and got a standing ovation. No way could I leave."

However, 1990-91 saw promotion at the first attempt, with the Rumbelows Cup won as a bonus. It was then that the Ron Atkinson story took yet another controversial twist. "We'd won promotion, we won the League Cup, the reserves won the Central League and the youth team got to the Youth Cup final. But I'd always wanted to manage Villa. They came in strong again and I realised that if I didn't take the job then I never would. So I had a meeting with the powers that be at Sheffield, who I had a great relationship with, Dave Richards the chairman and the board, and we agreed to keep it all under wraps that I was leaving. Unfortunately it coincided with the civic reception, so it was a very emotive time and when I arrived at the ground it had leaked out. I think a local radio station had overheard a mobile phone call between my legal people and the Villa's accountants. This was in the days before mobile calls were digitalised, so that put me on the spot. There we were, on an open-top bus, with all this hanging over my head. I went back to Sheffield and I was a bit shell-shocked. They hit me with everything, and in the end I said 'Okay, I'll stay.' They were prepared to give me the earth at Sheffield. Then a couple of days later I was at home thinking it over when Doug and Steve Stride turned up on my door."

There were other possibilities for the job made vacant by Jo Venglos's departure, but only one man was ever in the running. Atkinson may have originally turned the job down, but when he changed his mind he was welcomed back to the fold with open arms. Doug Ellis, not for the last time, was accused of breaking the FA's code of conduct for appointing managers, and some supporters had reservations about the unethical way in which the new boss had been chosen. But players and fans alike were delighted that Ron Atkinson had finally become manager of the Villa.

On the day he was appointed, the man himself spoke of his joy at returning to his first football love. "As a youngster I was one of Villa's keenest supporters. I played there and I always believed that one day I would return as manager. This is a good day for me." And straight away Atkinson came out with a statement that had supporters dreaming of what was to come. "I hope to provide Villa with a taste of the good times," he said. "This club is potentially as big as you can get."

The players were pleased with the overdue arrival of Atkinson to Villa Park. Ian Olney remembers, "Better late than never. He raised the profile of the club like nobody else ever could." As Stephen Froggatt puts it, "He was everything you'd expect from Ron Atkinson. From the day he arrived he took over the club." The new manager wasted no time in appointing his backroom staff. Andy Gray returned once more to Villa Park as Atkinson's assistant, under a deal whereby he spent part of his time working for Sky Sports. Also arriving were long-time Atkinson assistant, Brian Whitehouse as youth team coach and Jim Barron, with Peter Withe now in charge of the reserves.

Atkinson at first stated his intention to hold on to David Platt, the subject of fierce debate as to his future. However, it soon became clear the new Villa manager had lost his first battle almost before it had begun. "When I arrived I thought I'd get a couple of players, have a look round and a chat with David, see how things go. I said to him, 'I appreciate you want to play abroad and I'm not going to stop you but let's give it a chance.' Then a week later I realised it was best not to have it hanging over us all year, because the player was never going to focus on events knowing he was leaving. I said to Andy Gray, 'Let's do it now, then we'll concentrate on getting our team together quickly.' Doug rang me when we were in Hanover on the pre-season tour, telling me the way the deal was progressing and I told him to be as hard as he could because the Bari people couldn't afford to lose face. I still think we got half a million less than we could have done."

In the end Villa received £5.5 million for Platt, a world record fee at the time. They also had an agreement with the Italian club whereby Villa kept the receipts from two friendlies played between the clubs and half of any profit Bari made from selling Platt. But when Platt later moved to Juventus for the exact amount Villa had received, plus two Italian B internationals who were judged to have been free transfers, it was obvious that Doug Ellis had been outsmarted by his Italian counterparts.

The money received for Platt spent little time gathering interest. Dalian Atkinson represented a club record fee when signing from Real Sociedad for £1.6 million, Steve Staunton cost £1.1 million from Liverpool, a fee which would prove in time to be a bargain. Also joining Villa from Sociedad was experienced midfielder, Kevin Richardson. "Kevin was a bonus", recalls Atkinson. "He was an Andy Gray-type inspiration because when we were bringing Dalian back, they offered us Kevin for £400,000. I'd always rated him in the Arsenal side, Andy had played with him at Everton, but he was an added bonus – a tremendous player."

In terms of comings and goings 1991-92 was one of the most hectic seasons in the club's history. Two dozen transfers were concluded between Atkinson's arrival and deadline day. Platt and Tony Cascarino, a £1.1 million departure to Celtic, were the biggest sales while Dalian Atkinson's record fee was soon overtaken by the £1.7 million paid to Oldham for defender, Earl Barrett.

The season had begun, with typical irony, at Hillsborough. The reception Atkinson expected led Andy Gray to refuse to sit next to him on the coach ("In case somebody tries to shoot him and misses" was the explanation), but in truth Atkinson's return was not particularly hostile and many Wednesday supporters applauded him as he emerged from the players' tunnel prior to kick-off. With six debutants in their line up the team not surprisingly went two down, but a second-half revival saw Villa start the season 3-2 winners.

The rest of 1991-92 produced little excitement. Wins at White Hart Lane, 1-0 in an FA Cup replay and 5-2 in the league, were the high spots of the season, eleven league games with just one goal was the low point. Villa reached the quarter-final of the FA Cup, but unluckily lost to Liverpool just as the club's modern-day cup hoodoo appeared on the verge of being broken. "On the day we were the better team. Then it would have been Portsmouth, who were in the second division, in the semi, then Sunderland who were also in the second, in the final. It was ours for the winning that season."

Villa finished eighth in the league, a reasonable enough finish during a season of upheaval. This was to be the last time (hopefully) that Villa played in the first division, for the following year saw the formation of the Premier League. Football was becoming fashionable again, money was pouring into the game from sponsorship and television deals and Ron Atkinson's club were perfectly placed to be at the forefront of the brave new world. "We had to do things quickly the first summer because the team had struggled under Venglos. One or two of the players appeared to be past their best or they'd played well above themselves. There had to be surgery done straight away, so I bought with the Platt money, then I started to do it a bit slower. We needed a right-sided midfielder so I got Ray Houghton in. He was superb, brilliant, an inventive player, similar to Gordon Strachan. He could always pull something out of the bag. When you were chasing a game you always wanted him to have the ball because suddenly the adventure would come out. Then we wanted a centre forward. Cyrille Regis did a smashing job in that first year holding the fort but his ankle was giving him stick, and to go the next stage we needed a top striker."

Behind the scenes, Andy Gray was forced to step down from his job after Doug Ellis made it clear that Gray's commitments at Sky were incompatible with his position as Atkinson's assistant. Gray preferred to take the Sky gold and his replacement was the former Manchester United and Chelsea manager, Dave Sexton.

A month into the season it became clear that a goalscorer was indeed essential if Villa were to progress and Atkinson had the Liverpool striker, Dean Saunders earmarked as his number one target. How he went about signing him was a classic piece of Atkinsonian showmanship. "We were able to get into his mind; he wanted the move. I had him round my house for five hours one Sunday afternoon: he'd had his problems with Liverpool, he didn't get on with Graeme Souness and he couldn't play with Rushie. We agreed everything, the player was up for it and then the chairman suddenly messed around. It should have been put to bed overnight because we had the money, but it dragged on for about three weeks."

What had happened was that Atkinson and Liverpool manager Souness had agreed a fee of £2.3 million - another Villa club record - for Saunders. Doug Ellis had then insisted that the Villa offer be reduced by £200,000, with Liverpool chairman, John Smith promptly upping his club's demand by a similar figure. Atkinson recalls the deadlock that this sudden intrusion caused. "We lost to Chelsea 3-1 at home. Doug had messed around so much, he was getting stick from all over. He rang me and asked what the situation was. I told him it was the same as it had been for two weeks but the player was getting fed up. I was trying to keep him sweet, but Doug rang me on the way to one match and asked if it was still on. I said yes, and that was the day Dean played against Chelsea and injured Paul Elliott. So I'm driving to the match and I knew what was going to happen. If we didn't get a result the fans would turn on the chairman, the players would use that as an excuse, if you like, for ducking their responsibilities. So I spoke to Steve Stride, who incidentally is the best secretary I ever worked with, asked him to get me a microphone and the deal was for me to say, 'Get behind the team, we're doing the deal and we'll have a top class striker here next week.' We beat Palace 3-0, and the deal was done. I'd got everyone together. Doug loved the idea when I told him what I was going to do, but it was to tell the fans to get behind the team, the deal's being done."

Saunders was the catalyst that inspired the Villa to take off. He clicked with Dalian Atkinson immediately, scoring twice in his home debut, a 4-2 win over Liverpool. While Saunders was banging in goals regularly, the quality of Atkinson's strikes made him just as spectacular. His solo effort at Wimbledon deservedly won the BBC's Goal of the Season and suddenly Villa were the most talked-about team in the country.

For five months Villa looked on the verge of winning the inaugural Premier League title. Not only were they regularly topping the table, they were doing so in style. Atkinson and Saunders were the stars of the team but everyone else played his part. The Big Ron philosophy of attacking football put a smile on the face of everyone at Villa Park, and the crowds began to flock to the ground. Stephen Froggatt, who had broken into the team during Ron's first season in charge, tells of how Atkinson approached the title challenge. "He was never a great tactician, but his attitude was always 'Go on, entertain me. Do something to make me smile.' He didn't need to bother with team talks, we were playing great football in front of big crowds and everyone was enjoying themselves. He made us feel like world-beaters"

Ron recalls this golden period of his management career. "You never know how things happen, but Dalian's last game in 1992 was at Sheffield Wednesday. He hit two thunderbolts and I would have said that Dalian and Deano, with the help of Steve Froggatt, were the best pair in the league. They had a great rapport, they were good friends and they gelled together. Then Dalian got injured, but we kept the thing together and the only time when I first thought we might not win the league was that day we drew at home to Coventry."

The afternoon of Villa's home game with Coventry has gone down in the annals of Villa Park folklore. Not because of what went on at Villa Park, a goalless draw being notable only for Coventry's spoiling tactics and their obvious delight at preventing Villa from winning, but because of the events that unfolded at Old Trafford. Manchester United, by this time Villa's only rivals for the title, were a goal down to Sheffield Wednesday as the game entered injury time. "Sheffield were winning at Old Trafford. I've since been told by their players that the ref said there were two minutes left. Six minutes later they're still winning one-nothing and you get the impression that it was play until United win."

Indeed, that was to prove the case; two late goals giving United a win that was to prove the springboard to their first title success since 1967. From that moment on, United seemed to have every piece of luck going their way. "We went to Arsenal on the Monday and won. United beat Coventry with a poxy penalty, and a shot of Roy Wegerle's hit both posts and came out behind Schmeichel. Then we got beat at Norwich when we battered them, ripped them apart. We beat Forest and you had the feeling that if they'd have stuttered, we'd still have been in there. Oldham beat them on the Tuesday and we drew with Spurs the night after, when they kicked one off the line that was ten yards over. But that day against Wednesday was the defining moment. You can still see those pictures of Ferguson and Brian Kidd racing on to the pitch."

One criticism made of Atkinson was that during the final stages of the title race he kept faith with Dean Saunders, who was out of form, and allowed Dalian Atkinson to reclaim his place when returning from injury, at a time when Dwight Yorke had been playing well and scoring regularly. "You can say that. Yorkie had played okay, but in the first four games Dalian came back we won three. Dalian had been the hottest thing in the league, Dean had a spell when the goals stopped going in, but it may be that the onus was too much on him with the absence of Dalian."

United went on to win the title by ten points, a margin that did not reflect Villa's keen challenge until a fall away in the final three matches. And there was still much to be proud of. Villa were back in the big time, with a manager and team who looked set to emulate successful Villa sides of the past. Martin Swain remembers, "Ron was the right man in the right place. The Premier League took off, Ron could attract big names and Villa were as glamorous as any team in the country. Because of Ron, Dalian, Saunders, the general swagger of their play. That's what's so annoying about the next ten years. They had the right man in the right position in the right time but didn't cash in on it"

The summer of 1993, however, showed that the difference between Manchester United and Aston Villa was a lot more than ten points over the course of the season. United broke the British transfer record in signing Roy Keane, Villa bought Andy Townsend from Chelsea and Portsmouth's promising goalscorer, Guy Whittingham. Although, as Atkinson points out, in terms of experience Townsend was ahead of Keane, there is no doubt who would have been his number one target had finances allowed. "Two players I'd have loved were Keane and Alan Shearer. We chased Shearer for ages when he was at Southampton. To be fair, you can't spend what you can't afford and Blackburn were paying something like 15k a week when our top players were on three or four. I would never criticise Doug or anyone for that." And therein lies the difference. Villa have never been able to counter the fact that players of the calibre of Roy Keane will not come to Villa Park. And if Atkinson couldn't get them, nobody could.

The opening months of 1993-94 saw results go the Villa's way even if performances were not always hitting the heights of the previous season. The team were second in the league just before

Christmas, without ever looking capable of putting together a sustained run to challenge for the title, while defeat at the hands of
Spanish side, Deportivo La Coruna in the UEFA Cup second round
saw Ron storming angrily out of a television interview immediately
after the match. A poor run of home defeats in December began a
run that saw Villa slide down the table and out of contention.
Ironically, this run was started by a defeat at home to Southampton,
whose two goals were scored by long-time Atkinson target Matthew
Le Tissier. "I would have loved to sign Matt. There were times when
it looked like we might get him, Ian Branfoot couldn't handle him
and I kept knocking on the door. He would have been the icing on
the cake, he could have done for Villa what Cantona did for United.
And I'd have got him to play for me."

But Le Tissier stayed at Southampton, and Villa began the
sequence of results that would have such disastrous consequences
for Ron Atkinson. Stephen Froggatt believes that there was one main
factor in this downturn of form: "The players were tired. We'd put
more or less the same team out for eighteen months and they were
starting to feel the effects. The money should have been made available the previous summer to improve the squad, but for whatever
reason – maybe the board thought that Ron could work miracles
again - we didn't get the sort of signings that would take us to the
next level."

Fortunately, the domestic cup competitions provided a distrac-
tion. Villa went out of the FA Cup in round five following defeat at
first division Bolton Wanderers, but this was sandwiched between
the two legs of a tumultuous Coca-Cola Cup semi-final with
Tranmere Rovers, also of division one. Villa were three down in the
first leg at Prenton Park and seemingly out of the competition, until
Dalian Atkinson scored in the dying minutes. Again at Villa Park
they seemed out of contention when Atkinson levelled the scores
with seconds remaining. Mark Bosnich, lucky to still be on the pitch
after upending Tranmere's John Aldridge in the penalty area in the
first half, proved the hero of the hour when saving three penalties
in the sudden-death shoot out. Ron Atkinson, whose job was reported to be on the line around this time, remembers the tie well. "I
never gave a thought about job pressure then. In a funny way, we
battered Tranmere up there. We must have had twenty corners early
on; they scored two in a minute by players who had never scored in

about four hundred appearances. Aldridge got one that was a mile offside, then when Dalian volleyed one in, our dressing room was happier than theirs. If they'd have known before the game they were going to beat us three–one they'd have been on springs, but they knew we'd got back into it.

"Second leg, most people to this day would say it was one of the most dramatic matches they've ever seen. We got back to 3-3 on aggregate early on, they got the penalty with the Aldridge incident when Bossie might have gone, to be fair. Then Dalian got that one, O'Brien hit a shot with the last kick of normal time: he hit the bar, it rolled along the line and you're thinking someone must get that in but they didn't." And with Bosnich performing heroics in the penalty shoot out, Villa were off to Wembley for the first time in a competitive final since 1977.

Villa faced Manchester United in the final. For United it was expected to be the first leg of an unprecedented domestic treble. For Ron Atkinson, it was to prove his finest hour, as he sent out the most tactically astute team of his career. Often described as a manager who produced teams to win cups rather than league titles, his record bears this out. "Strangely, we had one eye on the final and we weren't playing well in the league. One of my regrets was that there were lads who played their hearts out for me over the time we'd been together, who I'd had to leave out because their form wasn't good enough. Garry Parker and Ray Houghton for instance, regulars for me who were nowhere near the top of their game, and we had to do something. I'd seen Arsenal play – another one of those myths: me doing TV affected the job at Villa - they played Man U, Cantona got sent off and they played with Alan Smith up front and Ian Wright and Kevin Campbell to the sides. I thought we could get away with that if we used Dalian and Tony Daley in a wide and strong, physical, midfield. They had Ince, Keane, Cantona dropped back, and we didn't have anyone who could go man to man with them. So I thought we could take them in numbers, force Cantona to drop deep where maybe he'd be less effective. I said to the fast lads on the wings, 'If their fullbacks start coming forward, come back with them or make them run backwards.' And I said to Deano, 'Run your socks off,' which was never a problem with him, 'see what happens'. Graham Fenton must have been the most surprised man in the world when I told him he was in the team in midfield. He was a bit of a softy, Fenton. He could have been a great but he had a bit of a soft centre,"

Atkinson's plans worked superbly. Villa dominated the match from the first whistle to the last, running out 3-1 winners thanks to goals from Dalian Atkinson and two from Dean Saunders. For Ron Atkinson, the victory completed a unique hat-trick as he became the first manager to win major trophies with three different clubs. Villa's first trophy for twelve years now safely in the boardroom, Atkinson could start to look forward to rebuilding his side. "It was a strange situation because I wasn't used to getting into Europe so early in the season. We'd got no chance of winning the league so I started to give the youngsters a chance. Ugo, the Germans, Froggy when he was fit, Dave Farrell. I said to them never mind about making mistakes, show me what you can do. So I started to look at them with an eye on bringing them into the team for the next season."

In hindsight this policy, laudable though it might have been, was a mistake. Results continued to dip and Villa ended the season in tenth place, with supporters starting for the first time to question Atkinson's actions.

The summer of 1994 saw Ron embroiled in more controversy. The sales of Tony Daley and Stephen Froggatt, together with the departures of promising German youngsters, Matthias Breikreutz and Stefan Beinlich, seemed strange, although in time they were justified. Froggatt and Daley both rejoined Graham Taylor at Wolves, where a succession of injuries meant that they were unable to recapture their earlier promise. As for the Germans, as Atkinson explains, they were unwilling to remain in England. "I didn't want to get rid, but their contracts were up and they could walk out, so rather than risk messing with tribunals I said to the chairman to accept what was offered and take it. Then Beinlich ended up playing for the national team and in the Champions League."

The lack of incoming new players was widely perceived to be, in part, due to Atkinson's involvement as part of the ITV commentary team at the World Cup in the USA. He was criticised by many supporters for appearing to care more about his television commitments than his day job, most notably by Shareholders Association chairman Buck Chinn, and the war of words between the two men spilled over into a heated argument during the club's AGM. Villa did eventually sign new blood: Phil King from Sheffield Wednesday while 19 year old Nii Lamptey arrived from Anderlecht. The biggest name newcomer was John Fashanu, a £1.35 million purchase from Wimbledon. This was seen as a strange move, as Fashanu was heavily involved in outside commitments and believed to be winding down his career. The signing was criticised at the time, but Fashanu's transfer is defended by Atkinson. "Look at his track record. The Villa had some good results when he was in the side, and they got most of the money back with the insurance."

The team started off the 1994-95 season well, but soon found themselves suffering the worst run of results in the club's history. Just one point came from nine games, and a memorable UEFA Cup first round victory over holders Inter was followed by away goals elimination at the hands of little-known Turkish side, Trabzonspor.

Atkinson still retained the backing of most Villa supporters, who were of the belief that he needed more time to put things right. By now the Evening Mail was receiving pages of letters, of the 'more in sorrow than in anger' type, asking that Ron sort out the problems the team were facing and perhaps devote less time to his growing television commitments.

Doug Ellis may have seen this as a sign the manger's popularity was on the wane. The day after Villa had let a 3-1 lead slip in going down 4-3 at Wimbledon, Atkinson found himself the latest victim of Ellis's axe. Ron remembers the fateful day. "I never gave a thought to losing my job. The Saturday before, Doug did an interview on Football Focus when he said I was one of the three best managers in the game. There was a contract offer we were discussing. And then I was sacked in about five minutes. For one of the few times when cameras are around, Doug left by the back door that night."

The circumstances surrounding Atkinson's departure bordered on farcical. The gates of Villa Park were locked while Abdul Rashid, the club's commercial manager, nervously read out a prepared statement. Supporters were furious, swamping the local media with calls for Atkinson's reinstatement, but Ellis defended his actions by pointing out the bare facts: "The reason is self-evident and it is essential that the recent disastrous run is reversed as soon as possible. 34 games, won 8, drawn 9, lost 17." As if to pre-empt the usual criticism of the Villa board, Ellis continued, "The buck stops with the manager, who had complete control of the playing staff, including those he bought and sold in the last 3 years."

There is little doubt that Ellis had read the mood of the supporters completely wrong, as he faced the greatest furore of his time in
office. Equally, it can be said that Atkinson's team had enjoyed a
spell of diabolical luck, as he himself admits. "We played some
European games on Thursdays, and we lost at West Ham and
Newcastle the Saturdays after. We were taking penalties and Kevin
Keegan was doing the TV and he came into my office at midnight,
telling me that his players had been in bed for three hours as mine
were getting showered. To be fair, though, it was big money for the
club and that was one of the reasons for being in Europe. During
that spell, I felt the quality of our play was as good as any time I'd
been there. There was the game against Man United when we outplayed them and lost, we had some terrific performances, but things
weren't quite breaking for us. I wasn't concerned, I thought this will
change and we could go on a run just as easy. If we'd been playing
badly then you've got a problem. We just needed a little change of
fortune. That's why I wasn't too bothered about bringing in new
players when I knew they were only as good as the ones we'd got. I
said to the chairman 'Keep your money, these lads will see it
through, then we can spend big in the summer and take it to the
next step'."

Indeed, Ellis stated that he had offered Atkinson money for players but had been turned down, just as a few weeks earlier he had
offered the manager an extended contract and described him as one
of the best three managers in the country the previous weekend. So
why was Atkinson dismissed so soon afterwards, and with scarcely
a second thought?

It was obvious that Ellis and Atkinson didn't get on. However, the
ex-manager is keen to emphasise that the two men's working relationship was perfectly amicable: "It's a complete myth that we
couldn't work together. I took the Villa job because I'd had a big
affinity with the club as a kid. Few people could tell you more about
the Villa since the end of the war than I could. And I took the job.
In other jobs you always have a big affinity with the chairman: at
United I had a great rapport with Martin Edwards, and at other
places it was like that. I knew all about Doug, our paths had crossed
and I wanted to do the job in my way. I didn't want a big social relationship with him. I said, 'I'll handle the football, you keep doing
your job.' I think he's done well in developing the ground, his

organisation of the club has been excellent. But in many ways he's a frustrated manager. I made it clear that he had his domain and I had mine. And that worked most of the time pretty well. I never criticised him in public when I was at the club. If I had anything to say, I'd say it to him. But one of the reasons he gave when he finished me, he said I spent too much time at the training ground, which I found strange."

The reason why Atkinson was forced out of Villa Park can, on one level, be explained away simply: His team were losing too many matches. There were, though, other theories abounding at the time. The popular perception was that Villa Park had become a rest home for ageing footballers, with Atkinson's favourites being able to more or less do as they pleased. He had always been a manager who remained loyal to players who had done well for him in the past, even if this loyalty had been misplaced on occasions. It had happened at Old Trafford and history was now repeating itself.

Atkinson was accused of spending too much time engaged in outside activities, particularly in his television career. And the manager's public treatment of Ellis, however good-humoured the intention, grated with the chairman. Ellis may well have decided long before the axe fell that he would take his revenge at the first available opportunity.

Following his dismissal, Atkinson spent a few months out of the game before joining Coventry City. Here he worked in tandem with Gordon Strachan, first as manager and then Director of Football, to provide the Sky Blues with a taste of the high life and relative success as Coventry found themselves regulars in the middle of the Premiership. "I didn't spend really big money, the most expensive player I bought was Noel Whelan. They had some good buys they made big money with later on, though."

Atkinson left Coventry in 1997, and this was followed by a successful, if strange, return to Sheffield Wednesday. As he recalls, "I went there when they were bottom, but the points tally from then on was European qualification standard. We beat Arsenal, Man United, stayed up without a problem. I honestly don't know why I left there, I still don't know. I'd signed Alexandersson, Emerson, I got a fresh contract, Dave Richards asked me to stay on and wanted me to groom Nigel Pearson as manager. Then I got a call from Carlton Palmer one Saturday; he told me he'd heard I was off. So I rang

Dave Richards and he couldn't really say what he wanted to. I told him I was off to Barbados the next day." Ron never was one to lick his wounds.

A short period at Nottingham Forest followed. The team were doomed, victims of ferocious cost cutting and internal player feuds. "It was good fun, a big challenge. We had no chance but we took 17 points from 16 games and at least we wound up with a decent team and a decent bunch of lads. There were so many problems there: the van Hooijdonk situation when he wouldn't play with the rest of the team and no money available, and there was no chance. Three months earlier I'd agreed a full time contract with ITV and I went there at the end of the season in 1999. Mind you, when I see the sort of money John Gregory was getting at the Villa..."

And there ended one of the most colourful careers in managerial history. Ron now plies his trade on ITV, where his double act with whoever finds themself playing second fiddle is always worth watching, regardless of the game. Ron Atkinson remains one of the great characters in English football, and there is no doubting his popularity. This is a man who truly can walk with kings and dust-men and retain the common touch. Twice he has left clubs with their supporters furious at the method of his leaving only to return, with those same fans now welcoming him with open arms. He managed the Villa during the worst run of results in the club's history, yet supporters were in uproar when he was dismissed. What is it about Ron Atkinson that inspires such devotion? Maybe it's because, whenever Ron's around, there's always something going on. In the words of former Villa club photographer, Terry Weir, "When Ron was manager, the Villa got the publicity they deserve."

A big club needs a big manager. And they don't come much bigger than Ron Atkinson.

18

Brian Little

November 1994 - February 1997

Anyone who watched the Villa during the seventies is entitled to get misty-eyed at the mention of the name Brian Little. Here was a player as talented as any in the game, yet also seemingly cursed. With an England career over almost before it began and a succession of injuries that forced him out of football when his team was on the verge of their greatest triumphs, Little was a footballer as unlucky as he was gifted.

Born on 25th November, 1953, the day when England were being taught a lesson by the Jimmy Hogan-inspired Hungarians, Little first set foot inside Villa Park as a nervous fifteen year old, one of the first recruits of Tommy Docherty's youth policy. His mercurial talent saw him make his first team debut at the age of eighteen, shortly before playing alongside brother Alan in the FA Youth Cup winning side of 1972.

Little's star continued to gather momentum, a solitary England cap coming against Wales in the Home Internationals of 1975. His playing career at Villa Park is well documented. Little's career would be blighted by injury, forcing him out of the game prematurely in 1981, at the age of 27. By then, however, his place in the Aston Villa hall of fame was assured. If Dennis Mortimer later on was respected and Paul McGrath worshipped, then it is fair to say that Brian Little was loved. Rarely has a Villa player inspired such devotion in those lucky enough to have witnessed him in action.

His playing career over, Little first worked for the club's promotions department, then later on he became youth team coach. However, this first stab at staying in the game was soon over, as he explains. "I came back as youth team coach when Tony Barton was in charge. When Graham Turner arrived, I felt I knew the club inside out, knew the players, and Graham never used to ask me a single thing about anything. We get on well now, but I used to disagree with him and I realised I shouldn't be working with him. We

had a few young lads going through into the first team, but Graham
never asked me about them. And one day something was going on -
Graham backed the chief scout Don Dorman - and so I walked out.
I thought Graham could have used me as an ear to listen to, with me
knowing the players, but that never happened."

Little was almost lost to the game for good, but took a job as youth
team coach at Wolves, spending two months during 1986 as caretaker manager, doing well but losing out when Graham Turner was
given the job on a full-time basis. Little then moved to
Middlesbrough, another club in financial difficulties, where he
worked for his former Villa team-mate Bruce Rioch as youth and
reserve team coach. Hankering after another chance to be a manager, Little took over at fourth division Darlington after two years with
'Boro. "Leaving Wolves had disappointed me, we'd been doing
quite well and I wanted to prove I could be a manager. I took over
at Darlington in February 1989 and they were already going out of
the league. My first two jobs - sacked at Wolves after nine games and
out of the league with Darlington, I thought I could be finished, but
Dick Cordon, the chairman, backed me totally."

Few of his playing colleagues had thought of Little as a potential
manager. In the worlds of Neil Rioch, "I didn't think he would be a
manager. Then again, I never thought Chico Hamilton would be a
fully-qualified FA coach with a specialist subject of attacking head-
ers either." Yet Darlington's relegation to the Conference was the
springboard from which Little would soon be regarded as one of the
most promising young managers in the game.

Darlington bounced back immediately, becoming the first team to
win the Conference and fourth division titles in successive seasons.
With the Villa job vacant after the dismissal of Jo Venglos and Little
starting to prove himself as a manager, it was only natural that a
return to Villa Park was mooted. "After we went straight through to
the third division I was being talked about as a future Villa manager, but I couldn't really say much about it. I had at the back of my
mind that I was always well thought of as a player, Villa fans have
always been fantastic to me, and I worried about changing those
memories. People become very unforgiving to managers."

Little did move from Darlington that summer, when the top job at
Leicester became available. "Going there was a great step," he
recalls. "Martin George, their chairman, rang me, he flew straight

up in his helicopter. They'd just avoided relegation the year before but I got them to the play off final, three years in a row before we finally went up.''

Little did indeed transform a Leicester side that had been on the verge of relegation to the old third division, taking them to three successive play-off finals before finally emerging triumphant in 1994. Staying in the Premiership was always going to be difficult for the East Midlands side and their manager until fate, in the dismissal of Ron Atkinson, took a hand. What followed was yet another controversial managerial appointment by Doug Ellis, although he could claim that, for once, he was the victim of circumstances. Little explains, "It was an absolute joke. Everybody at that time was worried about losing face when a manager left a club. There are two sides to the story, but everyone was cagey about making sure they came out of it without looking silly and I was the one who got hammered. I'd been offered the Villa job. I didn't think I could turn it down even though it might not have been the best time to take it. That's usually the way in football, things tend happen at the wrong time. I told the Leicester directors that if they didn't let me go it would damage our relationship, and I might think about walking out altogether. They agreed that I could go and they'd get compensation but, as it turned out, that wasn't the case. Certain parts of a letter were leaked; I've got my suspicions, but when they took me to court they didn't have a defence because they'd given me permission to talk to Villa. It just came out in such a way that it made me look bad, which I'm not sure I was. Maybe it would have been better to come out and say to the fans, 'I've had this opportunity and I have to go'.''

Allan Evans, who had been Little's assistant first at Darlington and then at Leicester, was a witness to the way in which the appointment was made. "Leicester wasn't a stepping stone, no way, we went there and it was never a case of wanting the Villa job. Brian wanted to be successful. If he'd stayed at Leicester and done well he'd have been happy. It was expected that he'd be considered at Villa, but the only time we talked about it was when there were rumours that Ron was under pressure and Brian would get mentioned. When Ron eventually got sacked, Martin George made the most of an awkward situation. You might say he was trying to keep hold of his staff, but he handled things the wrong way. If you've got a guy doing well and a massive club wants him, you accept it. Same as a player who wants to move. It wasn't right, the chairman was out of order. He printed this letter in the Sun, Brian saying he wasn't going to Villa, but the letter had been handed to him some days before, and he'd been given another one afterwards, which didn't say Brian wouldn't go to Villa. It got messy, I got a restraint against me, Brian had an attempted injunction against him."

Little resigned as Leicester manager on 21st November and was appointed manager of Aston Villa four days later. Of his appointment, Little stated, "I don't just want to be manager of Aston Villa, I want to be successful." Also joining was John Gregory, with whom Little had worked at Leicester and who had resigned the day after Little had walked out of Filbert Street. Allan Evans left Leicester a few days later and was immediately appointed Little's assistant. Leicester's response was an attempted injunction on Little, preventing him from managing the Villa.

The court cases were eventually settled, and Brian Little was free to take on the job that had for years been his destiny. However, it was far from a dream appointment. The playing staff were unsettled, the team's league position showed the club 19th in the league. Worst of all, the Villa Park crowd that idolised Little the player seemed not to want Little the manager. The situation mirrored the position Vic Crowe had found himself in all those years earlier, when Little was still an apprentice. A populist manager - in Crowe's case, Tommy Docherty - had been dismissed and any replacement was bound to suffer a backlash. The fact that both Crowe and Little were Villa men to the core was neither here nor there. They had replaced popular managers, therefore they were cast as villains.

In the circumstances it was not surprising that Little's side failed to make an immediate improvement. However, things gradually started to turn round until the arrival of Leicester City to Villa Park almost proved the club's undoing. 4-1 down with ten minutes to go, Leicester's fightback brought them three goals and an unlikely point, as well as beginning a sequence of results that almost saw Villa relegated, safety only being assured with a 1-1 draw at Norwich on the final day of the season. Of this period, Little remembers, "I found it pretty difficult to start with. I'd had surgery on my back the summer before and I wasn't as active and sharp as I might have been so I couldn't get involved on the training ground.

There was no real problem with the team, it was just that some of the players were getting older, they'd all been good players but they weren't gelling any more. The game was changing rapidly, becoming more mobile. There weren't many older players around, and that was showing at Villa. We had too many older players and they were getting found out. We got out of trouble, then we found ourselves sucked right back in and in the end we just survived. Major surgery was needed, which was something I'd done at all my other clubs. So I brought in the lads I wanted, while the ones I'd already signed were growing up a bit."

Little had brought in several players, the Derby County pair of Tommy Johnson and Gary Charles being the most notable, alongside Ian Taylor from Sheffield Wednesday. Now, with relegation only just avoided, the manager knew that he had to make the right signings if his return to Villa Park was not to become an embarrassment. Unfortunately, early attempts to strengthen the squad were doomed to failure: Les Ferdinand, Denis Bergkamp and Paul Gascoigne were just three of the players who turned the Villa down during the summer of 1995. With supporters beginning to despair, Little suddenly broke the club's transfer record twice within the space of a week. Gareth Southgate, a relatively unknown midfielder from relegated Crystal Palace, arrived for £2.5 million. Days later came one of the most controversial Villa players of recent years. The bandanna-wearing, model-marrying figure of Savo Milosevic arrived from Partizan Belgrade for a fee of £3.5 million with a promise to score thirty goals a season. As an encore, long-time Villa target, Mark Draper joined from Leicester City, who obviously thought that £3 million was an adequate enough amount to quell the anger of losing their star player to their new hate figures.

Useful though these three new signings might have been, they were hardly thought likely to be the calibre of player to take the Villa back to the top. Neil Moxley, who was covering the Villa for the Evening Mail, recalls the time. "The summer of '95 was a busy one for us. It seemed to follow a similar pattern - Draper and Southgate from teams that had been relegated. Brian had done the deal earlier for Ian Taylor. People were wondering what sort of quality he was bringing into the Villa. Nobody had really heard of Savo and there were a few players from other teams that hadn't pulled up any trees. Johnson, Charles, Alan Wright. Brian was putting his stamp on it and in fairness to Doug he spent a fair chunk of money."

Allan Evans says of the preparations for the 1995-96 season; "When we got there we knew players had to be moved on. Brian was always fair; if a player wanted to leave then, if it was right for the club, they could go. There was always an honesty about him, he'd tell the players if they had a future or not and always wanted the players to leave on good terms. But he would never back away from what needed doing." Of the reports that Ron Atkinson had allowed discipline to become lax, Evans says, "People had got set in their ways, they almost did their own thing a lot of times. I'm not criticising Ron for that, because every manager's different, but at Leicester we'd held players on a tight rein and we had to do that at Villa to have any chance."

Villa supporters approached the opening game of the season, at home to Manchester United, with trepidation. Dean Saunders had moved to Galatasary, while Dalian Atkinson followed his strike partner to Turkey, joining Fenerbache. Other players, many of whom had formed the backbone of Ron Atkinson's successful side, were either sold or, in the case of John Fashanu, retired from the game altogether. In their place was a collection of unheralded journeymen and signings from relegated sides. As kick-off against United approached, Villa fans in the crowd expected a difficult afternoon that would be a precursor to a season of struggle.

Forty five minutes later they were giving their team a deserved standing ovation. Three goals up, Villa had exceeded even Little's wildest dreams. Dwight Yorke, usually played in midfield or on the wing under Atkinson, had scored and was showing the touch that would transform him into one of the finest strikers in the Premiership. Villa eventually ran out three-one winners, and the match was just the first in a season that was as marvellous as it was unexpected. Of the afternoon, Little says, "Wonderful. Savo was outstanding, Dwight was there. I like to think I helped him and Gareth. I like to help individuals, push them in the right direction. Gareth Southgate, I never shouted and told him how to play as a centre back, just gave him the licence to play there. I don't go overboard, I tend to say things in odd situations to players. We did a lot of pattern work in those early days, giving the team an idea how to play. I enjoyed it and it was great to see Dwight and Gareth breaking through."

Neil Moxley recalls how the opening day set the stamp for the rest of the season: "Turning Dwight into a central striker was a touch of genius. Brian used the same system as he had with Leicester and Darlington, and after a while the side picked itself. Despite what they did, Villa underachieved that season. Brian had filled the dressing room with really good characters who got on with each other. There was that blend as well, young players who wanted to make their name and experienced players who helped them along. What really helped was that great opening day. 'Brian Little's New Model Villa' I called them in my report. And they were. If they'd had more self-confidence and conviction they could have won the league."

Villa were regulars in the top six all season, but saved their best performances for the cups. Franz Carr made a bit of history when scoring the only goal against his former team Nottingham Forest as Villa won their first FA Cup sixth round tie since 1960. However, the semi-final at Old Trafford saw the team out of luck as Liverpool were second best for most of the game yet won 3-0.

The Coca-Cola Cup, however was a different story. Villa progressed through the early rounds with ease, then found themselves two down at Highbury in the first leg of the semi-finals. This, though, was the night when Dwight Yorke showed the world how good a player he was to become, scoring twice as the game finished level at 2-2. The return leg was goal-less, and after a nerve-wracking two hours Villa were through to yet another final of their favourite modern-day competition.

The final against Leeds was, for neutrals, an anti-climax. Howard Wilkinson's bizarre team selection played into Little's hands and Villa ran out convincing 3-0 winners. Lifelong Villa fan, Ian Taylor crowned his climb from Holte Ender to hero with a fine goal, but this was overshadowed by the opening strike from Savo Milosevic. Criticised for his ungainly style, the Yugoslav international had been constantly defended by his manager, who insisted that Milosevic would score the most important goal of the season. Not only was it important, it was also the most spectacular, one of the finest individual goals ever seen at Wembley.

The season had been a strange parallel with Little's finest period as a player, nineteen years earlier. As in 1977 the Villa had won the League Cup (albeit under a different name), enjoyed a lengthy FA

Cup run and finished fourth in the league. Both times this league placing would have almost certainly been higher had the team not suffered a lacklustre run-in. The amount of games played took its toll on a tired squad that in 1996 was also demoralised by a serious injury to wing-back Gary Charles as the season drew to an end. They had played with style, and such a young squad was thought to be of great promise. Martin Swain remembers the time well. "That team was great. Still my favourite Villa team, they should have won the league. Ferguson called them the team of the year. They could have won it in 1995-96, and, bless his heart, had Savo taken a fraction of the chances he had, they'd have won it. But it's still my favourite Villa team. Dwight came through, McGrath was still great, Draper was brilliant, the midfield was a great combination."

The team had, indeed, been a revelation. Little had played throughout with a three-man central defensive unit. Paul McGrath was coming to the end of a great career, yet was still capable of playing his part alongside Ugo Ehiogu and Gareth Southgate, originally tried out as a stop-gap defender yet who grew into the part so well he was selected for England in the position. Andy Townsend, disappointing during the earlier part of his Villa career, became, under Little, the dominating figure Villa's midfield had lacked since the halcyon days of Dennis Mortimer. Up front, Yorke and Milosevic not only scored goals, they looked capable of playing together for a long time. With English football basking in the glow of a successful Euro 96, the future looked brighter than it had done for years

Allan Evans, though, ever the perfectionist, was still able to find fault. "I was never confident that we could win the league. The team were never as tight as we were in 1981. The problem was that the game had moved on, everyone was a star, bigger egos were around and that's the hardest part of any manager's job at that level, keeping the players together."

The title was won by Manchester United, in a race with Newcastle that will be remembered for the way in which Alex Ferguson totally psyched out Newcastle manager, Kevin Keegan as Keegan's team managed to blow what seemed an unassailable lead. Evans is convinced, though, that had Villa been in Newcastle's position, the situation would have been different. "Brian wouldn't have gone head to head with Ferguson and his mind games, that just wasn't in his character. Publicly he wouldn't have demonstrated how upset he was, it would never have got to him. People might think he didn't care, but that wasn't the case. He just didn't do it in public. He would have coped with a title challenge; he'd have loved it."

Villa were strongly fancied to challenge for the title in 1996-97. Little signed Fernando Nelson to replace the injured Charles, then broke the club's transfer record once more in buying Sasa Curcic from Bolton Wanderers for £4 million. Curcic was undoubtedly a talented footballer, but his arrival at Villa Park now appears to have been a mistake. Little says of the player "He never hit it off here. He could have been terrific but he never made it and I'm sure he regrets it now."

Neil Moxley, though, is less circumspect. "Curcic was the beginning of the end for Brian. His temperament was suspect and we were starting to hear stories about him being out all hours. He was a real oddball and gradually it all started to wear down the momentum. There was that Arsenal equaliser in about the fifth minute of extra time and after that Villa were never the same, they never had the same cohesion and balance. Sasa was lazy, he upset the dressing room harmony but at £4 million Brian had to play him and the players seemed to resent that." And the player himself made little attempt to hide his disquiet, soon stating that joining Villa had been the biggest mistake of his carer.

Villa, as they have done so often in the recent past, played well during the 1996-97 season without ever appearing capable of challenging for honours. They went out of the domestic cups in the early rounds and their return to Europe ended in an embarrassing first round defeat at the hands of Swedish part-timers, Helsingborg in the UEFA Cup. A good run of results in the run-up to Christmas culminated in a 5-0 victory at home to Wimbledon. Savo Milosevic was now in the best form of his Villa career; Little says of his one-time record signing. "He was a young lad, he'd come from a war zone and didn't speak English. If he'd put away five or six more chances in that first season he'd have been a big hero, but the media saw him as a target, making out that the fans got on his back when in fact they were pretty much behind him."

There had been two significant departures during the season. Paul McGrath, unquestionably the finest defender seen at Villa Park since the war, had been unable to command a regular first-team place and had moved to Derby County. Also leaving was first team

coach, John Gregory, who became manager of second division
Wycombe Wanderers. Gregory's departure was a greater loss than
was thought at the time as he and Allan Evans had been invaluable
aides to Little, the ebullient Gregory working well as a foil to the
less demonstrative Evans.

Had Villa made the right signing at that time and, with English
football in the best financial state it had ever enjoyed, they could
certainly have afforded it, the league title was theirs for the winning.
Instead, as has often been the case, they settled for what they
already had and finished fifth in the league. This in itself had been
something of an achievement, Little being the first Villa manager to
record consecutive top five finishes. But against a backdrop of so
much expectation, it is a sign of how quickly the team had improved
that a side tipped for relegation the previous season were now
regarding fifth in the Premiership as disappointing.

It was generally thought that the Villa needed a new striker. Yorke
was still on top form but Milosevic was not yet scoring the goals that
would win the championship, and the Villa's midfield, solid though
it may have been, were not netting as often as they should. A
goalscorer was required and, on paper at least, one man fitted the
bill. A strange 24 hours ensued with the Villa player of the year
awards taking place at the Grand Hotel in the city centre amidst
rumours that Stan Collymore was in the hotel and his signing was
imminent. The team then flew off to an end of season tour of
California, and while they were in the air it was indeed announced
that Collymore was to join the club for a record fee of £7million.

Stan Collymore was intended to be the final piece of the jigsaw. A
misfit who had scored goals and made headlines in equal measure
wherever he played, Collymore's arrival from Liverpool to the team
he claimed to have supported from childhood caused massive interest in the Villa. Unfortunately, the column inches generated by Stan
the Man were in inverse proportion to the team's performances. The
worst start to a season in the club's history saw the first four matches of 1997-98 result in defeat. Although results improved from this
point, the recovery was never sustained and Villa Park was once
more the scene of seemingly perpetual crisis. Little recalls: "At that
time everyone kept saying we weren't as strong as other teams, we
needed another forward. We brought Sasa in to get more goals, but
it never worked. We were going down the right road but we were

maybe running ahead of ourselves. We'd become like the team I inherited, good players but the balance wasn't right."

Little is honest enough to admit the big mistake that he made. "I disrupted the balance to go one step further, but it was probably the wrong step. I should have been keeping the same formation but changing the personnel from time to time. Managers have learnt that now. I don't think it was wrong for any of those players to come in, I just probably made the wrong decision, and I didn't give myself enough time. The problem was that I didn't utilise the three forwards. Looking back there were ways to have moved them round; I could play the three every now and again but not all the time. There wasn't too much wrong with Stan, we just made the decision to change the team at the wrong time."

Indeed, Little can be accused of tinkering with a winning formula. The 3-5-2 style that had worked so well was scrapped, initially in favour of playing with the three main strikers up front. When this didn't work, Little dropped Dwight Yorke, top scorer for the previous two seasons, into midfield. Again, the new formation failed to bring about the desired result and the tried and trusted three at the back unit was reinstated. By this time, though, it was too late to bring about a revival.

Things seemed to get worse for Little. Reports of dressing room splits, of Collymore being the cause of ever-increasing anger. Of the spirit amongst the players at that time, he says, "There were odd occasions when the lads were arguing, but they were still young lads. Money was coming into the game, just like in my time, so it was nothing different from the problems Ron Saunders faced in one respect, but the media exaggerated it. If Stan had a cold the press would say he was off through something else. Stan's a lovely man, a lovely lad. He's just made one or two bad decisions."

Little's nadir surely came at Ewood Park as Villa went down 5-0 in a game where the scoreline seemed of secondary importance to what happened on the pitch, or rather, on the running track. Little had cut a forlorn figure standing by the dug-out, seemingly unable to prevent his team from being outplayed by a Blackburn side who were scarcely world beaters themselves. Supporter anger had been mounting all afternoon and reached a crescendo as Savo Milosevic missed a straightforward chance and appeared to spit in the direction of fans who had turned on him. The aftermath of the incident saw fans at first critical of Milosevic, but then the player received a great deal of sympathy after revealing, somewhat spuriously, that his gesture had been aimed at a group who, he claimed, he recognised as having abused him all season.

Of the day Little now says, tellingly, "The Blackburn defeat hurt me, I thought, 'This isn't my team'. I thought it was for the best to go before things really went wrong."

Little hung on for a few more weeks that must have been almost as painful for those who idolised him as a player as they were for the manager himself. A 4-0 FA Cup victory at home to the Albion was followed by defeat in the following round by Coventry, who gained their first-ever victory at Villa Park. The following week a two-goal defeat away at Wimbledon, which left Villa 15th in the league, six points above the relegation places, proved to be Little's swansong. On February 24th it was announced that Brian Little had resigned as Aston Villa manager. The news was greeted with surprise. Fernando Nelson described it as "like a bomb." Little had not publicly stated his disillusionment with the job; indeed, the previous evening had seen him at a Shareholders Association meeting where he had talked openly about his plans for the following season.

For Allan Evans, the news of his long-time colleague's departure was no surprise. "From the first time I met him, I knew his character. If things got to a stage where he was being wound up that much, he'd walk away. And it didn't matter what it was. That was why he left. I was watching Athletic Bilbao on the Sunday but my flight got delayed and I was two hours late back to Birmingham. I always say that if I'd been around, if that flight had been on time, I like to think I might have been able to do something about it. But once Brian makes up his mind, that's it."

Little now says of the time, and of the theory that things had been going wrong since the departure of John Gregory, "We had one or two really disappointing games where I wasn't overly happy. I never thought I was outstaying my welcome, but John had left. I wasn't disappointed because it was his chance and I'd never stood in his or Allan's way. As a threesome we worked well together but once John left we never got it quite right again. As a coach John was bright, laughing and joking and the players loved being round him. But I always said, if you get chances, I'd never stand in your way."

Theories abounded as to why Little left. It was rumoured he had refused to accept the board's proposal to ask Gregory to return. Another story says that the final straw came when Little saw an article written in the Sun by his former team-mate, Andy Gray, criticising his management. Little, though, gives a far simpler reason as to why he walked out of Villa Park. "I wasn't going to ask John to come back as coach, there might have been talk of it, but he was a manager then, he wouldn't have come back." Little also denies that Andy Gray played any part in his departure. "I can't really remember the article. Things were just building up. I'd never had a break from football and I wanted one. I could maybe have survived if it was the summer, but I was getting closer to leaving. Then one day I got up and I just knew that this was going to be the day I left Aston Villa. I wasn't pushed, I just thought that it was the best for all concerned if I was to leave."

Supporter reaction to Little's departure was curious. He had been receiving the sort of criticism that was ridiculous considering he had produced two years of high league places and won a trophy. However, for some reason Little had never been truly accepted as Villa manager. Despite his successes, there were those who played down his strengths and were only too quick to gloat about his failings. The spectre of Ron Atkinson still loomed large over Villa Park, as many supporters claimed that Little's success was purely down to the fact that he had inherited such a good squad from his predecessor - which can be disproved by looking at the teams Little picked. He says, "I suppose I was an easy target for people. Ron can shield himself with his persona, but I'm not like that, I won't put on that ebullient charade. I'll soak it up rather than hit back."

The team Little left behind was without doubt a talented one. Yet at the time of his departure it was in 15th place in the league and fighting relegation. So why did things go so wrong, so quickly? Leon Hickman, whose time with the Evening Mail had begun when Little was a teenager fighting his way into the Villa team, comments, "The Little era sums up the Villa over the past two decades. He was the best young manager in the country, talked about as a prospect for the England job. He'd put together a very good side. Then two years later he was a defeated man, his career at the top level was over. You have to wonder what happened."

Little himself is guarded about his side's decline. "That team was closer than people thought to the finished article. A lot of people had question marks about Savo, but if I'd left him and Dwight alone that might have been the key. But I kept tinkering, trying to find someone else to play with them. I tried with Sasa, I tried with Stan. Nowadays you can have those three in the squad, there's nothing wrong with leaving a star player out to balance the side, but this was early on in the use of players. The thing I got wrong was that I had a good three and I tried to play them together, played Dwight behind the other two. With hindsight I should have left Dwight and Savo alone. That's not to say I shouldn't have signed Stan, you always need a change. It's just that people now are clever enough to change a team, to realise that players can't perform at that level every game."

And Little remains proud of the team he put together. "It was a good side, it didn't play in straight lines, it had a lot of flair. Draper and Taylor played well, Andy Townsend was outstanding for us. Dwight and Savo, Charles and Wright enjoyed their freedom with the three at the back. When you look at it, that team would do well in any era. It was a good side."

The local press were undoubtedly sympathetic towards Little. Neil Moxley remembers: "The things that had carried them so far were their downfall. The team spirit had been the bedrock of their success. That had gone. The players were split, the cliques were there: Bossie, Yorke and Ugo, then Collymore was friends with them for a bit. Townsend was finishing, McGrath had gone and there was nobody there to take the responsibility that those two had. Collymore and Curcic were playing up. And also this was the time when players were getting big money, they knew that they were going to be seriously rich. Suddenly the balance of power shifts, the manager can't tell the players what to do anymore. Maybe Brian wasn't strong enough to deal with these new millionaires; they needed Brian to be more firm with some of the players who were stepping out of line, but things were going on in his private life that prevented that."

There has long been a suspicion amongst Villa supporters that the club never really want to challenge for honours. The phase 'comfort zone' is often bandied around to describe the position where Villa usually find themselves - on the verge of European qualification, with the occasional cup run to provide a touch of excitement, but lacking the inclination to take the final step towards challenging the top clubs. Never has this position been more apparent than under Brian Little. When Little was manager of the Villa, the club were more capable than at any time since the early eighties to enter the elite of English football. The advent of the Premier League meant that the profile of the game had never been higher, and the failings of their local rivals meant that Villa were uniquely positioned to challenge for the hearts and minds of a large area of the country. Moreover, the money was available: from a successful share flotation, from increased gates and commercial revenue, and from financial institutions falling over themselves to lend money to a sector with which they had fallen in love. Yet once more, the club failed to make that final step, buying decent enough players when they should have been in the market for world class.

The blame for this lack of ambition has traditionally been placed with Doug Ellis. Yet he and Little enjoyed a closer relationship than most Villa managers have enjoyed with their chairman. Martin Swain recalls, "The day after Brian resigned, the press went up to Doug's house. He called Brian in to do a 'It wasn't Doug's fault' piece. We had to sit through Brian and Doug with Brian at pains to point out that he had no complaints about Doug's behaviour, and to be fair Brian doesn't bad mouth the chairman to this day. But that was a surreal experience." And indeed, Little still speaks highly of his former chairman. "I like him. He's one of those who love the club, he's accessible to all. We didn't need top of the tree players, we needed players who could come in and help us get the best out of the ones we had already. I agreed with the club's policy of not spending heavily. In fact, I influenced it."

Little began the following season at Stoke where, with a new stadium and money promised for players, he expected to do well. The team had a good start, topping the second division for a while, but promised funds never materialised and they slipped out of the promotion hunt. Little resigned at the end of the season. "It was great at first, then things caught up with us. There wasn't a lot of money around. We had players playing above themselves and they just weren't good enough. There were rumours that the Icelanders who had bought the club were bringing their own people in, so I walked away. Stoke was the one club where I was there at the wrong time."

From the Britannia Stadium, Little moved to another club struggling to recapture past glories, West Bromwich Albion. He got the team off to a good start at the beginning of the 1999-2000 season but, once more, things started to go wrong. "I should never have gone there. Every time we lost I'd have the Villa thing thrown at me. There were problems with the board, players were sold without my knowledge. I brought in £7 million for Kilbane and Maresca but I still couldn't buy players - although Gary Megson ended up signing some of those I hadn't been able to. I got the impression that from day one I never had a chance there. I didn't enjoy it."

Little's left the Hawthorns in March 2000, his next move a month later seeing his managerial career come almost full circle. The man who had started out at Wolves when the club was in danger of extinction and then Darlington, who were relegated to the Conference, moved to Hull City, in the third division and going into administration. "I loved it there. It was such a disappointment when I left, I wanted to show that I could work my way up from the bottom again. The club was in administration, there was no money, we'd go to away games where we had to keep stopping the bus to put water in the radiator, but I took them to the play-offs." Indeed, Little worked a minor miracle in taking Hull, who at one point were in such financial difficulties that he was telling players to leave the club for their own well-being, into the third division play-offs. However, when the club's money problems were eased, Little found his own troubles taking a familiar path. "A new chairman took over and I was out," he says candidly.

Brian Little is currently working for Sky Sports, enjoying life and hoping to get back into management one day. "I'd love to go back into it. I've been offered a couple of third division jobs but in truth I can't afford to work at that level."

Little's time as Villa manager curiously mirrored his playing career. There was an all-too-brief moment of glory, when anything seemed possible. Then the fates conspired to bring him crashing back down to earth again. Little will go down as the manager of a very good Villa team. More than any other Villa manager since Ron Saunders, it was tantalisingly close to being a great one.

19

John Gregory

February 1997 - January 2002

Brian Little's departure led to the usual round of speculation as to who would be the new manager. Ruud Gullit, who had recently left Chelsea, was the popular choice, with Kenny Dalglish and Terry Venables among the other fancied candidates. Whoever they wanted, though, supporters were united in the desire to see a big name arrival and of the opinion that it might take some time before Villa could attract a manager of sufficient calibre. Which was why the events of the next twenty-four hours were all the more surprising.

In response to Little's resignation, Doug Ellis had stated that the club were already in the process of securing a new manager. This was seen as an indication that an appointment would not take as long as might have been thought. Nobody, though, expected the news that emanated from Villa Park on the afternoon following Little's surprise leaving. Not only had the board made their minds up already, it was announced that the job had been taken by John Gregory, last seen heading out of Villa Park some eighteen months previous, and whose previous management experience had been confined to his spell with Wycombe and a brief period at Portsmouth almost a decade earlier. It later transpired that Gregory had been offered the job within hours of Little's departure. Steve Stride, a close friend of the new manager, had reminded Ellis of the decline in the team's fortunes since Gregory had left Villa Park and persuaded the chairman that here was a gamble worth taking.

Everyone, from supporters to pundits, were stunned at the news. Gregory had not been in the running for the job: indeed, bookmakers hadn't quoted odds on him at all, although they now responded by reducing Villa's odds on being relegated. The new man, though, was not overawed by his rapid promotion. "I'm a disciplinarian," he stated at his first press conference. "I expect players to behave themselves and conduct themselves properly. If they aren't playing well, I don't expect them in the side". This was a reference to one of the accusations made about Little, that he had allowed discipline to slip and been guilty of picking his favourites regardless of performance Curiously, the same charge had been levelled at Ron Atkinson and Little had promised to get rid of much the same culture when taking over in November 1994.

Gregory made it clear that he believed the side he had at his disposal to be good enough to survive in the Premier League and that, although he intended to play attractive football, winning had to be the first priority. "We are talking about survival and I will do what it takes to win a game," was his blunt message, although he added, "But I like to be entertaining."

That Gregory had been appointed to one of the top jobs in football was, in retrospect, no great surprise. He may have lacked experience at the top, but John Gregory never lacked confidence in his own abilities. Neither could he have been accused of not making the most of his own attributes. Gregory was born in Scunthorpe, in May 1954, and was married with three children. As a player he had worked his way from Northampton Town, via a utility berth at Villa where he was notable for playing in all ten outfield shirts, to a place in the England team. He had moved from Villa to Brighton for £250,000 as part of Ron Saunders' clearout during the summer of 1979, spending two years on the south coast before a £300,000 transfer to Queens Park Rangers. Four years at Loftus Road saw Gregory make six England appearances and he moved to Derby in 1985, for a fee of £100,000. Gregory then moved to Portsmouth in 1988, where he became assistant manager to Alan Ball, taking the manager's job when Ball was dismissed the following year. His own sacking took place in 1990, after which he spent time out of the game before joining Brian Little first at Leicester and then Villa until he joined Wycombe in 1997, managing to keep them in the second division after the departure of Alan Smith.

On the afternoon Little left the Villa, Gregory had been preparing his Wycombe side for a league game at Bristol Rovers. Steve Stride tracked the team down and offered Gregory the Villa job on the spot. Unsurprisingly, his team subsequently lost 3-1 that evening. His next league game would be the following Saturday, against Liverpool.

Before the match, Gregory spoke of the difficulties faced by Stan Collymore that season, and appeared sympathetic. "He seems to have had the thin end of the wedge," was the Gregory verdict on the tortured genius from whom he was now expected to get the form of which the England striker was capable. "He's an exceptional talent. Let's get him back to what he does best." Of his own baptism of fire, Gregory was candidly honest. "The fact that it's my first game is secondary; it's a big game for Aston Villa. The club is bigger than any individual."

Any doubts Gregory may have harboured that the supporters would be against him were banished by the time it took him to walk from tunnel to dug-out, accompanied by a thunderous ovation. However, when Liverpool threatened to take Villa apart from the first kick of the match, Gregory may have wondered just how long he would remain in charge. The visitors went a goal up after four minutes and although Collymore equalised soon after with a miss-hit shot that took a deflection off a Liverpool defender, Villa were in danger every time the visitors touched the ball. Gregory's team held out until half-time, however, and the second half saw a complete transformation. Villa destroyed Liverpool, with man of the match Collymore scoring again and proving a constant threat. Three points were Villa's and the Villa supporters belonged to John Gregory.

The game was the opening of a sensational run that saw eight wins from ten games, an enthralling UEFA Cup quarter final against Atletico Madrid where Villa were unlucky to go out on away goals, and an unlikely European qualification achieved via a final league placing of seventh. John Gregory had performed his first miracle. But now the hard work really began.

Hardly had the season ended than Collymore was front-page news following his assault on his girlfriend, television personality Ulrika Johnson, in Paris, during the World Cup. To make matters worse, the incident had taken place in a bar full of Scottish supporters. Gregory found himself under fire from all quarters ranging from the media, for whom Collymore was always good for a headline, to feminist groups demanding that Gregory make a stand against his wayward genius.

As the Collymore story went the same way as other media-driven events, Gregory continued with the more mundane business of managing a football club. Bolton's Alan Thompson was signed for a fee of £4.5 million, while several of Little's squad players were moved on. Steve Staunton became the first Bosman free transfer between two English clubs when Villa were unable to match either Liverpool's wages or the lure of a return to Anfield. David Unsworth signed from West Ham for £3 million then moved to Everton within weeks because his family found settling in the Midlands difficult, or because he had not known at the time of his move that Everton wanted to buy him - depending on which story you believe. And most significant of all, Alex Ferguson decided that he wanted Dwight Yorke for Manchester United.

The Yorke saga reached its climax in the first week of the new season. He played in the first game, away at Everton, and was criticised by Villa supporters for a lack of effort. The conclusion was inevitable - Yorke moved to Old Trafford for £12.6 million, while Gregory responded, "If I'd had a gun I'd have shot him." Not for the last time did the Villa manager respond to a tricky situation with a soundbite guaranteed to win over the fans.

Not that he needed any help to win the fans over as the season progressed. Villa went top of the league after three matches, and created a club record of twelve games unbeaten with a 4-1 victory over Southampton at the Dell. Gregory marked this achievement by arranging to have a team photograph taken on the pitch after the match. Although he was at pains to stress that this was purely for his own use, the gesture backfired when it was seen as a highly premature celebration.

The Yorke transfer money had been spent on Dion Dublin, a £5.75 million capture from Coventry and Paul Merson, who cost an additional £1 million from Middlesbrough. Dublin made an immediate impact with seven goals in his first three appearances for the club, while Merson struggled at first to justify his transfer fee.

Celta Vigo had knocked Villa out of the UEFA Cup in the second round, while Gregory treated the Worthington Cup with as much significance as did most top managers and sent an understrength side to get beaten by Chelsea. The league, though, was a different matter. By the time Arsenal came to Villa Park for a televised Premiership clash two weeks before Christmas 1998, Villa were second in the table behind Manchester United on goal difference with thirty points from sixteen matches. With goalkeeper Mark Bosnich out injured for much of the season, Villa regularly fielded an all-English team. Such a policy, accidental though it undoubtedly was

- Gregory himself admitted that to improve the squad would mean buying players from abroad - made Villa a popular side amongst those who were wary of the growing influx of foreign players into the English game and led to Gregory being spoken of as a future England manager.

The game with Arsenal was one of the most dramatic seen at Villa Park for many years. Two down at half time, Villa staged a revival in the second half. Substitute Stan Collymore was instrumental in the fight-back that saw Villa score three goals to take the points in a game made all the more dramatic when the second half was delayed following an accident which almost cost the life of a parachutist injured when hitting the Trinity Road stand roof at half-time.

Mixed results over Christmas saw Villa return to second place in the table but as the new year dawned, no-one could deny that 1999 had belonged to John Gregory – "the stuff of fantasy" he called it. Martin Swain had seen the whole dramatic period unfold. "He inherited a fantastic core talent, but they were underachieving when he arrived and nobody knew why, least of all John. But you get moments like that Liverpool game: it all could have gone wrong if he hadn't won the first game, he'd have never got that flying start. Collymore produced that performance that some would say was a tribute to Brian Little and others would say was an insult, because he certainly hadn't played like that while Brian was there. But Stan took on Liverpool single-handed, dragged Villa away from that bad start. Then there was that fantastic run in the league and they ended up in Europe. By the next Christmas everyone was waiting for things to go wrong and wondering how John would cope. Maybe it was bluster on his part, but his attitude was, 'Why do people at this club think it has to end? When I crack that, I've cracked the club.' Which sums it up – there's a feeling of second best that we carry around with us. But everyone was waiting for it to go wrong."

And things did start to go wrong early on in the New Year. Prior to Villa's shock FA Cup defeat at home to second division Fulham, Stan Collymore drove away from Villa Park after refusing to be listed as substitute, then claimed to be suffering from depression. Gregory had by now clearly lost all patience with the club's record signing and made several disparaging remarks in public, questioning how a highly-paid, talented footballer could be depressed. At the same time, Paul Merson was continuing to struggle with the demons that plagued his career, taking an unscheduled break from training to fly to New York and failing to live up to his reputation on the field. Mark Bosnich was in open revolt with his manager after making it clear that he would be following Steve Staunton on a Bosman free when his contract ran out at the end of the season. Injuries mounted and the team that had made such a flying start to the season now found themselves unable to win a game.

In the midst of this poor run came an incident that was to cause irreparable damage to the often-fragile relationship between the Villa board and supporters. The Brazilian star Juninho, a long-time target of Gregory's, was photographed leaving Villa Park as negotiations for his transfer from Athletico Madrid reached a climax. Supporters who had long suspected that the club were never entirely serious about buying at the top end of the market briefly thought that circumstances had changed and a world-class player was about to sign for the club. When the transfer broke down, following a dispute over personal terms, there was a feeling that, yet again, the club had shown a lack of desire. For Gregory, already feeling the frustrations of wanting to sign players that the board were unwilling to pay for, this was another setback in his plans to build a side that could challenge for the title. As Martin Swain puts it, "Juninho. That's when he realised what he was up against. He worked for the deal; we don't know whether or not it would have worked, but the point was that they didn't do the deal. And at that time everyone had the feeling that this was fools gold after all. You can say that what kept John going from then until he walked out was his sheer determination never to give Ellis the excuse to sack him. But it was to the detriment of Aston Villa."

As results continued to worsen, Gregory was finally allowed to strengthen what was by now a paper-thin squad. Veteran defender Colin Calderwood joined from Spurs for £250,000 while Nottingham Forest winger Steve Stone cost £5.5 million – a much higher valuation than expected for a player who had only recently recovered from serious injury.

Villa finished the season in sixth place, a final-day defeat at Highbury meaning that a team that had been in Champions League contention a few months previously missed out on qualification for even the Intertoto Cup. Gregory was now facing the first criticism of his reign. The brashness that had appeared so refreshing twelve months previous was being described as arrogance and there was barely-restrained glee that the new boy wasn't finding Premiership management as easy as it had first appeared.

During the AGM at the start of the 1999-2000 season, Gregory claimed that he had spent his first eighteen months in charge at Villa "fighting fires". But that summer he could, at least, see that he was finally making headway. Mark Bosnich, to no-one's surprise, moved to Old Trafford on a free transfer. His replacement was Liverpool's David James, a gamble for Gregory bearing in mind the goalkeeper's reputation for inconsistency. George Boateng signed from Coventry for £4.5 million. The Boateng deal also marked the end of Gregory's perceived preference for buying English players. The manager himself has stated that he never consciously under-took such a policy, but whatever the reason, from the time he signed Boateng until he left Villa Park, Gregory would never again sign a big-money British player.

Villa were also in the hunt for Wolves' Irish prodigy Robbie Keane, only to lose out when refusing to raise their offer of £5.5 mil-lion by the extra £500,000 Wolves were asking. When Keane subse-quently moved to Coventry, Villa supporters yet again questioned the club's lack of ambition, despite Gregory's assurances that he had changed his mind about signing the player whatever the fee.

Ten points from the first five games of the season saw the team in second place in the league, but lower than expected crowds led to Gregory's first reported falling out with Doug Ellis following Villa's 1-0 win over Middlesbrough before a crowd of 28,728. Ellis blamed the negative football Gregory's team had been playing, while the manager doubtless pointed out that supporters had been disillu-sioned by the failure to sign Juninho and Keane.

Gregory now found his honeymoon period well and truly over, and, with it, much of the goodwill he had enjoyed since his arrival. A deal to sign Sheffield Wednesday striker Benito Carbone fell through when the Villa, once more, could not agree terms with the player, although he later joined in a loan deal until the end of the season. Stan Collymore returned from a loan spell with Fulham, missed training, and became involved in such a bitter public dis-pute with his manager that the PFA were called in to mediate. Paul Merson published his autobiography, *Hero and Villain*, in which he attacked the attitude of certain of his team-mates as well as the defeatist culture of the club.

The team's form slumped, with three points from nine games. Gregory criticised Robbie Keane before Villa's game at Coventry; Keane inevitably scored the winner on a night when Gregory was reportedly offered a pen by a Coventry supporter, "to sign on with in the morning." The Villa manager was certainly not going out of his way to make friends during this period. Gregory claimed that the injured Ugo Ehiogu, absent at Coventry, "would have played if it had been a cup final." He also made a habit of criticising referees, one particular attack on Jeff Winter, following a defeat at Leicester, earning him a touchline ban during which time he found that he preferred to manage from the directors' box. It has to be said, though, that Villa were certainly finding themselves at the wrong end of several important decisions during their poor spell. And the media's favourite sources of news over the previous two seasons found that his past reputation as the most approachable manager in the game counted for little as the press pack scented blood. Gregory admits that he found his relationship with the press strained. The journalists who had supported him in the past were now talking as though his departure were inevitable. Yet to his credit, Gregory still appeared to be the same ebullient character who had blazed a trail to the top of the league twelve months previous.

Despite protestations to the contrary, Gregory now found his team entering a sequence of games that would decide his future. Luckily, fortune had endeavoured to favour the brave. The FA Cup third round saw Villa beat third division Darlington 2-1 with an unimpressive display, while Worthington Cup quarter-final defeat at West Ham was followed by the news that the game would have to be replayed as West Ham had fielded an ineligible player. Finally, Villa played Sheffield Wednesday, without an away league win all season, in a Premiership match at Villa Park. One down at half-time, the team turned in a second-half performance that may have saved Gregory's job. Paul Merson, in particular, was magnificent as Villa ran out 2-1 winners despite Dion Dublin suffering a broken neck bone in a horrific collision with a Wednesday defender towards the end of the game.

From that point onwards, Villa's form turned dramatically. Gregory's decision to play a 3-5-2 formation may not have made for entertainment, but it certainly produced results. 23 points came from a twelve game spell in the league as the team eventually finished in sixth place, with runs to the semi-finals in both cup competitions an added bonus. Leicester City knocked Villa out of the Worthington Cup, while Bolton Wanderers were defeated on penalties in a poor game at Wembley to send Villa to their first FA Cup final since 1957. That the Villa's winner was scored by Dion Dublin, completing a remarkable recovery from the injury that could have left him crippled four months earlier, added to the drama of the occasion.

By this time Gregory's biggest headache had left the club. Stan Collymore moved to Leicester for a nominal fee, and the general feeling was one of sorrow that such a talent had been wasted, mixed with relief that Villa were rid of one of football's more persistent problems. Gregory had long since given up on getting any sort of return from Collymore's undoubted ability; indeed the manager appeared to go out of his way to publicly criticise the player at times, to the point where it was said that Gregory actually played a part in Villa's inability to obtain a decent transfer fee for Collymore.

The second half of the season had seen championship form from the Villa, losing just two league games in eighteen. Sadly, they could not carry this form into the cup final. The game with Chelsea has gone down in history as one of the worst finals on record, and Gregory's tactics were heavily criticised. In attempting to stop Chelsea from playing he seemingly forgot to remind Villa to score. Chelsea won the game by a single goal, scored by Roberto di Matteo following a defensive mix-up for which David James took the blame; but the way in which Gregory sent the Villa team onto the Wembley turf in such a negative frame of mind remains the abiding image of the day.

Villa played four matches in semi- and finals during the season. Paul Merson and Benito Carbone, in particular, were disappointing, while the team as a whole struggled to get a single shot on target in all four games. Gregory would never shake off the reputation for dull, uninspired football that he gained as a result of these performances. In doing so he lost the last reservoirs of goodwill he had built up amongst supporters and would from now on be judged solely on his current efforts. He had, however, signed a contract shortly before the FA Cup final that had made him the best paid manager in the club's history at a reputed million pounds a year. It was, as

Gregory himself pointed out, a long way from his time working on market stalls ten years earlier.

The summer of 2000 was, by Gregory's standards, a relatively quiet one. Alan Thompson moved to Celtic for £2 million while another of Gregory's big money signings, Steve Watson, moved to Everton for barely half the £4 million Villa had paid Newcastle for him less than two years earlier. Benito Carbone was unable to agree a permanent deal and also left Villa Park. Arrivals included Turkish defender Alpay Ozalan, experienced Belgian international striker Luc Nillis on a free transfer and, most surprisingly of all, David Ginola signed from Spurs for £3 million in a deal that was reported to be hatched when Doug Ellis met the mercurial Frenchman whilst on holiday.

Villa approached the 2000-01 season with the battle lines beginning to be drawn up once more. Gregory by now knew that the board would never countenance the spending he felt was necessary to take his side into the Champions League spot that was by now becoming the Holy Grail of all ambitious Premiership clubs. The scene was set for a war of attrition that affects the club even to this day. Martin Swain, who was Gregory's closest confidante at this time, recalls, "He felt that the moment he had another bad run he'd be gone. And that explains how results became a priority. John was still inexperienced at this point; he'd still only been a top-flight manager for two seasons. He needed to be able to use the chairman's experience, but he felt that Ellis would see this as more evidence that John wasn't up to the job. So the competitive Gregory emerged and you had two years of pretence whereby the board pretended to back him, he pretended to be getting on with the job and all the time one foundation after another was wasted. It was just sad, achingly sad, that something that started with so much fire and passion should end up in such a nasty, poisonous air that still has repercussions years later."

As was becoming the case, Villa drifted to the top of the league without ever looking capable of staying there. Luc Nillis began the season promisingly, yet within a month had suffered the broken leg that would force him into retirement. With a replacement desperately needed the club failed to act, once again showing to the world the lack of ambition that has become an Aston Villa trademark over the years and has caused frustration to so many managers.

Ugo Ehiogu had been sold to Middlesbrough for £8 million, victim of a personality clash between himself and Gregory. Gareth Southgate, as honest and intelligent a player as has been seen at Villa Park for many years, asked for a transfer, claiming that the club lacked ambition. Gregory himself admitted to a growing empathy with Southgate and with the supporters who were now taking their protests both into the ground on matchdays and around the city with a poster campaign aimed at embarrassing Doug Ellis into buying new players.

With this in mind, Gregory's interview with Joe Lovejoy of the Sunday Times in December 2000 must rank as one of the most remarkable ever given by a serving manager. He accused Doug Ellis of "living in a time warp", talking of having to drag the chairman "kicking and screaming" into the 21st century and describing how penny-pinching had become a fact of life at the club. Gregory apologised for his outburst almost immediately, and escaped with what he described as a "Don't let it happen again" warning. Although the affair subsided, no-one who knew Doug Ellis imagined for a second that it was forgotten. Again, Martin Swain is able to offer an eye-witness view of the situation. "John took his eye off the ball. The time warp attack was ill-conceived, but typical of his mindset at that time. His obsession with Doug was starting to get in the way, but if you can't deal with Doug you can't do the job. I'm sure Doug had good reason to feel that same way about John; after all we're not talking about an innocent victim here, and the Ellis camp would have their own view of what trouble John was causing." Indeed, the board may well have believed that Gregory was using his own particular brand of populism to get the supporters onside, even though many of them were tired of his style of play. While some fans were orchestrating pro-Gregory, anti-Ellis protests, there were many who were now stating that they would be glad to see the back of both men. Petulantly, Gregory told at least one critical supporter to watch their football at St Andrews if they weren't satisfied with his approach to the game.

After a typically drawn-out saga, Colombian striker Juan Pablo Angel was signed from River Plate for £9.5 million, smashing the club record fee in the process. Angel was seen by many supporters as 'their' player, bought as a result of matchday protests, and this feeling undoubtedly helped as he took some time to settle into his role as Villa's saviour. Gregory certainly showed great faith in his record signing, regularly stating that the player would show the form that had made him one of South America's top goalscorers.

Villa finished the 2000-01 season in eighth position, which was either a model of consistency or a sign that the club had no great desire to improve, depending on which view you took. Gregory himself stated that it had been the 'Lost Season', when the opportunity to capitalise on the advances of the previous two years had been wasted. It can certainly be said that this was the time when Villa's flirtation with the elite of English football, which had started out so promisingly under Brian Little, finally halted. Whether it was Gregory's fault that Villa were stagnating, or whether he was the reason why they had stayed in contention for so long, are matters for more complex debate.

As the season ended, one event of seemingly minor significance took place when Graham Taylor announced his retirement from full-time football and accepted a position as a non-executive director at Villa Park, stressing as he did so that he had no desire to return to management. The summer's personnel changes saw Gareth Southgate join Middlesbrough for £6 million, although his departure was in part due to his being yet another player to fall out with the manager. Assistant manager Steve Harrison and goalkeeping coach Paul Barron also moved to Middlesbrough. David James, who had enjoyed a mixed relationship with Gregory, was sold to West Ham, his surprise replacement being Peter Schmeichel, previously thought to have been winding his career down with Sporting Lisbon. Gregory was also able to spend heavily on Coventry's Mustapha Hadji, Swedish defender Olof Mellberg from Spanish side Santander and promising Croatian striker Bosko Balaban from Dinamo Zagreb, for a combined cost in excess of £12 million.

Villa, as usual, moved to the top of the table prior to a slump in form amidst player unrest. Gareth Barry asked for a transfer claiming that he had been frozen out by Gregory. David Ginola, virtually ignored since his arrival at Villa Park, announced that he intended to take legal action forcing Villa to pay up his contract should he not be picked for the first team. Gregory now asked for more money to cement the team's place at the top of the league. He targeted Leicester's Muzzy Izzet as the player he wanted, and believed that a fee of £8 million would be necessary. Doug Ellis, predictably, refused to sanction the purchase, stating that, "all managers think they need two more players" and claiming, in tandem with finance director Mark Ansell, that the club had no money left for signings.

Supporters, naturally, agreed with Gregory although there remained a sizeable element who held that enough money had been wasted by a manager whose transfer dealings seemed no better than when he first arrived at Villa Park. That Bosko Balaban had failed to start a league game since his £6 million arrival, while Mustapha Hadji was hardly justifying a £4.5 million tag, added weight to their argument.

The club was again at war with itself, yet the events of late-January 2002 were still a bombshell. Two days after a 2-1 victory at Charlton, Gregory announced his resignation as Villa manager. Initially described as the biggest sensation to hit Villa Park since the departure of Ron Saunders, this parting of the ways was, in hindsight, inevitable.

As ever with the board and John Gregory, there were conflicting reports as to why he quit. The official club line was that the manager had told the board he was quitting, after finding the pressures of the job too great. This story was denied by Gregory, who had gone to New York on holiday immediately the news of his resignation broke. Again, Martin Swain offers the clearest view of proceedings. "John said 'You're not going to change me, I'm not going to change you. Let's call it quits, agree not to say anything in public, shake hands and walk away. I took you over in fifteenth, I'm leaving you in seventh, my conscience is clear, let's call it a day'."

One thing that is certain is that Gregory had, within a week, been offered and accepted the job of managing Derby County, fighting against relegation to the first division. Taking another position so quickly after leaving the club he always regarded as a marriage inevitably led to accusations that Gregory had been approached to take over at Derby while still at Villa. It is, however, an accusation he has always denied.

Supporters reacted to the news of Gregory's resignation with unprecedented fury. Although there were many who were privately relieved that the manager had gone, these tended to keep their thoughts to themselves. Protest meetings were held, marches organised by what was once famously described as "the ever-growing number of spokesmen for the ever-growing number of Villa protest groups" and the first game of the post-Gregory era, a goalless draw at home to Everton, saw thousands of supporters noisily demonstrating their opposition to Doug Ellis. Throughout his dealings with the board, Gregory had been able to play on the Villa supporters' growing disenchantment with Doug Ellis, particularly after his 'timewarp' statement, and was now seen as a martyr to their cause.

Gregory was unable to keep Derby in the Premiership, and they struggled against further relegation during the following season. With supporter unrest mounting, it was announced that Gregory had been suspended as manager of the club in March 2003, following allegations that were believed to have referred to the treatment of injured players. This time there was none of the fury that had accompanied his departure from Villa Park. Gregory had never communicated with the fans at Derby in the same way that he had with Villa supporters and the subsequent announcement that he had been sacked came as no surprise. Gregory appealed against this decision and when his dismissal was upheld by the Derby board, he responded by launching a legal action for breach of contract.

By now, though, Gregory was making more headlines for his off-the-field activities. Rumours had been rife throughout football for some time that Gregory's transfer dealings were not as watertight as they might have been. In December 2002 Villa announced that they had asked the FA compliance unit to investigate transfers made during his time at the club, although they were keen to emphasise that Gregory himself was not under investigation. Of particular interest were the purchases of Balaban, Angel and Alpay, where it was alleged that the selling clubs had received only a fraction of the total transfer fee.

The satirical magazine Private Eye then ran a story drawing attention to the fact that many of Gregory's transfers had been conducted through the Proactive Sports Management agency, in which he was a shareholder. Gregory denied this charge and the agency's owner, Paul Stretford, began legal proceedings against the magazine. The FA were showing no great urgency in investigating Villa's complaint and with the future of their compliance unit in doubt at the time of writing, the full story of the transfers that were a cause for such concern may never be revealed. Whilst there has never been any evidence of wrong-doing, and Gregory has always categorically stated his innocence, to date he has for legal reasons been denied the opportunity to clear his name.

No manager has ever split Villa supporters in the way that John Gregory did, and continues to. Since the day of his departure he has aroused strong feelings. His supporters claim that he was restrained by a backward-thinking board, and that with the right backing Champions League qualification would have been achieved. Detractors point to the often-tedious football played under his charge and say that no Villa manager has had so much money available, yet he could not be said to have improved the team to any great extent. He certainly made mistakes in the transfer market, Bosko Balaban being the most obvious example, and paid far too much for players who gave distinctly average service to the club. The Hodgson Report into the business workings of the club, published during the summer of 2003, described "the vast majority" of Gregory's transfer dealings as "unfortunate." There has further been an underlying implication by club employees that the money spent by Gregory on transfer fees and wages for such players has been the real reason why Villa have been unable to compete at the top end of the transfer market since his departure.

Yet Gregory himself would claim that he was rarely allowed to sign the players he wanted. In his autobiography, The Boss, Gregory spoke of supporters "wanting Ginger Spice in a basque and suspenders. I had given them Nora Batty in tights." He spent £71 million, far more than any other Villa manager in history, even allowing for the inflationary transfer market of the time. Naturally, those who defend him will say that over £50 million of this figure was raised by the sale of players and he was only ever allowed to buy replacements for those who had already left, rather than to strengthen his squad.

Equally, for every slump in form there was an unbeaten run offering hope that Gregory was finally close to success. To reach the FA Cup final of 2000 was either a marvellous achievement or resulted in such an embarrassment that it would have been better had Villa been knocked out in the earlier rounds.

It's hard to argue with the point made by Stephen Froggatt, who by the time of the manager's departure was covering Midlands football for the BBC, "For the amount of money he spent, John should have improved the team more than he did." But one suspects that, despite the mountain of evidence offered by both sides, the answer to the question of whether or not John Gregory did a good job as Villa manager depends on whether or not you liked him.

20

Graham Taylor

January 2002 - May 2003

When Graham Taylor announced his retirement from full-time football at the end of the 2000-01 season, Doug Ellis wasted no time in persuading the former Villa manager that his experience could be utilised back at Villa Park. Taylor agreed to become a non-executive director of the club, joking that one of his roles would be "to keep an eye" on Ellis. The role was not greatly defined, but one thing Taylor was certain of was that his managerial days were over. "I have retired," was the adamant reply, but Taylor now elaborates on his decision. "I found myself saying yes to a lot of things and one of them was to become a non-executive director at Villa. I made it very clear to Doug that no way was I coming back for him to sack John Gregory and for me to become the manager. I guaranteed him that, should that happen, I wouldn't take the job. I tried to gain the trust of John and his coaching staff so that I could help behind the scenes. It took me a long time to gain John's trust, which is understandable, but I certainly wasn't rushing up to Bodymoor Heath while John was in charge. In fact, I only visited there twice. My involvement was very minimal. I attended four board meetings, watched a few games and I was happy with that."

After finishing his second stint at Watford, Taylor had settled into life as a respected elder statesman of the game. He had been awarded the OBE for services to football in the New Years' Honours List of 2002, and was presented with an award by the Football Writers Association for his outstanding contribution to the game. Taylor had also begun a second career as a media pundit, working for BBC Radio Five Live.

However, this decision changed with the resignation of John Gregory. While names such as Alan Curbishley and former Spanish national boss Javier Clemente were mentioned, there was a lack of available obvious candidates. Taylor explains how the situation developed. "I was on holiday with my wife, walking in the Yorkshire

Dales, when I switched television on and saw on teletext that John had walked out. I was as gobsmacked as anyone. When we got back from holiday, Doug asked me to become manager. I was most reluctant, because it would look as though it was planned. At first I turned it down, one Sunday lunchtime, then about four hours later I thought, 'Graham, this could be the biggest regret you'll ever have'. I knew that I had no part to play in John's resignation, I hadn't tried to get his job, so why was I worrying? I remembered the saying that it's not what you do that you regret, it's what you don't do. And I knew that I would always regret not taking the chance. So I phoned Steve Stride and asked him to tell Doug that I'd take it. I signed a contract for the rest of that season, and for two more years. I'd never signed one for less than three years, and perhaps the reason I signed for two years was that I had a gut feeling things weren't right."

Most supporters were prepared to give the returning hero a chance, but there were those for whom Taylor's acceptance of the role was tantamount to treason. Some saw the appointment as a cynical decision based on appeasing the fans rather than what was best for the club, and it is true that the protest movement that had sprung up when Gregory walked out vanished almost as quickly as it started. Navid Nazir, chairman of the Aston Villa Independent Supporters Association, described the move as, "a short-term appointment designed to get the chairman off the hook." Others felt that Taylor had been appointed because he would be more amenable to the demands of Ellis and Mark Ansell that the club cut back on wages and spend less on new players.

"When I'd joined in 1987, it wasn't a split club, there was just nothing there. The second time you'd got the staff and the players but talk about splits. It wasn't just one group here and one there; there was splits all over the club. At the Academy level for instance, Tony McAndrew and Kevin McDonald had both at some stage coached the first team. Then John Deehan had coached the first team and under his spell Villa went top of the table. Three weeks later Stuart Gray walks in, unannounced to John or anyone but John Gregory and Doug. I inherited all that. But remember I didn't know about Stuart and it wasn't just that I was a director, but Stuart was captain when I was manager, so some supporters must have felt I influenced that appointment when in fact I knew nothing about it."

Taylor soon realized the extent to which the club was plagued by in-fighting. "I walked into a club wracked by division. There was the Alpay situation, where he'd gone off to a clinic in Germany, Angel still angry about how he'd been treated when he first arrived. It was amazing that the club had been anywhere near the top of the table; there was such division. The youngsters were getting no opportunity, little or no interest was being shown in the youth side at all. I'd smelt all this as a director, but I had no idea how deep all of these divisions went. And I have to say that there was no respect between the dressing room and the boardroom. You had players like Peter Schmeichel; he was used to much better situations that this."

At the press conference to announce his appointment, Taylor was in typically ebullient mood. "I'm coming back to try and finish what I started here," he announced, stating that he intended to use the rest of the season to look at the Villa squad.

Taylor had never been under any illusions about the politics that frequently ravage the club. But even he must have been shocked at the savage reaction to Doug Ellis during a supporters' forum that took place within weeks of the manager's appointment. As expected, Ellis bore the brunt of criticism based on the departure of John Gregory and the general air of under-achievement that had dogged the club for years. Taylor, in an attempt to take the heat from the situation, spoke of his ambitions for the club: "I'm looking for Champions League football," and summed up the situation that had led to such discontent amongst supporters: "You're bored with finishing sixth." Taylor says of that evening, "In 1987 Doug Ellis had a small minority of supporters against him. When I came back I realised that it was no longer a small minority, there was in fact a large number who intensely disliked him, and that seemed that if the club had a good message to give, he was the wrong messenger. Too many people now will not accept him."

The biggest criticism leveled at Taylor was that he would be using outdated tactics. The 'long-ball' image that had haunted him since his early days at Watford was reinforced when his first signing was Portsmouth's giant forward Peter Crouch. Never mind that Crouch was actually a talented player better on the ground than in the air, the old clichés were available to be dusted down once more.

Under Taylor, Villa's season petered out, and they eventually finished eighth in the league. There were encouraging signs in the way that Taylor had given an opportunity to promising youngsters such as Finnish goalkeeper Peter Enckelman and German midfielder Thomas Hitzlsperger, as well as the opening form of Peter Crouch. That the club's under-18s had won the FA Youth Cup also added to the general air of optimism around Villa Park at the time. Taylor had made a start on getting Bodymoor Heath modernized and addressed personnel issues that had dogged the club in previous seasons. However, he soon found himself a victim of circumstances beyond the control of any manager.

Football had found itself caught up in a wave of hyper-inflation fueled by television money and the supposition that the good times would never end. The collapse of ITV Digital, together with a downturn in television revenues throughout Europe, caused a crisis of confidence in the game and led to an overnight collapse in the transfer market. Villa, with several players on lucrative long-term contracts, were harder hit than most as Taylor struggled in vain to offload players who he felt didn't want to play for the club or who hadn't been performing. "They'd spent all their money," is Taylor's frank assessment of the situation.

Taylor found himself with little money to spend and consequently brought in players that may not have been of the high quality he would have liked. Ironically, one player who was happy to move on was the most popular Villa player of the previous few years, Paul Merson, whose quest for first-team football took him to Portsmouth on a free transfer. Also moving from Villa Park was George Boateng, who joined the growing ex-Villa colony at Middlesbrough for a fee of £5 million.

The 2002-03 season started with a disenchanted Villa Park dressing room. Worse, Taylor had lost the backing of many fans still smarting from the loss of their hero Gregory, or who felt that the manager was deliberately trying to drive their favourites from Villa Park. It was hardly surprising that performances suffered from the off, with three defeats in the first four league games and elimination from the Intertoto Cup. Taylor consequently never managed to regain the goodwill from either fans or players that was necessary to turn the club round. As Stephen Froggatt puts it, "If he'd known what he was getting himself into, I don't think Graham would have gone anywhere near the job. Everything was in disarray, from the players to the supporters. His summer signings weren't immediate successes and he never really got over that. One or two players needed their careers re-starting and Graham either couldn't, or wouldn't, do that for them."

Performances during the season usually ranged from mediocre to abysmal. With Juan Pablo Angel suffering from the effects of a pre-season injury, and with new signings Crouch and Marcus Allback out of form, goals were hard to come by and Villa frequently lost matches that they should have won comfortably. Taylor sums up the season, "In a nutshell, we didn't score goals and we weren't com-petitive away from home." A humiliating defeat at St Andrews, remembered chiefly for a mistake by Peter Enckelman, was a typi-cal example - Villa lost 3-0 but had enough chances to have reversed the result. There was enough quality in the Villa side to ensure the odd encouraging display - a 1-1 draw at Old Trafford and a 2-1 vic-tory at home to Chelsea being the highlights - but it seemed that every time the team put together a couple of good results they would inevitably be followed by a disappointing one. Angel, the club's record signing, appeared particularly out of sorts. Taylor speaks of the problems he faced with the player: "As much as he can play, I'd gone round his house; we'd appointed Lorna McClelland who speaks Spanish, Italian and French as the club's welfare officer, but he couldn't get out of his mind how he'd been treated two years previous. The biggest thing, though, was the injury he suffered pre-season against Walsall. When he came back and played with Allback, I kept them together for the first Birmingham game. They'd done well before then, but in the first half against Birmingham I couldn't believe how badly they played. And players will always look for something else to explain their performance."

"We finished sixteenth and our defensive record was acceptable. If five of our 1-0 defeats had been 1-0 wins we'd have finished sixth. My frustration was that I knew there was a team inside those play-ers but they just couldn't put the ball in the net. Then when we beat Middlesbrough and Blackburn, we went one up against Fulham and I thought we could finish in the top eight. But the players got com-placent, got into a comfort zone. They thought they were better than the position they were in and when we had those two wins they thought they'd cracked it and results would just come from then on. If anything disappointed me it was that attitude, because from then on we went on this lousy run that included the Birmingham return."

Taylor seemed at times to be totally disenchanted by the attitudes he had found on his return to top-level club football. Within a month of the 2002-03 season starting he talked of Villa Park being "a political minefield. There are hidden agendas all over the place." During one interview he gave the revealing opinion, "The Premier League has been responsible for many marvellous moments but the fun's gone out of it." Increasingly he seemed like a man out of his time. The celebrity-driven ethos of the Premier League was a new experience, and not, it appeared, a pleasant one.

Villa had been in the lower half of the table for most of the season, and a disastrous spell of four consecutive losses - one of them another defeat to Blues, in a Villa Park clash marred by violence on and off the pitch - led to Taylor suffering vitriolic criticism. "After that game I had the first thoughts of packing in. Not because we'd lost but because the atmosphere, the game, represented everything I've ever stood against. And I questioned then whether I wanted to be part of that situation."

When Premiership safety was finally ensured with a win over already-relegated Sunderland in the final home game of the season, Taylor attempted to address the crowd, only for his words of apology for what he described as a disappointing season to be drowned out by a torrent of abuse. "What you have to do as a manager is to look at yourself. Towards the end of the season I asked the chairman what money was available for the following season. Initially he said there was none and I said that we had to tell the supporters. At the end of the meeting there was £ 4 million to spend. I asked Steve Stride afterwards where the money had come from and he said he had no idea. And I thought, 'You can't manage this. Nothing's changed'.

"Other things were eating into me. When a player's name was suggested, you could tell whether the chairman and the other directors fancied that player by how much they were prepared to pay. If they didn't fancy him the money wasn't available but if they liked him then there were efforts to get the money and offer a decent salary. I wasn't prepared to accept that situation, I deserved more than that."

Villa finished the season in sixteenth place, only the second time since the formation of the Premier League that they had finished in the bottom half. The post-mortem on the season had hardly begun when, two days after the final match (a 3-1 defeat at Leeds where, yet again, Villa had had enough chances to win), Taylor announced his resignation. "Playing results are not the reason for my resignation, he stated, going on to say, "Modern football involves much wider issues than mere playing matters and those are a major factor in my decision.

He now says of his decision to resign, "In 1987 I had the desire to fight all this silliness. I needed to fight it and I wanted to fight it. I was after bigger and better things. At the end of 2003 I asked myself if I had the desire to fight all this crap and no, I hadn't. Did I need the job? Well, I was on more money than I'd ever been on. That was nice, but I'm not going to be desolate without it. Most importantly, did I want the job? Once I looked in the mirror and there was any hesitation, I decided to pack it in. I wasn't being fair to myself, to my wife and family or to the club. One of the things I remember was that last game in 1990 at Everton. Then when I came back with Watford there was a standing ovation as I walked from the tunnel and also the response when I came onto the pitch for the Chelsea game, my first game back. I couldn't stay in the job if it wasn't right for me because you're not being true to yourself and to other people."

The following week, Taylor elaborated in the Daily Telegraph on his reasons for leaving: "I was under no pressure to resign as Aston Villa manager - but have become increasingly unhappy at how the club as a whole was run. There are fundamental problems at Aston Villa that are preventing it from becoming a top-four football club." Taylor spoke of the transitional period he had overseen, pointing out that thirteen players had made Villa debuts over the course of the season, including five aged twenty or under, and remarked that such players needed a manager who would be able to devote more time to their development than Taylor, who had just one year left of his contract. He now says, "I'm disappointed that I couldn't finish the job as I said I wanted to do. But I hadn't got the time left on my contract so it was best to leave it to others. By me sacking the board rather than the other way round I hoped to send a message that things had to change. The interesting thing was that when I told Doug I was leaving he asked first if it was about money, and then he was worried that I might do a hatchet job on him. His only concern was for himself."

Taylor's managerial return to Villa Park happened at an inopportune time. Everyone at the club, from players to supporters, seemed unhappy at the perceived lack of ambition from a board who had boasted for years that their cautious approach would be proved correct when football's boom period ended, yet who appeared unprepared when it actually did end. The whole club needed revitalising from top to bottom, in the way that it had when Taylor first took charge in 1987, yet for a variety of reasons he was unable to perform such a task for a second time. As he put it, "There are some great people working at Villa. But when I came back I realised that there are some there who owe their job to the chairman, and they work for Doug Ellis rather than for Aston Villa. You can't say anything to them for fear that it might be reported back. It didn't make for a healthy atmosphere."

It would be unrealistic to deny that Graham Taylor's second spell as Villa manager was anything other than a disappointment on the field. Performances were poor and the club seemed further away from the high-flyers of the game than they had at any time since he took the England job thirteen years earlier. Much of what Taylor did can be seen in hindsight to have been wrong - such as Merson and Boateng leaving without being replaced - but he also ensured that in many ways his successor would inherit a better situation than he did himself. The youth policy that had begun to reap such rewards was maintained as several young players were given the opportunity to shine; the long-overdue appointment of a welfare officer to help players, particularly from overseas, to settle at the club was made and improvements to Bodymoor Heath took place. "When I left in 1990, it was as good as any training ground in the country. By the time I came back it was nowhere near good enough, way behind the top Premiership clubs. I had to convince Doug to spend £350,000 just on getting the surfaces right."

In looking back at Graham Taylor's overall time at Villa Park it is probably best to remember his first three seasons, when he set in place much of the foundations for the success that subsequent managers enjoyed, and to draw a discreet veil over the results during his return. Such a fine servant to Aston Villa, and to football in general, deserves no less.

21

David O'Leary

June 2003 - present

Graham Taylor's resignation may not have come as a great surprise, but it still left a vacancy that needed to be filled as soon as possible. Even those supporters who had not backed Taylor were galvanised by his parting shots, while Dennis Mortimer said of the departure, "This incident with Graham Taylor is the last straw. So we keep Doug and lose Graham. That might be someone's idea of a bargain but it isn't mine. The real reason Taylor has gone is because he is a man of integrity. But you have to question the integrity of people who are still at Villa Park."

Ellis had stated that the board were prepared to wait up to two months to get the right man, but there was little doubt that the pressure was on for him to come up with a suitable replacement, and quickly.

Once more there were no outstanding candidates, although the out-of-work duo of George Burley and Bryan Robson were both regarded as possibilities. Leicester boss Micky Adams was favourite for the position, but his club's compensation demands were thought to have ruled him out of contention. David O'Leary's appointment was therefore seen as a surprise, although as betting on the identity of the new manager had been suspended during the afternoon O'Leary was unveiled as Villa boss, word had obviously leaked out somehow.

Born in Dublin in May 1958, O'Leary signed for Arsenal on his fifteenth birthday and stayed at Highbury for almost twenty years, moving to Leeds United on a free transfer in the summer of 1993. His time at Highbury saw O'Leary make 558 first team appearances, winning two championship medals and 67 caps for the Republic of Ireland. He played just ten times for Leeds before announcing his retirement from playing in October 1995, staying on at Elland Road as coach and then assistant manager to his former Highbury boss, George Graham. When Graham left Leeds to join

Spurs in October 1998, O'Leary was appointed manager and at first enjoyed a measure of success, steering the club to regular European qualification and a place in the Champions League semi-final of 2000-01.

However, O'Leary came under criticism for spending heavily and for his handling of Leeds players. His book The Trial Of Leeds United came out shortly after Leeds players Lee Bowyer and Jonathan Woodgate had been tried on serious assault charges and was felt to have had an effect on Leeds' poor performances during the 2001-02 season, at the end of which O'Leary was sacked.

O'Leary's time at Leeds raised mixed feelings. He put together a side who played attractive football and who had some success. However, the image of the club at the time was not as it could have been and for all O'Leary's big spending, Leeds failed to win a trophy during his tenure. As the transfer market collapsed, the club were also revealed to be in serious debt - which was generally regarded as being the result of the excessive spending undertaken by O'Leary with the encouragement of then-chairman Peter Ridsdale.

O'Leary therefore came to Villa Park in the unique position of both being an experienced manager and of having something to prove. His Leeds side had been a good, albeit ultimately unsuccessful, one. He did, though, need to be able to show that he could put together a team without access to unlimited funds, Villa having announced record losses of £11.6 million shortly after O'Leary's appointment.

When he was appointed, the new Villa manager spoke of "waiting for the right opportunity at the right club, and that has come along." In reference to his time at Leeds he said, "One thing I took this job for was to show that David O'Leary doesn't need money."

Swedish international Marcus Allback, signed by Graham Taylor the previous summer, was of the opinion that: "I think he will do good things for us. Now it is important that we all pull together in the same direction." O'Leary himself acknowledged this problem when he described attempting to reunite a fragmented dressing room as "a job and a half".

Villa started the 2002-03 season with a squad reduced in number from the one that had performed so poorly the previous year. The only new arrivals were midfielder Gavin McCann and goalkeeper

Thomas Sorensen, both signed from newly-relegated Sunderland for a combined fee of just over £4 million. These were more than offset by the losses of several players on free transfers, amongst them the long-serving trio of Ian Taylor, Alan Wright and Steve Staunton.

Hassan Kachloul, epitome of the high-salaried madness that had enveloped English football in the wake of the Bosman ruling, moved to Wolves on loan, while a similar deal took Peter Crouch to first division Norwich City. The Crouch move was to give the oft-derided young forward first team experience, the others seemed purely for the benefit of reducing Villa's wage bill, which, although large, was nowhere near the size of some Premiership clubs. O'Leary therefore had the restraints of the job made clear to him early on. If he were to succeed at Villa Park, nobody would, indeed, be able to, accuse David O'Leary of needing money to achieve success.

A few weeks into the start of the new season, rumours of takeover bids from mystery foreign consortia were already making the manager's job more difficult than it could have been. O'Leary spoke of the warnings he had received from others in the game prior to accepting the post. "A few people told me not take the job because of everything that apparently goes with it, but I haven't seen anything that would've frightened me off and I'm delighted and proud to be here. There is plenty to do and it could be that one or two wouldn't fancy it because there's a lot of hard work involved, but I'm already enjoying the challenge and determined to put things right. It's a fantastic opportunity for me to put the club back where it belongs."

Of the politics that regularly bedevil the club, he seems utterly unconcerned. "There is certainly more interest in that side of things from the media than I expected. I had been warned that politics is a big part of this club but I don't see it as any more significant here than anywhere else. Anyway, it's not an area that I need to get involved in. I'm here to manage the team and I will be judged on results and performances. Whatever else happens around me is up to other people."

And the manager was certainly aware of the size of the task in front of him, stating that: "A club this size should be in Europe every year, but it will be a long hard job to make that happen and all-round improvement has to be the first part of the plan."

How he performs in the claret and blue hot seat, only time will tell. But every Villa manager going back to Jimmy McMullan would agree that David O'Leary will need every ounce of his undoubted managerial ability, plus a large slice of luck, to cope with the unique pressures of the job.

Bibliography

Children of the Revolution – Richard Whitehead (Sports Projects)
Pinnacle of the Perry Barr Pets – Simon Page (Juma)
Aston Villa, The First 100 Years – Peter Morris (Naldrett Press)
The Team Makers – Peter Morris (Pelham Books)
Football with a Smile – Gary James (ACL & Polar Publishing)
The Sack Race – Chris Green (Mainstream Publishing)
Kicking & Screaming – Rogan Taylor (Chrysalis Books)
The Boss – John Gregory with Martin Swain (Andre Deutsch)
Big Ron, A Different Ball Game – Ron Atkinson (Andre Deutsch)
Stride Inside the Villa – Steve Stride with Rob Bishop (Sports
Projects)
The Head Bhoys – Graham McColl (Mainstream Publishing)
Prophet or Traitor, the Jimmy Hogan Story – Norman Fox (Parrs
Wood Press)

===

Also available from Heroes Publishing

FROM ONE SEASON TO THE NEXT
An Astonian Odyssey
by Dave Woodhall

A season-by-season guide to Aston Villa Football Club from 1975
to 2002.

From One Season To The Next looks at the rollercoaster ride that
is Aston Villa and includes supporter reminiscences of the good, the
bad and the downright distressing.

"A fascinating trip through the club's recent history" (Sporting Star)

176pp fully illustrated. Price £9.95   ISBN: 0-9543884-0-2